# Sunset

# Home Repair Handbook

BY THE EDITORS OF SUNSET BOOKS AND SUNSET MAGAZINE

Lane Publishing Co. ■ Menlo Park, California

Book Editor
**Cynthia Overbeck Bix**

Research & Text
**Karen A. L. Boswell**
**Beverley J. DeWitt**
**Marianne Lipanovich**
**John McClements**
**Susan E. Schlangen**

Technical Editor
**Donald Rutherford**

Coordinating Editor
**Suzanne N. Mathison**

Design
**Joe di Chiarro**

Illustrations
**Rik Olson**
**Mark Pechenik**
**Bill Oetinger**

## All through the house . . .

The next time a leaking faucet or a squeaky floor in your house signals the need for repair, why not fix it yourself? Let the *Sunset Home Repair Handbook* show you how, with step-by-step drawings that walk you through these and dozens of other common repair projects, from the roof to the basement.

Is it an emergency? Turn to the front of the book for concise, practical advice. Are you unsure of what tool to use for a particular job? In the second chapter we offer a description of basic tools and how to use them, along with practical suggestions for materials you'll want to have on hand.

In the following chapters, we focus on specific repair jobs throughout the house—inside and out, upstairs and down—including repairs to your plumbing, electrical, and heating and cooling systems. Charts help you pinpoint causes and remedies for problems you may encounter.

To keep your house in top shape the year around, follow the maintenance routine outlined in the back of the book. Here, you'll also find a glossary of home repair terms.

In preparing this book, we've drawn on the talents of many knowledgeable professionals. For their generous help and technical advice, we'd like to thank Les Shipnuck, architect/builder; Joyce Berkowitz, general contractor; Home Plumbing Supplies; Dan Littleton, ICOM Mechanical, Inc.; Al Kelsey, Home Electrical; Rick Meyer, Meyer Electric; David L. Curtis, Stuart Floor Co.; Bud Hopkins, Hopkins Plumbing; Mitch Stuart, Heart Construction; Tom Chaney, Chaney's Paint & Wallcoverings; Rand Haas, United States Gypsum; Lambro Barbas, Schlage Lock Co.; Jeff Kicksmiller, Kelly-Moore Paint Co., Inc.; Todd R. Zabelle, California Shingle & Shake Co.; and Fire Inspector John Garibaldi, Menlo Park Fire Protection District. Thanks also to Scott Atkinson and Brian Smith for lending technical advice.

Special appreciation goes to Fran Feldman for developing key sections of the manuscript, and for thoroughly editing all the copy; to Kathy Oetinger for the many hours she spent cutting color screens for the illustrations; and to Diane Dyson for editing "Major Appliances."

**Cover:** Photograph by Nikolay Zurek. Design by Lynne B. Morrall. Step-by-step instructions for replacing ceramic tile appear on page 94.

Sunset Books
Editor, David E. Clark
Managing Editor, Elizabeth L. Hogan

Second printing January 1987

# Contents

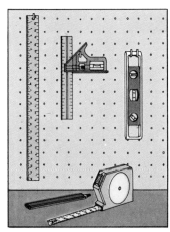

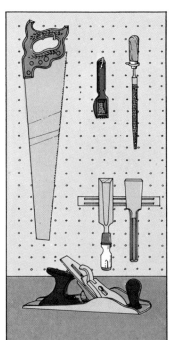

# Household Emergencies

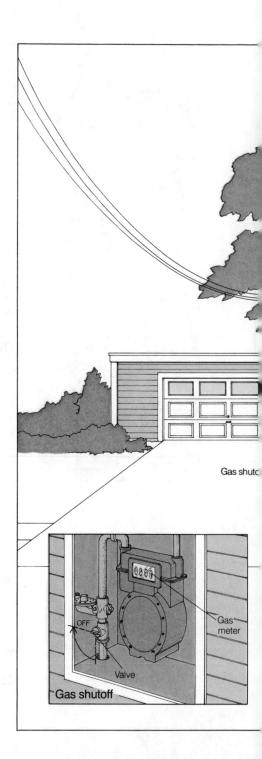

Gas shutoff

Gas meter

OFF

Valve

Gas shutoff

At some time, you may have to face a household emergency that requires you to shut off the supply of water, gas, or electricity to your home. This chapter explains how to locate and use these important shutoffs (shown below), so you can act promptly if necessary. You'll also learn safe ways to handle specific emergencies, such as a grease fire or a toilet overflow.

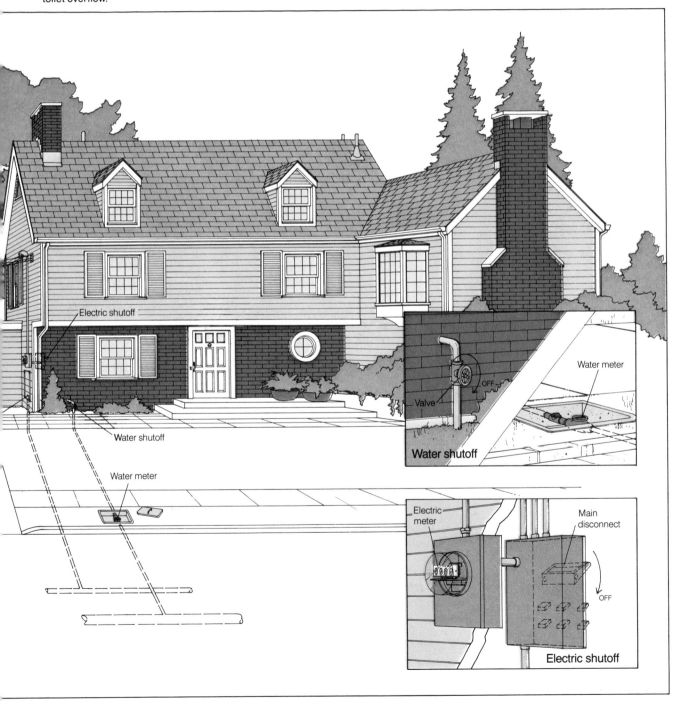

Electric shutoff

Water shutoff

Water meter

Water meter

Valve    OFF

**Water shutoff**

Electric meter

Main disconnect

OFF

**Electric shutoff**

# Home Emergencies

At one time or another you'll probably have to face an emergency situation in your home. The most common household emergencies and what to do about them are described below and on the following pages. It's important to read this section now *before* an emergency occurs. Be sure every member of your family knows and understands the steps to take in case of a fire, and familiarize everyone with the shutoff valves and switches that control the flow of water, electricity, and gas into your home. (If special wrenches are required to turn the valves, keep them close to the shutoffs.) Post emergency telephone numbers by each phone.

In the event of a natural disaster such as an earthquake, flood, tornado, or hurricane, you may need to shut off the gas, electricity, and possibly the water. It's a good idea to have some basic emergency supplies—a portable radio, a flashlight with extra batteries, and a first aid kit with instructions for its use—on hand at all times.

## Fires

In the event of a fire in your home, immediately take the following steps:

- **Get everyone out of the house.**
- **Call the fire department from a neighbor's house.**

Protect yourself and your family from fire-related injuries by taking precautions ahead of time. With your family, map out escape routes from your house, particularly from bedrooms, and have a central meeting area so everyone can be accounted for. Be sure to have safety ladders near windows if your home is more than one story high.

Smoke detectors provide an excellent early warning about fires; they're your first line of defense against fires that break out at night. Install one or more detectors on every floor of your house near the exits and adjacent to the bedrooms. Test the detectors once a month and replace the batteries when needed (usually once a year).

Equip your home with a portable fire extinguisher; it's useful for fighting such small, contained fires as an upholstery fire or a fire in a wastebasket. Extinguishers are classed by the type of fire they're designed to put out. If you have only one extinguisher, make sure it will extinguish all types of fires; if you have more than one, choose ones that will be effective against the type of fire likely to occur in the particular area where the extinguisher is stored. Learn how to operate your extinguisher *before* you need to use it.

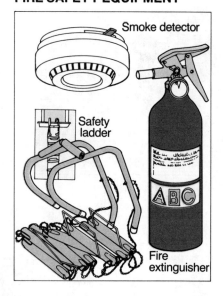

**FIRE SAFETY EQUIPMENT**

Smoke detector

Safety ladder

Fire extinguisher

ABC

---

### Kitchen grease fires

Here's how to extinguish fires that result from cooking:

- **Small grease or oil fire in a pan:** Turn off the heat and immediately cover the pan with a lid. DON'T pour water on a grease or oil fire—water will cause the fire to spread.

- **Oven fire:** Turn off the heat and let the fire burn itself out. DON'T open the oven door—this will let in more air, feeding the fire and causing it to continue to burn.

---

### Chimney & roof fires

A chimney fire occurs when the soot and creosote deposits inside the flue ignite, making a loud roaring noise and causing flames and sparks to shoot out of the chimney. A roof fire results from sparks traveling up the flue and igniting the roof; often, such a fire burns through the roof before it's discovered. In the event of a chimney or roof fire, get everyone out of the house and call the fire department.

To prevent such fires, observe the following precautions:

- **Keep your chimney or stovepipe clean** (page 38).

- **Do not burn large amounts of loose newspaper** or other paper in your fireplace or wood stove.

- **Install a spark arrester** (page 38) on the top of your flue.

# Plumbing Emergencies

In a plumbing emergency, you'll need to stop the flow of water quickly. To do this, you and each member of your family need to know the location of the shutoff valve for every fixture and appliance, as well as the main shutoff valve for the house, and how they operate (see at right). To learn about your plumbing system and how it works, turn to page 112.

If the emergency involves a specific fixture or appliance, first look for its shutoff valve and turn it clockwise to shut off the water to that fixture or appliance only. The valve is usually located underneath a fixture such as a sink or a toilet, or behind an appliance, such as a clothes washer, at the point where the water supply pipe (or pipes) connects to it.

If the problem is not with a particular fixture or appliance or if there's no shutoff valve for the fixture or appliance, use the main shutoff valve to turn off the water supply to the entire house. You'll find the main shutoff valve on the inside or outside of your house where the main water supply pipe enters. (In cold climates, look just inside the foundation wall in the basement or crawl space.) Turn the valve clockwise to shut it off. If you need a wrench to turn the valve, keep one, specially labeled, near the valve so it's handy.

If the main shutoff valve itself is defective and needs to be repaired, call your water company; they can send someone out with the special tool that's required to shut off the water at the street before it reaches the valve.

## WATER SHUTOFF VALVES

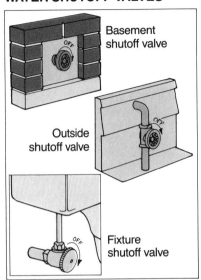

Basement shutoff valve

Outside shutoff valve

Fixture shutoff valve

---

**A leaking or broken pipe**

- Turn off the main shutoff valve to prevent water damage.

- Make temporary repairs to stop the leak (page 135); the pipe will have to be replaced as soon as it's convenient to do so.

---

**An overflowing toilet**

- Reach inside the toilet tank, push the tank stopper down into the valve seat, and hold it there.

- Turn off the water at the fixture shutoff valve underneath the toilet. If

there's no valve there, turn off the main shutoff valve.

- Unclog the toilet using a funnel-cup plunger or closet auger (page 132).

---

**A stopped-up sink**

- Shut off any faucet or appliance (such as a dishwasher) that's draining into the sink.

- Unclog the sink using a plunger or snake (pages 122–123). DON'T use a chemical drain cleaner if the blockage is total.

---

**A faucet that won't shut off**

- Immediately turn off the water at the fixture shutoff valve underneath the sink. If there's no valve there, turn off the main shutoff valve.

- Repair the faucet (pages 113–118) or, if necessary, replace it.

---

**A steaming hot water faucet**

- Open all the hot water faucets to relieve the overheated hot water heater.

- Turn off the gas or electric supply to the heater.

- Let the faucets run until cold water flows from them (this indicates that

the water in the heater is no longer overheated); then close them.

- Call in a professional to make any necessary repairs to the heater's thermostat and pressure relief valve.

# ...Home Emergencies

## Electrical Emergencies

Whether it's a power failure throughout the neighborhood or simply a malfunction in an electrical appliance, at some time you may have to cope with an electrical emergency. It's important to familiarize yourself with the information below *before* the emergency strikes.

You should know how to turn off the electrical power during an emergency, as well as when you need to make electrical repairs. NEVER WORK ON ANY LIVE CIRCUIT, FIXTURE, RECEPTACLE, OR SWITCH. Shut off the power first and test the circuit carefully with a circuit tester (page 22) to be sure it's not live.

You can shut off power to your entire electrical system at the main disconnect (illustrated at right and discussed on pages 152–153); it's almost always at the service entrance panel.

The panel may be located on the exterior of your home below the electric meter or on an inside wall directly behind the meter.

Be sure everyone in your family knows where the service entrance panel is and how to shut off the power in your particular type of disconnect. You should also know how to turn the power back on once it's safe to do so.

Whenever you work with electricity, observe the safety precautions on page 153. If you have questions or concerns about the wiring in your home, call an electrician.

Keep a supply of fuses on hand (if your system is equipped with them) so you can replace any that have blown. Also have flashlights with extra batteries, as well as candles and matches, handy in case of power failures.

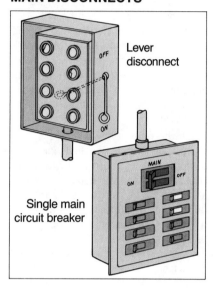

**MAIN DISCONNECTS**

Lever disconnect

Single main circuit breaker

---

### A power failure

If the electricity fails suddenly in your house, determine first if it's just in your home or throughout the neighborhood.

- **If the outage affects the neighborhood,** notify the utility company.

- **If the problem is just in your home,** check for blown fuses or tripped cir-

cuit breakers. Replace any blown fuses or reset any tripped circuit breakers (pages 152–153). If the outage recurs immediately, test for a short circuit or overload (page 155).

- **To retard food spoilage,** don't open the refrigerator or freezer during the outage unless absolutely necessary.

---

### A smoking or sparking appliance

- **Immediately unplug the appliance** or shut off the wall switch that controls it. DON'T touch the appliance itself. Turn off the power to the circuit if you can't unplug the appliance or shut off the wall switch.

- **When the appliance cools off,** take it to a repair shop or ask a service rep-

resentative to come to your home to make the needed repairs.

- **If the appliance catches fire,** get everyone out of the house and call the fire department from a neighbor's house. DON'T use water on an electrical fire.

---

### A smoking or sparking appliance plug

- **Unplug the appliance** (pull by the cord) and allow the plug to cool off. Check the plug and cord for signs of damage; replace them if they're defective (pages 156–157).

- **Check for a blown fuse or tripped circuit breaker;** replace the fuse or reset the tripped breaker (pages 152–153).

- **If the plug and cord are in good condition** and if the circuit is okay, plug another appliance that you know is in good condition into the receptacle. If that plug sparks, replace the receptacle (pages 160–161). If there are no sparks, the original appliance is faulty and should be repaired or replaced.

## Gas Leaks

If you ever smell gas anywhere in your house, take the following precautions:

- Get everyone outside the house immediately.

- Call your gas company or the fire department from a neighbor's house.

- DON'T light a match and DON'T turn on any electrical switch—the danger of fire or explosion is severe. You should leave as many windows and doors open as possible to help clear the gas from the house.

Once everyone is out of the house, you can turn off the main gas supply at the gas shutoff valve (or you can wait for the utility company to do it). The valve is located on the gas inlet pipe next to the gas meter. To shut off the valve, use an adjustable-end wrench to turn the valve a quarter-turn (in either direction) so the valve is perpendicular to the pipe, as shown at right.

DON'T turn the gas back on until you've discovered the source of the problem and corrected it.

In the event of a natural disaster, you may have to turn off the gas supply yourself. Make sure that you and all the members of your family know the location of the gas shutoff valve and how to operate it. It's a good idea to keep a specially labeled adjustable-end wrench in an accessible location so it will be close at hand in the event of an emergency.

### GAS SHUTOFF VALVE

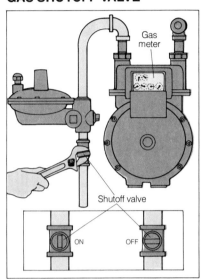

## WHEN SHOULD YOU CALL A PROFESSIONAL?

Deciding whether to tackle a repair project yourself or have a professional do the work involves an honest assessment of three factors: your time, your tools, and your skills. If your assessment convinces you to hire a professional, give careful consideration to your choice.

**Have you the time?** If a repair must be made immediately to protect people or property, such as tightening a loose banister or unclogging a backed-up toilet, and you can't do it right away, call a professional.

Where timing isn't critical, consider the size and scope of the work. A project that might take a professional a day or two could take you two or three weeks, working in your spare time. Weigh the inconvenience of living with a repair in progress against the cost of having the work done immediately. And decide, too, if you have the time to do the job.

**Tools you'll need.** Look into the cost of buying or renting any specialized tools required for a job, particularly if you don't expect to use those tools again. To repair your roof, for example, you may need special roof safety equipment; clearing a main drain clog may call for a power snake. The professional's investment in the right tools for such jobs is part of the fee.

**Your skills.** Be realistic about your knowledge and skills. If you aren't sure how to make a particular repair after reading all you can about it, it probably makes sense to have the job done professionally. The same is true if you're not comfortable tackling the job—working on the roof, for example.

When appearance counts, such as with finish carpentry details or repairs to wood paneling, it may also pay to call a professional if you don't have woodworking experience.

**Choosing a professional.** The best way to find a competent professional is to ask friends or neighbors for recommendations. You can also seek referrals from building materials outlets and community colleges or local groups that offer building classes.

The Yellow Pages lists professional repair services under "Fix-It Services." For a specific repair, look under the appropriate category, such as "Electric Contractor," "Glass," or "Roofing Contractors." Local newspapers often carry ads for individuals specializing in home repairs.

Before you begin working with a professional, establish the fee and be clear about the work included. If you're paying an hourly rate, ask for an estimate of the time needed to complete the job. For a major repair, ask for references and compare the fees and the quality of work of several professionals before making a decision.

# Tools & Materials

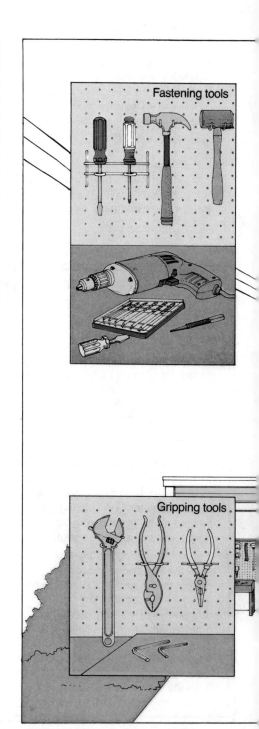

Fastening tools

Gripping tools

Hands can do amazing things. But to be "handy" in home repair means to have a good grasp of tools. Using a high-quality tool that's right for the job—and using it correctly—can help ensure the success of any repair. In this chapter we describe the basic tools and materials you'll need to keep your house in top shape. Organize them by use, as shown below, and store them in a place of their own, so you can easily find whatever you need.

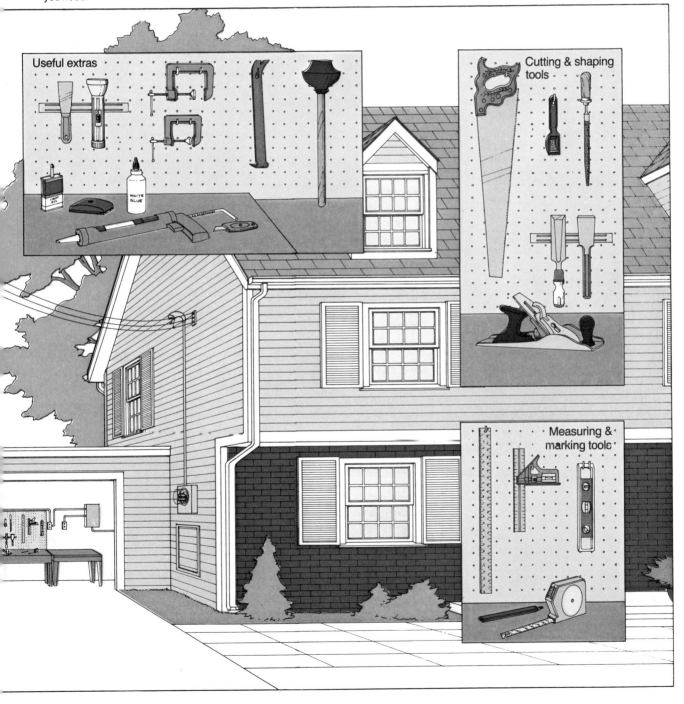

# Tool Selection & Safety

The shelves of a well-stocked hardware store or home improvement center display an impressive and sometimes bewildering array of tools, fasteners, and materials—many intended for a specific use. Often, knowing exactly what you need to make a particular repair can be your key to success. This chapter explains how to choose the right tool or material for your project and how to use it safely and properly.

## Choosing tools & materials

All of the basic tools and materials pictured on page 11 and listed in the chart below, as well as the more specialized ones described in this chapter, have been selected because they're the most versatile type in their category, they can be used in many kinds of home repairs, or they're required for a specific job. Except for the handy electric drill, all the basic tools are hand tools—the only ones you'll need for most simple repairs.

Before you shop, take an inventory of the tools you already have and their condition. Buy tools as the need for them arises—and then buy the best you can afford. Quality tools make the job easier and are safer than bargain-basement varieties. For one-time repairs, you can rent power or specialty hand tools.

Fasteners such as nails and screws, and materials such as sandpaper, caulks and sealants, lubricants, and adhesives are items you may want to keep on hand. An assortment of various-size fasteners and washers, for example, can come in handy when you need to make a minor repair. Buy specialized items for particular jobs as you need them.

This chapter is divided into four sections. The first describes the tools in the basic collection, as well as some special-purpose types in each category. In the second section are descriptions and illustrations of specialized tools for plumbing and electrical repairs. Information on basic fasteners—nails and screws—appears in the third section (for information on special wall fasteners, see page 95). The last section lists some of the basic materials you'll need and explains their uses.

## Using tools safely

Proper techniques and common sense are the basics of working safely with hand and power tools. While you're working, observe these tips:

**Position yourself securely** when working so you won't slip or fall if something unexpected happens. For tips on ladder safety, see page 30.

**Use sharp cutting tools**—they're safer than dull ones because they're easier to control. A dull cutting edge tempts you to apply extra pressure to compensate.

**Wear special safety equipment** when necessary:

- **Safety goggles** with plastic lenses are a must when you're operating power tools, chipping or grinding, working above your head, or striking metal against metal.

- **A dust mask** protects your lungs when you're sanding or doing other dust-producing jobs, or working with insulation.

- **A cartridge respirator** (rented or purchased) provides extra protection from paint and solvent fumes.

- **Gloves** protect your hands from chemicals, insulation, and abrasive or sharp objects.

- **Ear protection** is a good idea when you're working with noisy power tools.

**Work carefully with power tools,** always unplugging a tool when it's not in use (even temporarily) or when you're adjusting it. To guard against electric shock, check cords for cracks and breaks. Plug three-pronged tools into three-pronged, grounded outlets only; don't use an adapter unless you're sure it's properly grounded.

Turn off an overheated tool immediately and let it cool. Always stand on a dry surface when you're working and, to avoid shock, be sure not to touch a water pipe with any part of your body or with the tool you're using.

## THE BASIC TOOL KIT

| Measuring & Marking | Fastening | Cutting & Shaping | Gripping | Useful Extras |
|---|---|---|---|---|
| Steel tape | Electric drill & bits | Crosscut saw | Slip-joint pliers | Utility knife |
| Straightedge | Claw hammer & nailset | Bench chisel | Needlenose pliers | C-clamps |
| Torpedo level | Mallet | Smoothing plane | Adjustable-end wrench | Caulking gun |
| Combination square | Screwdrivers (assorted | Cold chisel | Allen wrench set | Plunger |
| Carpenter's pencil | sizes) | Perforated rasp | | Sanding block |
| |     Standard tip | File | | Putty knife |
| |     Phillips tip | | | Prybar |
| |     Stubby | | | Flashlight |
| | | | | White glue |
| | | | | Light machine oil |

# Basic Tools & Techniques

Having the tools you need on hand encourages you to tackle home repairs when they need to be done. This section is an illustrated guide to eight basic tool categories: measuring and marking tools; hammers and mallets; screwdrivers; drills; saws; pliers and wrenches; chisels, planes, files, and rasps; and special-purpose and miscellaneous items. You'll find out how to match the tool to the job, what to look for in a quality tool, and how to use common tools properly.

In addition to describing tools in the basic tool collection, this section explains tools you'll need for special jobs. You'll learn, for example, that a hammer is not just a hammer, but a claw, a ball peen, or a tack hammer—and each has its own specific use. Then compare your own tool collection with the one presented here so you'll know if you have the appropriate tool for your repair job.

## Measuring & Marking Tools

For the best results when you make repairs, always measure and mark carefully. To be sure everything that should be is straight, square, level, or plumb, use the right tools.

**Straightedges and tapes.** These may be either rigid or flexible:

- A **2-foot steel straightedge** allows you to measure short distances and mark cutting lines.

- A **12-foot flexible steel tape** is for long or inside measurements (see below). Look for a ¾-inch-wide tape with easy-to-read markings, a sturdy case, and a button that locks the tape in the extended position.

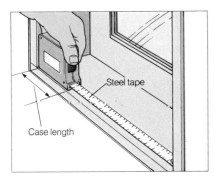

**For an inside measurement,** butt the tape's hook against one edge, the case against the other; measure and add the case length to the measurement.

**Squares.** Use these layout tools to position accurate cutting lines:

- A multipurpose **combination square** helps you check for square, mark boards for crosscutting (page 16), and measure both 45° and 90° angles. Use the spirit level (if your

**SELECTED TOOLS FOR MEASURING & MARKING**

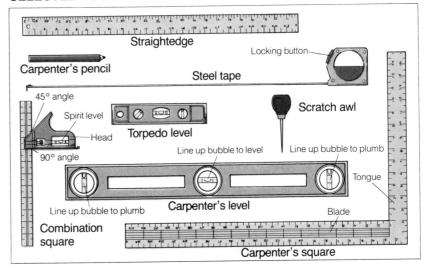

square has one) to check for true horizontal (level) and vertical (plumb). The square's removable sliding head can be tightened anywhere along the blade.

- A longer **carpenter's square** is handy for squaring or marking sheet or wide materials. The edges of the blade and shorter tongue are graduated for inside and outside measurements.

**Markers.** Accurate marking calls for sharp points, whether graphite or metal:

- A flat-sided **carpenter's pencil** won't roll when you put it down and sharpens to a fine, flat edge.

- A **scratch awl** or utility knife scribes a very fine, tight-to-the-line mark.

**Measuring and marking tips.** For accuracy, turn your measuring tool on edge. Mark distances with a V, placing its point exactly at the graduation on the measuring tool. Draw straight lines with a straightedge and an awl or pencil, tilting the tool slightly so the point is flush against the straightedge.

**Levels.** With a level, you can gauge whether a horizontal surface is level or a vertical surface is plumb.

- An **8-inch torpedo level** is good for leveling short spans.

- A **2 or 3-foot aluminum carpenter's level** measures longer spans and affords greater accuracy.

**To test a level for accuracy,** place it on a horizontal surface. Adjust the surface until the bubble is centered between the markings. Then turn the level end for end. The bubble should again be centered.

# ...Basic Tools & Techniques

## Hammers & Mallets

Though hammers and mallets are basically fastening tools, they also have other uses. A claw hammer is helpful for pulling out nails as well as for driving them; you can use a mallet to drive a chisel as well as to tap together a wood joint.

**Claw hammer.** The 16-ounce claw hammer is the most versatile hammer for home use. Look for a drop-forged steel head and a handle of wood, solid steel, or fiberglass (the last two may have cushioned grips that reduce vibration). The slightly crowned (bell) face allows a nail to be driven flush without marring the surface. The claws provide leverage for pulling nails.

CAUTION: Never use a claw hammer to drive a cold or other metal-handled chisel; the hammer's hardened steel face may cause metal chips to fly up.

**Other hammers ... plus mallets.** Use these tools for special jobs:

- A **ball peen hammer**—a special soft-headed steel type—is safe for working on metal, striking a cold chisel (page 19), and driving hardened masonry nails.

- A **tack hammer** with a magnetized head drives small brads and tacks.

- A **mallet**—wood, hard rubber, or plastic—can be used to strike wood-handled or cold chisels, tap dowels into their holes, and tap together stubborn joints.

**Hammering a nail.** Fast, accurate nailing comes with practice. Experiment on pieces of scrap wood until you get a feel for it.

To start a nail, hold it with your fingers near its head. Choke up slightly on the hammer handle and use wrist action to tap the nail partially into the material. If the nail is too short to hold, insert it through lightweight cardboard, hold it with needlenose pliers, or place it between your flattened index and middle fingers.

### HAMMERING TOOLS

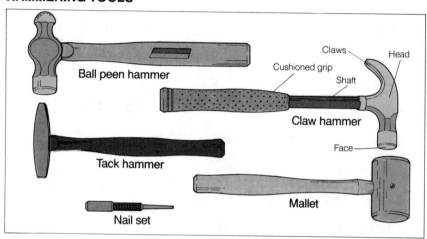

Ball peen hammer

Tack hammer

Nail set

Claws

Head

Cushioned grip

Shaft

Claw hammer

Face

Mallet

After the nail is started, grasp the hammer handle near its end. Keeping your eye on the nail, swing your hammer with the wrist, elbow, or shoulder as the pivot point, depending on the amount of force needed.

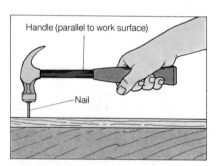

Handle (parallel to work surface)

Nail

**When the hammer hits the nail,** the handle should be parallel to the material you're nailing.

To prevent the wood from splitting when nailing near the end of a board, either blunt the nail tip by holding the head against a wood scrap and striking the tip gently with a hammer, or drill a pilot hole (page 15).

**Removing a nail.** When you're removing a nail with a claw hammer, slip a thin wood scrap under the hammer's head to protect the surface; for a longer nail, substitute a thick wood block for more leverage. Use a prybar (page 20)

when you need to pull out large, deeply driven nails.

CAUTION: Before using a hammer, check it: a loose head or cracked handle can cause injury.

**Using a nailset.** To sink nails so their heads can be concealed, you'll need a nailset. Sizes range from $1/32$ to $5/32$ inch; you can purchase them singly or in sets of assorted sizes.

Drive the nail to $1/8$ inch above the surface to avoid marring the material. Hold a nailset slightly smaller than the nail head firmly against it (see below); using a hammer, strike the nailset squarely to sink the nail. Fill the hole with wood putty or filler.

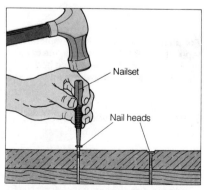

Nailset

Nail heads

**A nailset's tip** should be slightly smaller than the nail head's diameter. Sink the nail a distance equal to its diameter.

# Screwdrivers

A screwdriver that slips when you're driving a screw is both frustrating and dangerous; avoid this by choosing the right screwdriver for the job.

**Types of screwdrivers.** Choose screwdrivers with forged steel blades; plastic handles are the most durable.

- **Standard** (for straight-slotted screws) and **Phillips** (for cross-slotted screws) are basic screwdrivers. The square-shank type gives extra strength.

- A short-handled **stubby screwdriver** and an **offset screwdriver** are handy for work in tight spots.

- A **spiral-ratchet screwdriver** accepts many tips, so it replaces an assortment of screwdrivers. It's also a timesaver when you're driving or removing a number of screws, since pressure on the handle turns the tip.

- A variable-speed, reversible electric drill with a screwdriver bit (page 16) drives and removes screws quickly and effortlessly.

**Driving a screw.** It's easier to drive a screw if you drill a pilot hole first (see below). For maximum turning force,

## ASSORTED SCREWDRIVERS

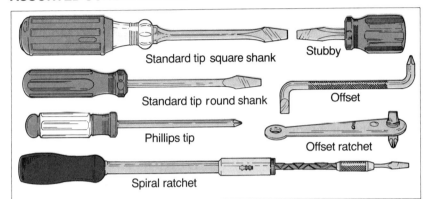

Standard tip square shank · Stubby · Standard tip round shank · Offset · Phillips tip · Offset ratchet · Spiral ratchet

use a screwdriver with the largest handle and longest blade your working space will accommodate. Make sure that the tip fits snugly in the slot (or, for a Phillips screw, the cross-slots) and is the same width as the slot. Lubricate the threads of wood screws with soap or wax before driving them.

**Removing a screw.** If a screw slot is clogged, clean it with the tip of the screwdriver or a nail. To remove a stuck screw, tighten it a quarter-turn; then unscrew and retighten it repeatedly. If that doesn't work, douse the screw with penetrating oil.

**PROFESSIONAL HINT**
MAINTAINING YOUR TOOLS

A light coating of machine oil keeps steel tools from rusting. Remove any rust spots with fine steel wool and oil.

Keep tools sharp for best performance. Sharpen some tools, such as chisels, knives, and planes, on an oilstone (page 20); saws and other tools are best sharpened by a professional.

## DRILLING PILOT HOLES FOR WOOD SCREWS

In all but the softest wood, it's best to drill pilot holes for wood screws.

Choose a drill bit the diameter of the screw's shank and drill only as deep as the length of the unthreaded shank. In hardwoods, also drill a smaller hole below the shank hole for the threads; it should be half as deep as the threaded portion is long. Use a drill bit slightly smaller in diameter than the screw's shaft.

Flathead screws (page 23) can be countersunk to sit flush with the

surface; sometimes the screw will be sunk deeper (counterbored) and the head covered with a dowel plug or with wood putty.

An electric drill's combination bit (page 16) creates pilot, countersink, and counterbore holes in one operation. But you can get the same result using three drill bits—one equal to the screw's shaft diameter (without threads), another equal to the screw's shank diameter, and a third equal to the screw's head diameter.

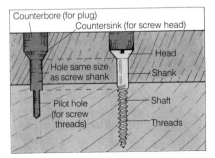

Counterbore (for plug) · Countersink (for screw head) · Head · Hole same size as screw shank · Shank · Pilot hole (for screw threads) · Shaft · Threads

**Drill** to accommodate the shaft, shank, and head of a wood screw; if necessary, counterbore for a plug or putty.

# ...Basic Tools & Techniques

## Drills

Many homeowners now use a portable electric drill instead of hand drills, except for the push drill (useful for starting small holes). Electric drills are classified by the maximum-size bit shank accommodated in their chucks (jaws). A good choice is a ⅜-inch variable-speed, reversible (VSR) drill. Purchase a double-insulated model.

**Drill bits and accessories.** A number of different bits are available for specific purposes:

- **Multipurpose twist bits** have two cutting edges and spiral grooves that lift waste out of the hole as the bits turn. For durability, choose high-speed steel bits.
- **A spade bit** cuts large holes speedily in wood.
- **A combination bit** drills pilot holes for screws (page 15).
- **Screwdriver bits** drive and remove screws.
- **A carbide-tipped masonry bit** (not shown) drills holes in masonry and ceramic tile.

### DRILLS & BITS

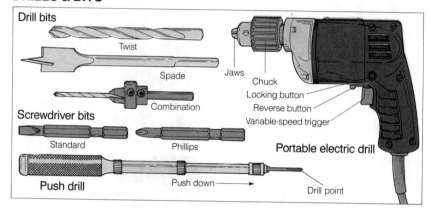

Drill bits — Twist — Spade — Combination — Jaws — Chuck — Locking button — Reverse button — Variable-speed trigger — Screwdriver bits — Standard — Phillips — Portable electric drill — Push drill — Push down — Drill point

Accessories range from sanding discs to paint stirrers. A plastic depth gauge will stop the drill at the correct hole depth.

**Drilling techniques.** Follow these tips for easy, safe drilling:

- **Wear safety goggles** when drilling.
- **Clamp materials** when possible.
- **Match the drill speed to the job:** highest speeds for small bits and soft wood, slowest for large bits and metal. As you drill, apply light pressure; leave the motor running as you remove the bit from the material.
- **Make a center hole** (use a nail point, an awl, or, in metal, a center punch) before drilling to prevent the bit from "skating."
- **Mark the hole depth** on the bit with masking tape or a depth gauge.
- **Release a stuck or binding bit** by turning the drill off, then reversing it.

## Saws

For most home repairs, handsaws are sufficient, though you may want to acquire a portable circular saw as well.

**Types of handsaws.** A saw's function is a product of its shape, blade size, and position and number of teeth. The lower the point size or the fewer the teeth per inch, the rougher but quicker the cut.

- **An 8 or 10-point crosscut saw** with a 26-inch blade, the most versatile choice, cuts boards across the grain; it also cuts plywood.
- **A ripsaw** (not shown), a specialized version of the crosscut, cuts with the grain. A ripsaw isn't essential—you can use a portable circular saw for crosscutting and ripping.

- **A back saw,** often used with a miter box, is for fine finish cuts on molding and other trim.
- **A keyhole saw** (also called a compass saw) makes cutouts in boards or wall panels.
- **A coping saw** cuts fine, accurate curves in thin material; its narrow blade can be inserted in a starter hole near an edge and then attached to the saw frame.
- **An adjustable-frame hacksaw,** which accepts blades of various lengths, cuts metal; it's handy for cutting off nail heads.

**Using a crosscut saw.** Brace a length of board securely on a sawhorse or work table; support a wide plywood panel by placing it across sawhorses bridged by scrap 2 by 4s. Position the board or panel good side up.

Place the saw blade on the waste side of the cutting line so your piece won't be short. (The width of the cut a saw makes—the kerf—is wider than the saw blade's thickness.)

Hold the saw nearly vertical and, resting the blade near its butt end on the board, pull the saw toward you slowly once or twice; guide the saw with the thumb of your free hand (see facing page). Lower the saw angle to 45° and, using a push-pull motion and gradually lengthening the strokes, apply light downward pressure to complete the cut. If the blade veers from the cutting line, bend it back; if it binds, use a nail to hold the kerf open.

Near the end of the cut, reach around and support the waste piece with your free hand; holding the saw vertically, slowly finish the cut.

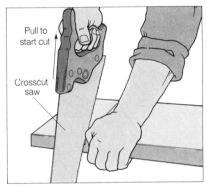

**Grasp the handle of a crosscut saw firmly,** but not tightly. Use your thumb to guide the start of the cut.

## A SELECTION OF SAWS

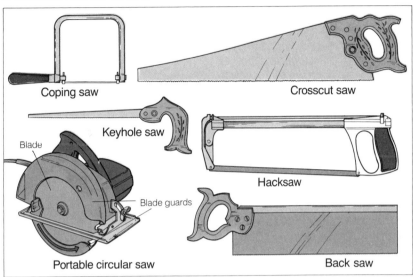

**Using a back saw and miter box.** The back saw's length must match the width of the miter box. The variety of angles you can cut depends on the box. Inexpensive boxes made from hardwood or plastic limit you to cutting 45° or 90° angles; more expensive metal boxes can be set to allow for cutting a greater range of angles.

To use the box, mark the material. (Place a piece of scrap wood under it to protect a wood or plastic box.) Butt the piece against the far side of the box and, holding the wood firmly, pull the saw toward you, tilting the handle up slightly. Level the saw and complete the cut (see below).

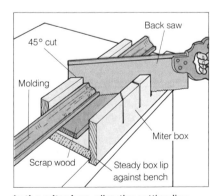

**In the miter box,** align the cutting line with the desired angle, offsetting the piece slightly so the saw's cut will fall on the waste side.

**Using a keyhole saw.** To make a cutout in wood, drill a starter hole, insert the keyhole saw, and start the cut. (Once started, you can switch to a crosscut saw for a long, straight cut.) Use a small 6 to 8-inch-long keyhole saw to cut gypsum wallboard. Here, you don't need a pilot hole; simply tap on the saw's handle end until the blade is started.

**Using a coping saw.** The blade may be positioned with teeth up, down, or to either side; rotate the blade holders to adjust the position.

For cutouts near an edge, slip the blade through a starter hole and then reattach it to the frame. For better control, clamp the material to a sawhorse or a vise. If you use a sawhorse, point the saw's teeth away from the handle and cut on the push stroke. When cutting material held in a vise, point the teeth toward the handle and cut on the pull stroke.

**Using a hacksaw.** Choose higher blade point sizes for thin materials, lower for thick metals. Since hacksaws cut on the push stroke, insert the blade in the frame with the teeth pointing away from the handle. Set the blade tension by tightening the wing nut.

Place the material in a vise. With the steadying hand at the top front of the frame, use both hands to apply downward pressure only on the forward stroke. Keep the blade as square to the work as possible.

When cutting thin sheet metal, sandwich it between two pieces of wood and cut through all three.

**Portable circular saw.** A circular saw cuts much more quickly than a crosscut saw. A good choice is a 7¼-inch saw equipped with both depth and angle adjustment levers and upper and lower blade guards. An all-purpose combination blade comes with the saw; job-specific blades are also available.

Before you start, check the blade's cutting angle and depth. For most cuts, you'll want the blade angled at 90° and protruding only ¹⁄₁₆ to ⅛ inch below the bottom face of the material you're cutting.

Place the material good side down and rest the saw's base plate on it, lining up the blade with the waste side of the cutting line. Release the safety button and let the motor reach speed; then, holding the saw firmly, slowly feed the saw into the material. As you reach the end of the cut, be sure you're in position to support the saw's weight.

CAUTION: Keep the power cord free of the blade and wear safety goggles.

# ...Basic Tools & Techniques

## Pliers & Wrenches

Pliers and wrenches let you reach, grasp, or turn things that your fingers alone can't. When you shop for these tools, pay the price for quality. Look for drop-forged tempered steel tools with jaws that operate smoothly.

**Pliers.** Most of the many types of pliers are used for gripping:

- **Slip-joint pliers** pivot on a bolt and have two jaw positions, one for gripping small objects, the other for large ones. Sizes range from 4 to 10 inches; the 7-inch size is a versatile first choice.

- **Needlenose pliers,** with their thin, tapered jaws, reach spots other pliers can't and are especially useful for making loops in wire. Choose a pair about 6 inches long, with insulated handles.

- **Smooth-jaw diagonal cutting pliers** are handy for cutting wire and small brads.

- **Locking-grip pliers**—straight jaw or, for pipes, curved jaw—perform the functions of pliers, a wrench, and a vise. An adjusting screw sets the jaws to the desired width; handles lock the pliers onto the work.

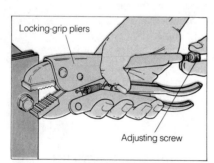

**To clamp locking-grip pliers,** turn the adjusting screw counterclockwise until the jaws grip the object tightly; squeeze the handles together to lock the pliers.

- **Rib-joint pliers** have a multiposition pivot that keeps the jaws parallel to better accommodate objects of different sizes and shapes. Before you exert any pressure on these pliers, be certain that the joint is engaged

### COMMON PLIERS & WRENCHES

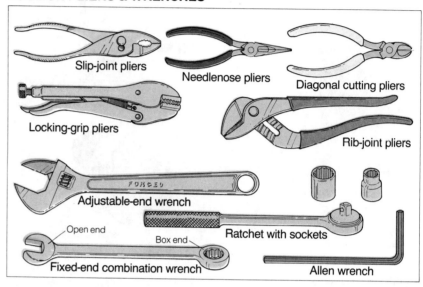

Slip-joint pliers

Needlenose pliers

Diagonal cutting pliers

Locking-grip pliers

Rib-joint pliers

Adjustable-end wrench

FORGED

Open end

Box end

Ratchet with sockets

Fixed-end combination wrench

Allen wrench

so you won't damage the pliers or injure yourself.

**Wrenches.** To grip and turn nuts and bolts, you'll need the following types of wrenches:

- **Adjustable-end wrenches** in 6, 8, and 10-inch lengths meet most household needs. To avoid skinned knuckles, size the wrench to the fastener head, seat the head all the way into the jaws, and tighten the jaws.

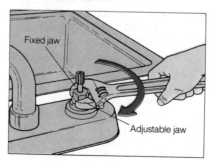

Fixed jaw

Adjustable jaw

**Always turn** an adjustable-end wrench toward its adjustable jaw.

- **Fixed-end wrenches** stand up under a lot of pressure, but you must have a size that exactly matches the fastener's head. These wrenches may be either box-end or open-end

types. Combination wrenches offer both types on one wrench.

- **A ratchet wrench** with interchangeable sockets does what fixed-end wrenches do, but a ratchet wrench is easier to work with and does the job faster. A lever on the handle reverses the turning direction of the socket, so there's no need to remove and refit the socket on the nut or bolt for each turn of the wrench.

- **Allen wrenches** loosen setscrews. You'll need a set that includes a range of sizes. When you're using an Allen wrench, be sure to tighten it by hand only; don't use pliers to apply pressure.

- **Pipe wrenches** are described on page 21.

---

**PROFESSIONAL HINT**
PROTECTING THE FINISH

To prevent the jaws of pliers and wrenches from marring decorative finishes on fasteners, fixtures, and hardware, wrap the jaws with electrician's tape or masking tape.

# Chisels, Planes, Files & Rasps

Chisels, planes, files, and rasps are used to smooth, shape, and cut wood, metal, and other materials.

**Chisels.** These tools are used for cutting and shaping:

- **A bench (bevel-edge) chisel** shapes wood, marks cut lines, and cuts mortises. Choose a blade slightly narrower than the area you're working.

- **Cold chisels** cut metal, masonry, or ceramic tile. Drive them with a mallet or ball peen (*never* a claw) hammer and wear safety goggles.

**Using a chisel.** Be sure to observe the following precautions:

- **Keep both hands positioned** *behind* the chisel's cutting edge; never cut toward yourself.

- **To mark cut lines or remove chunks of wood,** tap a plastic-handled chisel with a hammer, a wood-handled chisel with a soft-faced mallet.

- **For a shallow cut,** work with the beveled edge down. Turn bevel up for deep cuts. When marking a cut line or cutting up to a line, the bevel should face the waste material.

- **To cut a mortise** with a chisel, see page 71.

- **Keep your chisel sharp** so it won't skip. Hone it, beveled edge down, on an oilstone (page 20), holding the chisel at an angle that matches the bevel. Turn the chisel over and, keeping it flat against the stone and using a circular motion, remove any burrs.

**Planes.** These tools smooth and trim wood by removing it in very thin layers (see page 71 for instructions):

- **Bench planes,** used for with-the-grain finishing, include jack, jointer, and smoothing planes; the last is best for general use.

- **Block planes** shape and smooth end grain.

## SMOOTHING, SHAPING & CUTTING TOOLS

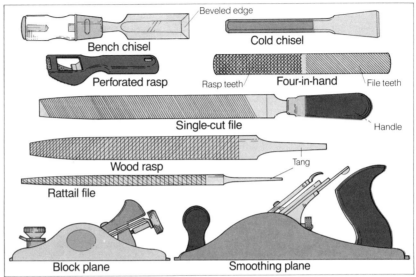

**Adjusting a plane.** To adjust a bench plane, remove the lever cap, cap iron, and cutting iron (blade). Loosen the screw and align the irons so the cutting iron projects about $\frac{1}{16}$ inch; tighten the screw and reassemble. Turn the plane over and sight down its sole. If the blade is out of square, use the lateral adjustment lever. To adjust blade exposure, turn the depth adjustment nut.

Block plane adjustments vary according to the model.

CAUTION: A dull cutting iron is dangerous. To sharpen it, stroke it on an oilstone (page 20) and bevel it down.

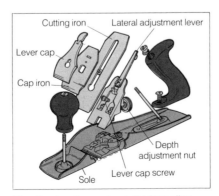

**To adjust a plane,** check the iron alignment and blade squareness and projection.

**Files and rasps.** Generally, files abrade both metal and wood; rasps are for wood only. Rasps differ from files in that they have individual, triangular teeth.

- **A perforated rasp** both removes and smooths wood, and, with the proper blade, gypsum wallboard, soft metals, and plastic.

- **A half-round single-cut file** and the coarser double-cut file (not shown) smooth both wood and metal.

- **A rattail file,** thin and rounded, smooths inside curves and holes.

- **A wood rasp** removes material from soft wood.

- **A versatile four-in-hand** is half-file, half-rasp.

**Using files and rasps.** Files and rasps cut on the forward stroke; lift them off the work on the return. With one hand on the handle and the other on the end, apply even, downward pressure. Keep the tool level and at a slight angle to the work.

NOTE: These tools are sold without handles. When you purchase a file or rasp, buy a handle to cover the sharp end, or tang.

# ...Basic Tools & Techniques

## Other Useful Tools & Equipment

Though you may not think of some of the items on this page as tools, you'd be hard pressed to complete many home repair and maintenance jobs without them.

**Knives and cutters.** This category includes tools both for cutting and for patching:

- **A utility knife** cuts everything from string to ceiling tile. Choose a metal one that has a button to retract the blade when it's not in use.

- **Putty knives** and taping knives (page 87) apply patching material and adhesive, and handle scraping chores. Choose a flexible taping knife about an inch wide and a narrow, stiff-bladed putty knife.

- **Tin snips** cut sheet metal or window screening; their blades may be straight or curved (use the curved ones for making irregular cuts). Don't use tin snips to cut nails or wire.

- **A glass cutter** with a small cutting wheel at its tip is used to score glass for cutting.

**Clamping devices.** Secure materials for cutting and hold glued materials while they dry with this equipment:

- **C-clamps**—a pair of 4-inch steel ones—are basic. Add other sizes to your collection as jobs require.

- **A bench vise** with serrated jaws clamps and holds pieces of wood as well as metal. Be sure to pad the jaws with scrap wood to protect your work when necessary. If you'll be using wood a lot, a woodworker's vise (not shown) is preferred.

**Sanding block.** For finishing, insert sandpaper in a rubber or plastic sanding block, or wrap the paper around a 2 by 4 wood block and secure it with staples.

**Prybars.** These tools are essential for demolition jobs both inside and outside your house:

### USEFUL EXTRAS

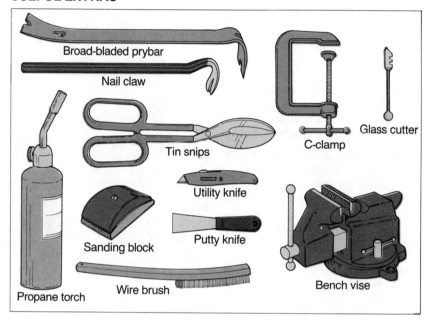

Broad-bladed prybar
Nail claw
Tin snips
Propane torch
Sanding block
Wire brush
Utility knife
Putty knife
Glass cutter
C-clamp
Bench vise

- **A nail claw** pulls large nails with its curved claw, saving wear and tear on your claw hammer.

- **A broad-bladed prybar** or a larger wrecking bar removes wall materials from studs, pulls large nails, and does a multitude of other removal and demolition jobs.

**Caulking gun.** For general maintenance and repairs, a half-barrel caulking gun (shown on page 11) that accepts disposable drop-in cartridges is best. See page 49 for details on loading and use.

**Staple gun.** Attach ceiling tiles, insulation, lightweight paneling, and window screening with a heavy-duty staple gun (not shown). Especially handy is one that accepts staples of various lengths.

**Propane torch.** To thaw frozen pipes or loosen resilient flooring for removal, you'll need a propane torch. Follow the manufacturer's instructions for lighting and using the torch. Protect the surrounding area with a fireproof shield.

**Oilstone.** To keep your tools' cutting edges sharp, use an oilstone at least 6 inches long with a fine and a coarse side (not shown). Apply a little light oil, preferably cutting oil, to the surface during use to keep the pores from clogging. Store the stone carefully; oilstones break easily.

**Other aids.** These miscellaneous items will come in handy:

- **A lantern flashlight or a trouble light** (not shown) frees your hands for work.

- **A wire brush** removes flaking paint, rust, and grime from metal.

- **Disposable plastic drop cloths** (not shown) are handy for painting jobs, but they don't hold up very well. Underlay them with canvas cloths for better protection.

- **Extension cords** (not shown) are often necessary when you're using power tools. Match the gauge and length of the cord to the tool's amperage rating (check the owner's manual).

# Specialized Tools

## Plumbing Tools & Materials

Tools you'll need for plumbing repairs include some that are part of the basic tool collection or suggested additions to it, as well as special tools and materials used specifically for fixing pipes and fixtures.

Among the basic tools are standard and Phillips screwdrivers for faucet screws, adjustable-end and open-end wrenches for nuts and bolts, and rib-joint pliers to remove some fittings. You may also need an offset screwdriver with standard and Phillips tips, a set of Allen wrenches for setscrews, and a hacksaw blade to cut off rusted bolts and nuts.

Specialized plumbing tools fall into three categories: drain-clearing tools, wrenches, and job-specific tools. You'll also want to have certain materials handy for temporary and permanent repairs.

**Drain-clearing tools.** These three tools are used to clear plumbing clogs in fixtures and drains:

- **A plunger** uses alternate pressure and suction to dislodge clogs in drains and plumbing fixtures. The funnel-cup type, shown at right, is designed for toilets, but it folds flat for drains. For tips on its use, see page 122.

- **A snake** (also called a drain-and-trap auger), available in lengths from 10 to 75 feet, stretches into a drain to clear a deep blockage. Locking the snake's thumbscrew and turning the handle drives the corkscrew-like tip into the clog.

- **A closet auger** is designed specifically for toilets; its bent shaft guides the 3 to 6-foot cable into the toilet's trap (page 132).

**Wrenches.** In addition to the wrenches mentioned above, you may need some more specialized ones.

- **A spud wrench,** with its wide, smooth jaws, is useful for unfastening extra-large nuts and fittings on sinks and some toilets.

### TOOLS FOR PLUMBING REPAIRS

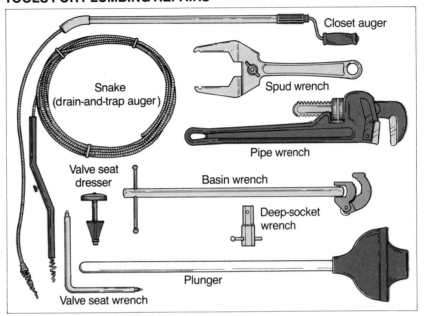

Snake (drain-and-trap auger) · Closet auger · Spud wrench · Pipe wrench · Valve seat dresser · Basin wrench · Deep-socket wrench · Plunger · Valve seat wrench

- **Pipe wrenches** have adjustable, serrated jaws for gripping fittings and galvanized or cast iron pipe. Always use them in pairs on threaded pipe, as shown below: one wrench holds one section of pipe stationary; the other turns the pipe or fitting you want to tighten or loosen.

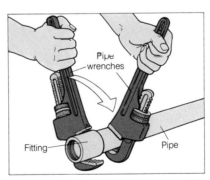

Pipe wrenches · Fitting · Pipe

**Pipe wrench at right holds** the pipe while the one at left tightens the fitting. To loosen the fitting, reverse the position and direction of the wrenches.

- **A basin wrench's** long handle reaches out-of-the-way couplings and nuts. Its reversible jaw can tighten or loosen nuts.

**Job-specific tools.** Certain jobs call for very specialized tools:

- **A valve seat wrench and valve seat dresser** are tools you may need if you have compression faucets (pages 113–114). The former has both a hexagonal and a square end to remove valve seats; the latter cleans corroded seats and smooths pitted, nonremovable seats.

- **A deep-socket wrench** removes the hard-to-reach packing nut on a tub compression faucet (page 120).

**Materials.** It's a good idea to keep certain items for plumbing repairs on hand. Plastic, electrical, or auto hose tape can be useful for a temporary repair of a leaky pipe or trap; to protect fittings, wrap tool jaws with electrical tape.

For permanent repairs, check your faucet sizes and stock assorted washers, brass screws, O-rings, and packing. You'll also need pipe joint compound to ensure a tight seal between threaded pipes and fittings. Keep penetrating oil handy for loosening stubborn or "frozen" connections.

# ...Specialized Tools

## Electrical Tools & Materials

For simple electrical repairs, you'll need basic tools, as well as a few specialized ones. Standard and Phillips screwdrivers are very helpful. Use needlenose pliers (preferably with insulated handles) to form wires into loops, diagonal cutting pliers to snip wire in tight spots, and Allen wrenches to turn setscrews. Have a flashlight or trouble light, too, since you may need to turn off the power to the room where you're working.

Specialized electrical tools include those for wires and testing circuits. You'll also want to stock assorted materials.

**Wire-handling tools.** Special tools often make working on wire easier:

- **A multipurpose tool** cuts wire and bolts, crimps wire, and strips wire insulation.

- **A wire stripper** removes wire insulation. Set the adjustment screw to the correct gauge, place the stripper on the wire at an angle, close the handles, and rock the tool.

- **Electrician's pliers** (also called lineman's pliers) are for gripping and to cut and twist wires.

**Testing devices.** With these devices you can determine if the power is on and if it's flowing properly:

- **A circuit tester** (120 to 240-volt range) tests whether a circuit is live or dead. Check it by grasping the tester's leads by the insulated areas *only* and, on a receptacle, for example, inserting the probes into the slots (see at right). If the tester's bulb lights, the circuit is live. NEVER WORK ON ANY LIVE CIRCUIT, FIXTURE, RECEPTACLE, OR SWITCH. Shut off the power to the circuit and test it again before doing any electrical work.

- **A battery-operated continuity tester** is used with the power off to test continuity of a circuit, switch, appliance, lamp (see at right), or fuse. To check

### TOOLS FOR ELECTRICAL REPAIRS

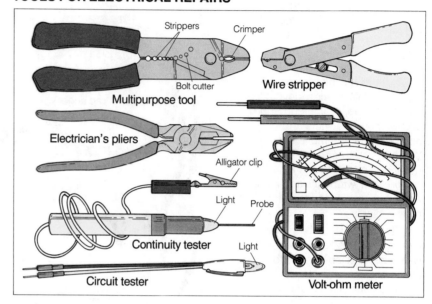

a cartridge fuse (page 152), for example, touch the probe to one contact, the alligator clip to the other. If the bulb on the tester lights, the fuse is not blown and can be used.

CAUTION: Shut off the power to the circuit or unplug the device you're testing before positioning the probe.

- **A volt-ohm meter** does the job of both testers and also measures voltage and ohms (resistance). It's use-

ful for testing appliances as well as electrical devices such as the transformer on a doorbell (page 162). For instructions on using the meter, read the owner's manual. CAUTION: Shut off the power when checking resistance or continuity.

**Materials.** If you have fuses, stock replacement ones of the proper type and amperage rating (page 152). Also, keep wire nuts of various sizes and plastic electrical tape on hand.

### TESTING ELECTRICAL CIRCUITS

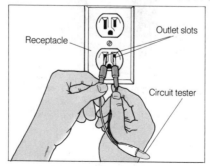

**Check a receptacle** with a circuit tester before doing any work. If the bulb lights, the electricity is still on. You must shut it off before working on the receptacle.

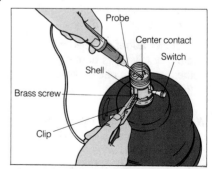

**With the lamp unplugged,** check its switch with a continuity tester. If the tester lights when the switch is turned on, the switch works.

# Fasteners

---

## Nails

Nails are quick and simple fasteners. Size—specified in "pennies" and abbreviated "d"—indicates length and diameter, and ranges from 2d (1 inch) to 60d (6 inches). When possible, use a nail ¼ inch shorter than the combined thickness of the materials it's fastening.

**Nails for general use.** Choose from among the following types of nails:

- **Common nails and thinner but similar box nails,** recommended for general use, have flat, broad heads that won't pull through. Coated ones have more holding power than uncoated ones.

- **Small-headed finishing or casing nails** are suitable for cabinets and trim. Casing nails hold better, but finishing nails leave a smaller hole.

- **Brads** (not shown) are tiny finishing nails used to fasten thin moldings and paneling.

**Specialized nails.** These improve holding power in certain applications:

- **Spiral-shank and annular-ring nails** have grooved shafts that act like screws for fastening flooring and subflooring.

- **Wallboard (or drywall) nails** (not shown) are used to hang gypsum wallboard.

- **Shingle nails** (not shown) are used to attach wood siding and roofing shingles.

- **Masonry nails,** made from hardened steel, penetrate and hold in masonry. When you drive these nails, wear safety goggles and use a ball peen hammer.

- **Roofing nails** have large, flat heads that resist pull-through. To prevent corrosion, use aluminum, not galvanized, nails on aluminum roofs and siding.

### TYPES OF NAILS

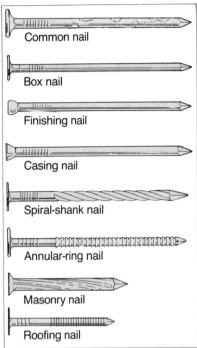

Common nail
Box nail
Finishing nail
Casing nail
Spiral-shank nail
Annular-ring nail
Masonry nail
Roofing nail

---

## Screws

When you need plenty of holding power, choose screws. They can be tightened or removed without damaging the material and, providing you make a pilot hole, they won't split wood.

Screws come in lengths ranging from ¼ to 6 inches and in diameters from #0 (1/16 inch) to #24 (almost ⅜ inch). Choose a screw that's ¼-inch shorter than the combined thickness of the pieces being fastened. In general, the thicker the diameter for a given length of screw, the greater its holding ability.

**Wood screws.** These screws have smooth shanks and are threaded about ⅔ of their length. Available with either straight-slot, Phillips (cross-slot), or one-way heads, wood screws come in three configurations:

- **Flathead screws** can be driven flush with the surface or counterbored (page 15) and concealed.

- **Roundhead screws** have heads that sit atop the surface and are the choice when the top piece is too thin to permit countersinking.

- **Ovalhead screws,** usually brass or chrome finished, are suitable for decorative applications.

Washers—flush for flathead screws, flat for roundhead screws, and countersink for ovalhead screws—can be used with any of these screws.

**Other types of screws.** These are for special applications:

- **Lag screws,** with square or hexagonal heads, range from 1 to 6 inches long and from ¼ to ½ inch in diameter. They offer extra holding power in wood. Turn them with a wrench.

- **Sheet-metal screws and self-tapping screws** have pan or round heads and threads from head to tip.

### TYPES OF SCREWS

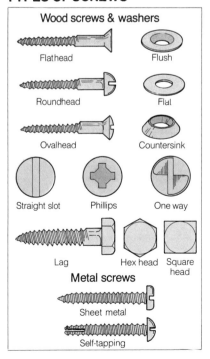

Wood screws & washers

Flathead      Flush
Roundhead     Flat
Ovalhead      Countersink
Straight slot  Phillips  One way
Lag    Hex head   Square head

Metal screws

Sheet metal
Self-tapping

# Basic Materials

Some simple home repairs, such as patching cracks in a wall or sealing air leaks around windows, require few tools. But they do involve choosing the appropriate materials. The information below will help you choose abrasives, adhesives, caulks, sealants, lubricants, and patching materials. Buy good-quality materials—they make the time and energy you invest worthwhile.

**Abrasives.** When you're removing small amounts of wood or paint, or smoothing a surface, you need an abrasive—steel wool or sandpaper. Steel wool can be used on wood or metal; grades run from 3 (coarse) to 0000 (superfine). Sandpaper comes in a variety of types (see chart below) and grades. The type is usually labeled on the backing, along with the following specifications:

- **Grade** is indicated by a grit number from 12 to 600; 50 (very coarse) to 220 (very fine) is the common range. Silicon carbide is available up to 600 grit. Coarse grades are for rough work, fine grades for finishing.

- **Backing** may be cloth or paper. Cloth-backed types can be used wet or dry; paper-backed types are usually for dry-sanding.

- **Coat**—open or closed—indicates grit density. Open-coat types resist clogging, but they cut more slowly than closed types.

**Adhesives.** Ranging from all-purpose white glue to special mastics, adhesives vary in strength, water-resistance, ability to fill gaps, and setting time (see chart on facing page).

**Caulks and sealants.** Caulking and sealing compounds are used indoors and outdoors for sealing joints and cracks. Most are available in drop-in cartridges for use with a caulking gun (page 49). These compounds vary in both price and composition; generally, the best are also the most expensive.

For information about types of caulks and sealants, see the chart on the facing page. NOTE: The chart lists major categories of caulks and sealants; many types are available within some categories. To choose the best type for a particular job, consult a building supply center.

**Lubricants.** You'll use these lubricants over and over again:

- **Penetrating oil** loosens rusted and balky screws and nuts. It's especially helpful for freeing stubborn plumbing connections.

- **Light machine oil** silences squeaky hinges and lubricates and protects tools; use it with steel wool to remove rust.

- **Powdered graphite** (without oil) is ideal for lubricating locks, because it doesn't attract dirt and dust.

- **Silicone spray** is an all-purpose lubricant that doesn't congeal during cold weather.

- **Paraffin wax** helps windows and sliding doors glide more easily and makes screws easier to drive.

- **Plumber's grease** is handy for lubricating some plumbing parts.

**Patching materials.** These materials are essential for both indoor and outdoor repairs:

- **Wood putty,** available in stick or paste form, fills gouges, cracks, and nail holes in wood. Putty can be sanded and painted over. You can buy putty in colors to match most woods, but you may have to add coloring to it to blend with a particular finish.

- **Patching plaster** fills large or deep holes and cracks in plaster and gypsum wallboard.

- **Spackling compound** fills small indentations, narrow cracks, and nail holes in walls.

You can also buy specially formulated patching materials, such as glazing putty for window glass; roofing cement; vinyl, epoxy, or latex concrete patch; grout for ceramic tile joints; stucco patching compound; butyl gutter seal; mortar for brick joints; and plastic metal fillers.

## ABRASIVES

| Type | Characteristics | Uses |
|---|---|---|
| **Sandpaper** | | |
| **Silicon carbide** (O/C) | Hard, sharp; cuts well but is brittle; can be used wet (black) or dry | Good for wet-sanding soft metals, joint compound on gypsum wallboard, glass, and plastic; good for dry-sanding wood and finishes on hardwood |
| **Aluminum oxide** (O/C) | Durable, sharp | All-purpose abrasive for wood and soft metals |
| **Garnet** (O/C) | Hard, sharp; medium quality | Good for wood |
| **Flint** (O) | Quick to dull; clogs easily | Removes finish from heavily painted or varnished wood |
| **Emery** (O) | Durable | Polishes metal (use with oil) |
| **Steel wool** | Flexible; very gentle (finest grades); can be used dry or with oil | Removes rust from metal, paint from glass; good for rubbing down finish coats on wood |

O = Open coat; C = Closed coat

## ADHESIVES

| Type | Characteristics | Uses |
|---|---|---|
| **White** (common household) **glue** (polyvinyl acetate) | Rigid bond; can be sanded; softens above 150°F; not waterproof | Good for general home repairs, except for metal and high-heat or high-moisture applications; bonds indoor wood joints (must be clamped); fills gaps between materials |
| **All-purpose** (household) **cement** | Moderately strong bond; dries fast; water-resistant | Good for bonding wood, some vinyl, metal, leather, and paper products |
| **Yellow** (carpenter's or wood) **glue** (aliphatic resin) | Rigid bond; dries clear and can be sanded; heat-resistant; not waterproof | Bonds wood (must be clamped); fills gaps between materials |
| **Contact cement** | Water-resistant; bonds on contact | Bonds thin materials to a base |
| **Epoxy resin** | Strong, rigid, permanent bond; waterproof | Different types available for bonding most like and un-like materials; some types patch water pipes, fill gaps between materials |
| **Urethane glue** | Strong, permanent bond (but not as strong as epoxy); waterproof | Good for bonding wood, metal, vinyl, and ceramic; fills gaps between materials |
| **Hot-melt glue** | Flexible bond; waterproof; applied with an electric glue gun | Bonds most materials; good for joints that can't be clamped; fills gaps between materials |
| **Mastic** (latex or solvent base) | Water-resistant (some are waterproof) | Different types available for bonding resilient, com-position, wood, and ceramic tile; resilient sheet material; paneling; and wallboard |
| **Resorcinol glue** (marine resin) | Strong, rigid, permanent bond; waterproof; dries dark | Good for bonding wood in high-moisture applications (must be clamped); fills gaps between materials |
| **Plastic resin glue** | Strong bond; water-resistant (but not as water-resistant as resorcinol) | Use on wood for a structural bond (must be clamped) |
| **Instant glue** | Instant, strong bond | Bonds nonporous materials such as metal, glass, porcelain, ceramic, rubber, and most plastics. CAUTION: Bonds quickly to skin |

## CAULKS & SEALANTS

| Type | Characteristics | Uses |
|---|---|---|
| **Elastomers** | | |
|   **Silicones** | Long-lasting, elastic seal; waterproof; not paintable, but available in colors | For interior and exterior use on metal, glass, masonry, tile, porcelain, and ceramic |
|   **Polysulfides** | Long-lasting, elastic seal; waterproof; avail-able in colors | Good for sealing cracks and for glazing; adheres to wood, masonry, glass, and metal |
|   **Polyurethanes** | Long-lasting seal; foam application | Seals interior and exterior cracks (use with primer on unpainted wood and masonry) |
| **Butyl rubber** | Very flexible seal (may shrink); water-resistant; paintable, but messy to apply | Joins like materials inside and outside; bonds well to metal |
| **Acrylic latex** | Somewhat flexible seal; paintable; avail-able in colors; adheres to damp surfaces, but not for use on permanently wet areas | Good for narrow interior joints and for exterior joints around painted doors and windows |
| **Nonacrylic latex** | Not very flexible seal; waterproof | Use on stable interior joints only |
| **Oil base** (includes rope caulk) | Low performance; dries hard | Use for temporary interior and exterior repairs, and on stable interior cracks |

# Roofing & Siding

Built-up roofing

Protecting your home against the effects of wind, rain, heat, and cold is a tough job requiring tough materials, in this case a concrete foundation, wood and brick siding, and an asphalt shingle roof. All are at the mercy of the elements. It's no wonder, then, that repairs become necessary in time. In this chapter, you'll learn just what steps to take.

# The Roof

Most homeowners don't pay much attention to their roof until rain or melting snow starts to leak through it—then it demands immediate action. But if you periodically inspect your roof, you can correct minor problems before they become serious enough to cause damage.

Understanding the structure of your roof (see below) is the first step toward diagnosing possible problems. On the facing page, you'll find directions for inspecting your roof from the inside and outside. If your inspection indicates that repairs are necessary, refer to pages 31–38.

CAUTION: Tile and slate roofs are extremely slippery, and the materials can break easily; metal and plastic roofs also tend to be slippery. If your house has one of these out-of-the-ordinary roofs, it's best to leave inspection and repairs to a professional roofing contractor.

## Understanding Roofing Structure

A roof protects a house from damage by the elements, especially water. Roofs are designed to shed water; the parts comprising a roof combine to direct water off the roof and away from the house.

### Anatomy of a roof

A typical roof (see illustration at right) begins with a framework of rafters which supports a roof deck (sometimes called a subroof) consisting of sheathing and underlayment. The roof deck, in turn, provides a nailing base for the roof surface material.

**The roof deck.** Though the type of roof deck used can vary depending on the roof surface material, most decks have both sheathing and underlayment.

Sheathing, the material that provides the nailing base for the roof surface material, ranges from solid plywood to fiberboard to open sheathing (used with wood shakes).

Sandwiched between the sheathing and the surface material is the underlayment, usually roofing felt. A heavy, fibrous black paper saturated with asphalt, roofing felt is thick enough to resist water penetration from outside, yet thin enough to allow moisture from inside the attic to escape.

**The roof surface.** The material on the roof must be able to withstand wind, rain, snow, hail, and sun. A wide variety of roof surface materials is available—the different types are discussed at right and on pages 31–33.

The surface of the roof is often broken by angles and protrusions, all

**ANATOMY OF A ROOF**

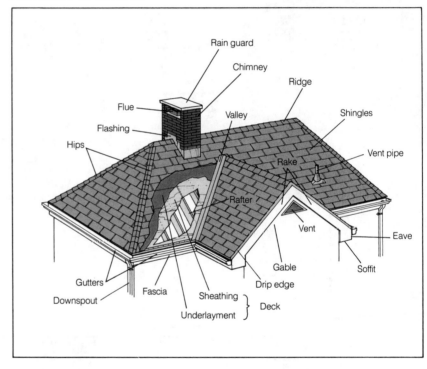

of which require weatherproofing—usually provided by the flashing. Made from malleable metal or plastic, flashing appears as the drip edge along the eaves and rakes of a roof, the collars around ventilation and plumbing pipes, the valleys between two roof planes, and the "steps" along a chimney or dormer. Less obvious flashing also protects other breaks in the roof, such as around some solar panels and skylights. At the roof edges, metal, wood, or vinyl gutters catch water runoff and channel it to the ground via the downspouts, which direct water away from the house and into the soil.

### Types of roofing materials

Roofing varies widely in size, shape, and material. Traditional sloping roofs are usually covered with overlapping layers of asphalt shingles, wood shingles or shakes, or tile, though you can find such roofs covered with slate, aluminum, or galvanized steel.

Flat or low-sloping roofs are most often surfaced with alternating layers of roofing felt and asphalt, with a layer of gravel on top. These are known as built-up, or tar-and-gravel, roofs. Some flat roofs are covered with insulating polyurethane foam.

## Inspecting for Damage

It's a good idea to inspect and repair your roof in autumn, before the hard weather hits. Then examine the roof again in spring to assess whatever damage may have occurred during the winter. If you discover problems, make the necessary repairs, following the instructions on pages 31–38.

**Inspecting from inside.** Begin an inspection in the attic, using a strong flashlight, a thin screwdriver, a knife, and a piece of chalk to examine the ridge beam, rafters, and sheathing. Look for water stains, dark-colored areas of wet wood, moisture, and soft spots that may indicate dry rot. Mark the wet spots with chalk so you can find them easily later on.

If it's necessary to remove fiberglass insulation batts to examine the sheathing, be sure to wear loose clothing, gloves, goggles, and a respirator for protection.

Next, turn off any lights. If you see any holes above you, drive nails or poke wire through them so they'll be visible from the roof's surface. (In a wood shingle roof, small shafts of light coming in at an angle indicate cracks that may swell shut when the shingles are wet.)

**Inspecting from outside.** When you examine the roof from outdoors, evaluate the condition of the roof structure, surface material, flashings, eaves, and gutters.

To check the roof structure, stand back from the house and look at the lines of the ridge and rafters. The ridge line should be perfectly horizontal, and the line of the rafters, which you can assess by looking along the plane of each roof section, should be straight. If either sags, call in a professional contractor—you may have a structural problem.

Next, inspect the roof's surface. Before climbing up on your roof, be sure to read the safety tips on page 30. If you're at all nervous about going up on the roof, make the inspection from a ladder, using a pair of binoculars. Don't walk on the roof any more than is absolutely necessary; you can easily cause more damage.

Inspect the flashings for rust spots and broken seals along the edges. If you have metal gutters and downspouts, look for rust spots and holes.

Then examine the roof surface for signs of wear, loose or broken nails, or curled, broken, or missing shingles.

Use a knife and screwdriver to test the boards along the eaves and rakes. Scrape out any damage caused by dry rot, treat with a wood preservative, and fill the holes with wood putty. If the damage is extensive, replace the boards and finish them to match the existing areas.

## Locating a Roof Leak

Roof leaks usually appear during storms, when you can't make permanent repairs. But you can take some steps to temporarily divert or halt the flow of water, as shown below.

Generally, leaks begin at a roof's most vulnerable spots—at flashings, where shingles are damaged or missing, in valleys, or at eaves. Often, the water shows up far from its point of origin after working its way through layers of roofing materials and down rafters to collect in a puddle on the attic or bedroom floor.

During a storm, trace the course of water from where it's dripping through the ceiling to where it's coming through the roof. Drive a nail or poke wire through the hole so you can find the hole later when you get up on the roof.

Once the roof is dry enough, check it thoroughly, looking for weak spots that indicate a source for the leak. Keep in mind that the point where a nail or wire is poking through may be below the actual source. Make permanent repairs as described on pages 31–33.

## TEMPORARY REPAIRS FOR A LEAKY ROOF

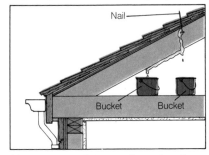

**Water diverter.** Drive a nail or poke wire up through the hole to direct some of the water into a bucket directly below; position a second bucket to catch runoff.

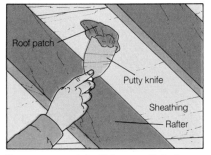

**Emergency patch.** Using a putty knife or caulking gun, apply special roof patch liberally to the hole from inside. Work the compound in thoroughly so it adheres.

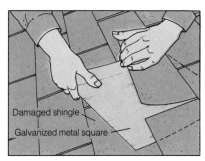

**Temporary shingle.** When the roof is dry, slide a 2-foot square of galvanized sheet metal under the row of shingles above the missing or damaged shingle.

# WORKING SAFELY ON THE ROOF

Before venturing up a ladder to repair roofing, siding, windows, or gutters, it's important to know and observe the following safety precautions.

## Ladder safety

Ladders for long reaches range from straight wooden types to aluminum extension ladders (one that extends to 20 feet is adequate for most houses). Be sure your ladder is strong, yet light enough to be handled easily.

Here are some tips for using a ladder safely:

- **Inspect your ladder** for cracks or weaknesses before you lean it against the house.

- **Place the ladder base** on firm, level ground at a measured distance from the side of the house, as shown below.

- **Get on and off the ladder** by stepping onto the center of the rung. Use both hands to grip the rails (not the rungs). If the ladder wobbles, back down and reposition it.

- **Keep your hips between the ladder rails.** Don't lean out to reach an area; instead, reposition the ladder.

- **Make sure that only one person** stands on a ladder at a time.

**To position a ladder:** 1) Set the base against the wall. 2) Walk the ladder into an upright position. 3) Move the base outward. 4) Set the base at a distance from the wall equal to ¼ the ladder's length.

- **Install rubber safety shoes** (available at home improvement centers) on the ladder feet if the ladder is to stand on a slick surface.

- **Don't stand on the top two rungs** of a ladder. If you're repairing a roof, at least two rungs of the ladder should extend above the eaves so you can step directly onto the roof.

- **Be sure the rung hooks of an extension ladder** are locked in place and that no section is extended more than three-quarters of its length.

- **Pull materials up a ladder** with a rope and have a place to store them at the top.

## Roof safety

Working on a roof requires extra caution. The surface is usually slick, sloped, and well above the ground.

**Safe work rules.** Below are some precautions to observe when you need to make roof repairs:

- **Don't walk on a roof** any more than is absolutely necessary; you may cause more damage. Don't walk on tile and slate roofs at all—they're slippery and breakable.

- **Let a professional make any repairs** on a steeply pitched roof— one that slopes more than 25° or rises more than 6 inches vertically for every 12 horizontal inches (a 6 in 12 slope).

- **Wear loose, comfortable clothing** and clean, dry, rubber-soled shoes with good ankle support.

- **Work on the roof only in dry, calm, warm weather.** A wet roof can be treacherously slick; a sudden wind can knock you off balance.

- **Never get on the roof when lightning threatens.**

- **Keep children and pets** away from the work area.

- **Be careful not to put your weight** on brittle or old roofing materials and rotted decking.

- **Stay well away from power lines** and be sure neither your body nor your equipment comes into contact with them.

**Special safety equipment.** The standard safety devices illustrated below help to distribute your weight evenly and provide secure footing. They're available from tool rental companies.

- **A metal ladder bracket** allows you to hook a ladder over the ridge.

- **Toe board jacks** nailed to the roof support you with a 2 by 6 plank. (Use strong, straight-grained lumber no longer than 10 feet unless you support the middle with another jack.) The jacks have notches in them so they can be slipped off the nails. Secure the jacks with nails long enough to penetrate the sheathing and rafters (to prevent leaks, set and caulk the nails when you're finished).

- **An angled seat board** lets you sit on a level surface while working. The angles on the sides must match the slope of your roof.

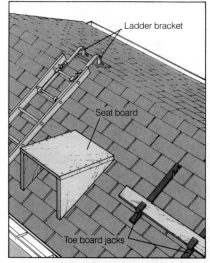

**Safety equipment** for working on roofs includes a metal ladder bracket, toe board jacks, and an angled seat board.

# Asphalt Shingles

Asphalt shingles are composed of mats made from organic or fiberglass material impregnated with asphalt, in which are embedded colored mineral granules. Organic-base asphalt shingles, also called composition shingles, have a felt mat made from wood and paper fibers. Fiberglass-base asphalt shingles, commonly called fiberglass shingles, have a fiberglass mat. Asphalt roofing is also manufactured in the form of roll roofing (page 33).

Though shapes vary, many asphalt shingles are notched at intervals to form tabs, giving the appearance of smaller units. They usually last from 15 to 25 years, depending on the climate and type of mat. Asphalt shingles that are aging may show bald spots; another clue to aging is a heavy accumu-lation of granules in the gutters, indicating crumbling shingles.

Check your roof's condition on a warm day when the shingles are flexible. Remove a tiny piece of the corner from one or two shingles on each roof plane; the core of the shingle should be black. Gently bend several shingles back to see if they're flexible. If a number of shingles appear gray and bloated, if the material crumbles easily, or if you see large bare spots or damaged areas, consider replacing the roof.

Cracked, torn, or curled shingles can be repaired, as shown below; replace any loose or missing nails. If some of the shingles are badly worn or damaged, replace them (see below). Use shingles that remain from the origi-nal roof installation. If you don't have any leftover shingles, you'll have to buy new ones—identical in brand, color, and size, if possible. Fasten the shingles with galvanized roofing nails long enough to penetrate all roofing layers (at least 1½ inches long).

Don't remove a damaged shingle that's on a ridge or along a hip; instead, nail each corner in place. Then apply roofing cement to the bottom of a new shingle and place it over the defective one. Nail each corner, then cover the nail heads with roofing cement.

When you repair asphalt shingles, do the work on a warm day when the shingles are more pliable; cold shingles are brittle and can break easily. Also, have roofing cement at room temperature so it will spread more easily.

## THREE SHINGLE REPAIRS

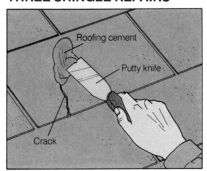

**Hairline crack.** Seal a very fine crack with roofing cement (or use asphalt paint). Apply the cement or paint along the crack with a putty knife.

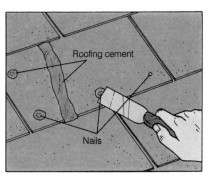

**Tear.** Liberally trowel roofing cement under the tear. Press the shingle in place; secure each side with roofing nails, covering nails and tear with roofing cement.

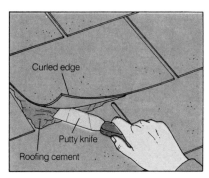

**Curled shingle.** To flatten a curled shingle apply roofing cement under the lifted portion; press in place. Tack with roofing nails and cover nail heads with roofing cement.

## REPLACING AN ASPHALT SHINGLE

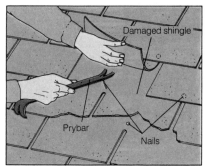

**1)   Lift the shingle tab** above the damaged one and, with a prybar, pry out both rows of nails holding the damaged shingle.

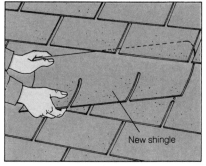

**2)   Slide the new shingle** into place, taking care not to damage the roofing felt (snip the top corners if the shingle sticks).

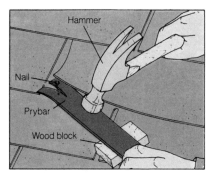

**3)   Nail on the new shingle;** if you can't lift the tab above it high enough to nail underneath, use a prybar as shown.

# Wood Shingles & Shakes

Wood shingles have a smooth, finished appearance; wood shakes have a rough-hewn look. Both are made from western red cedar. Shingles are sawn into lengths of 16, 18, or 24 inches. Shakes, which are thicker than shingles, are split by machine or by hand into 18 or 24-inch lengths. Both come in random widths.

Shingles and shakes are laid in overlapping courses, or rows. Shingles either have a continuous underlayment of roofing felt or none at all; shakes alternate with strips of felt. Both shingles and shakes may be laid directly on the sheathing or over an earlier roofing surface, such as asphalt shingles. They are attached with galvanized roofing nails.

Wood shingles and shakes usually last between 15 and 25 years, depending on the roof slope and the climate. If you suspect wear, inspect the roof for curled, broken, or split shingles, and for shingles that have been lifted by wind. Look also for shingles thinned by weathering and erosion, especially around areas where an attic inspection reveals pinpoints of light (page 29). Wood shakes show their age when the wood crumbles easily underfoot or between your fingers.

The extent of the defects you find will indicate whether you need to repair or replace shingles or shakes. If only a few shingles or shakes are split or wind-lifted, you can repair them; those that are badly splintered or curled or that have begun to crumble should be replaced (for instructions, see illustrations at right). If the damage is extensive, consider replacing the entire roof.

To remove the nails from a damaged shingle or shake you're replacing, either rent a shingle ripper or use a hacksaw blade. To use the ripper, slide it under the shingle and around a nail; then cut the shank of the nail with a hammer blow (see at right).

Since shingles and shakes are random widths, you'll need to trim the new ones to fit the space, using a roofer's hatchet or a saw. Leave a ¼-inch clearance on each side of every replacement piece to allow for expansion of the wood.

## REPAIRING A WOOD SHINGLE OR SHAKE

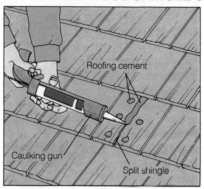

**Split shingle.** Butt the pieces together, drill pilot holes, and nail in place. Cover nail heads and joint with roofing cement.

**Wind-lifted shingle.** Press the shingle down and secure it with roofing nails. Daub roofing cement over the nail heads.

## REPLACING A WOOD SHINGLE OR SHAKE

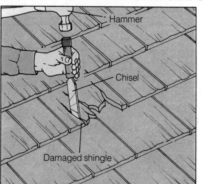

**1)  Carefully split the damaged shingle** along the grain and pull out as much of it as possible. Pry up the shingles directly above the damaged one to reach nails securing it.

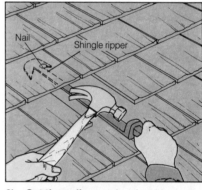

**2)  Cut the nails** securing the shingle to the roof deck, using a shingle ripper as shown (or saw nails off with a hacksaw blade). Don't damage the sheathing or underlayment.

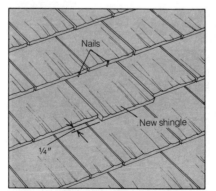

**3)  Insert the new shingle** so it protrudes ¼ inch below adjoining shingles; allow ¼-inch clearance on each side. Drive in two roofing nails at an angle just below the edge of the row above.

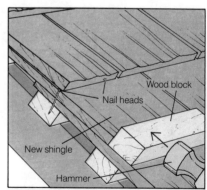

**4)  Drive the edge of the new shingle** even with the other shingles, using a hammer and wood block. The nails will bend, pulling the heads under the shingles above.

# Built-up Roofs & Roll Roofing

Homes with flat or low-sloping roofs usually have a built-up roof surface, also called a tar-and-gravel roof. Sheds, garages, and other out-buildings are sometimes roofed with asphalt roll roofing.

A built-up roof consists of several layers of roofing felt, each coated with hot or cold-mopped asphalt. The top layer is surfaced with crushed gravel or rock. These roofs generally last from 10 to 20 years, depending on the sun's intensity.

Asphalt roll roofing, made in the same way as asphalt shingles (page 31), has a lifetime of 5 to 15 years. Sometimes, roll roofing of a matching color is used to cover the valleys of an asphalt shingle roof.

Leaks in a flat roof are usually easy to locate—they tend to be directly above the wet area on the ceiling. Leaks may develop at flashings (page 34) or where wind has blown the gravel away to expose the surface. Leaks are also likely where weather and wear have caused blistered asphalt, separations between the roof surface and the drip edge, curling or split roofing felt that's exposed, and cracks or holes in the roof material.

Repairs are the same for both built-up and roll roofing. Fill in any cracks with roofing cement. If you're re-pairing a blister or small hole (see below), cut the patch you need from either a piece of roll roofing or an asphalt shingle. Use galvanized roofing nails to secure the patch. Any hole larger than a square foot should be patched by a professional roofer.

If your roof is beyond repair and must be replaced, it's best to call in a professional. Resurfacing a flat roof with layers of roofing felt and hot-mopped asphalt is beyond the scope of most homeowners because of the processes and equipment involved; moreover, working with hot molten asphalt is a messy, difficult, and even dangerous job.

## REPAIRING A BLISTER

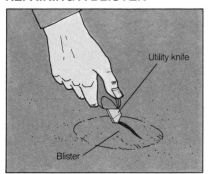

**1) Sweep all gravel aside,** using a stiff-bristled broom. Then, with a utility knife, cut into the asphalt and roofing felt until the pressure under the blister is released.

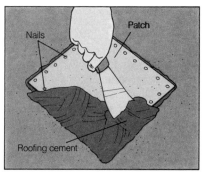

**2) Cover the cut** and an area 2 inches around all sides of it with a generous amount of roofing cement, applying it with a putty knife. Work the cement well under each edge of the cut.

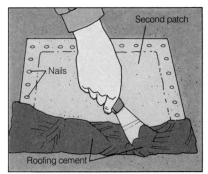

**3) Cut a patch** 2 inches larger on all sides than the slit and press it into the roofing cement. Nail the patch down, then cover the area with more cement. Replace the gravel once the cement starts to dry.

## PATCHING A HOLE

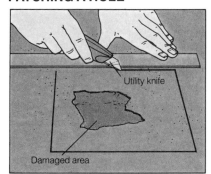

**1) Sweep all gravel aside,** using a stiff-bristled broom; then cut out a rectangle around the damaged layers of roofing. Remove the pieces, then cut a patch to fit the rectangle exactly.

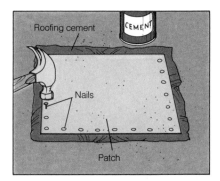

**2) Fill the hole with roofing cement,** spreading it over the surrounding area; nail the patch in place. Cover the patch with more cement, extending it 2 inches beyond the edges of the patch.

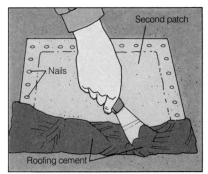

**3) Cut a second patch** 2 inches larger than the first. Nail it in place and cover it with another coat of roofing cement. Replace the gravel once the cement begins to dry.

# Roof Flashings

Flashing protects the roof at its most vulnerable points: in the valleys, at roof and plumbing vents, around chimneys, along the eaves—anywhere water can seep through open joints into the sheathing (page 28). As you might expect, the areas where flashings are located are the most prone to leaks.

Though you'll find flashings made from plastic, roll roofing, roofing felt, and rubber, the best choice for most homes is flashing made from rust-resistant metal, such as aluminum or copper. The joints may be sealed with roofing cement or caulking (for tips on caulking, see page 49). Cracked or crumbling cement or caulking is a major cause of leaks around flashings.

**Where flashing is found.** Flashing is found on shingled roofs wherever the courses of shingles are interrupted, whether by the intersection of two roof planes or by obstructions. Flashing is also installed around obstructions or protrusions (such as vent pipes) on built-up roofs (page 33).

■ **Chimney flashing** is installed in two layers to protect joints between the chimney and roof. Step flashing bends in an L shape to fit along the roof deck and up the sides of the chimney and is interleaved with the shingles. Cap or counter flashing is mortared or caulked into the chim-ney and bends down over the step flashing.

■ **Valley flashing** may be open, with shingles cut away to expose the flashing (see facing page), or closed, with shingles meeting or overlapping at the center of the valley.

■ **Vent pipe flashing** is installed over the course of shingles just below the pipe. The next courses cover the flashing.

■ **Skylights** that are self-flashing (see facing page) have built-in flanges that sit on the roof deck. A skylight mounted on a curb (a wood frame attached to the roof deck) requires flashing, much like that for chimneys, installed all around the curb.

■ **Drip edges** are strips of flashing installed under the shingles along the eaves and rakes and over windows and doors. They facilitate water runoff.

■ **Dormer flashing** is similar to step flashing found on chimneys; it extends under the siding on the dormer and under the roof shingles at the base.

**Repairing flashings.** Inspect flashings semi-annually. Renail any loose nails and cover all exposed nail heads with roofing cement. Look carefully for holes. You can plug pinholes with spots of roofing cement; patch holes up to about ¾ inch in diameter with the same material as the damaged flashing (see below). Replace the flashing if you find larger holes.

Check the all-important seals at the flashings' edges. If the roofing cement or caulking is cracked, dried, or crumbling, reseal the joints promptly (directions for the most common types of flashing appear on the facing page).

**Repainting a flashing.** To make the flashing less conspicuous, it's often painted to match the roof. Before re-painting, use a stiff brush and solvent to remove any flaking paint, rust, or corrosion from the flashing (keep solvent off asphalt shingles; it will dissolve them). Tape newspaper to the roof around the flashing. Apply a zinc-base primer, then spray on two or more light coats of rust-resistant metal paint.

**Replacing a flashing.** You'll need to replace any flashing that has large holes or is badly corroded. You can buy new flashing or fashion it out of aluminum or copper (use the old flashing as a pattern). To install new flashing, several courses of shingles as well as the flashing itself have to be removed; for instructions, see the *Sunset* book *Do-It-Yourself Roofing & Siding*. If you have no roofing experience, it may be best to hire a professional.

---

## PATCHING A HOLE IN FLASHING

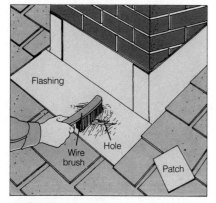

**1) Roughen the area** around the hole with a wire brush or sandpaper; clean. Cut a patch of flashing material 2 inches larger than the hole on all sides.

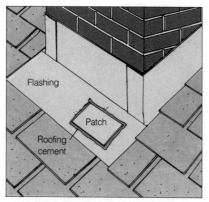

**2) Apply roofing cement,** then press the patch in place, and hold it for several minutes. Cover the patch with another coat of cement.

---

**PROFESSIONAL HINT**
REMOVING ROOFING CEMENT

Roofing cement works wonders on a roof, but when it gets all over you and the roof, it can create a mess.

Fortunately, roofing cement *can* be removed. Use kerosene and a rag to scrub unwanted cement from both the roof and you. Promptly wash any kerosene from your skin and dispose of the rag properly.

## RENEWING FLASHING SEALS

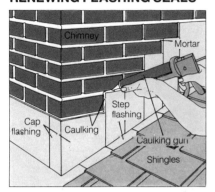

**Chimney flashing.** Chip out the old mortar and caulking along the cap flashing. Then caulk the joints between the flashing and chimney and between the cap and step flashings.

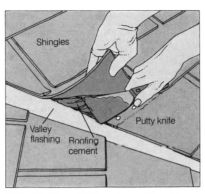

**Valley flashing.** Lift the edges of the shingles along the flashing and spread roofing cement on the flashing to about 6 inches in from the edges of the shingles.

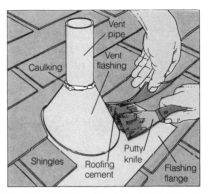

**Vent pipe flashing.** Caulk the joint between the flashing and pipe. Lift the side and back shingles; apply roofing cement to the joints between the flange and shingles.

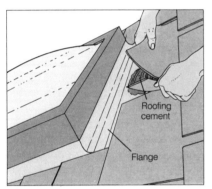

**Self-flashing skylight.** Lift the adjacent shingles and spread roofing cement liberally on the joints between the skylight flange and roofing felt.

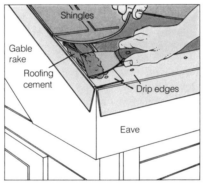

**Drip edge along a gable rake.** Lift the shingles and spread roofing cement on the top of the drip edge. Don't seal the drip edge along the eaves.

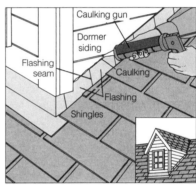

**Dormer flashing.** Remove any old caulking; apply caulking to the joints between the flashing and siding or shingles and between flashing seams.

## REPLACING VENT PIPE FLASHING

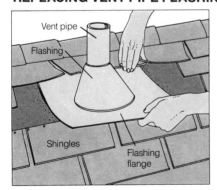

**1)  Remove the shingles** covering the flange at the back and sides. Using a hacksaw blade or shingle ripper (page 32), cut off the nails holding the flashing in place; lift the flashing off.

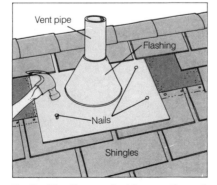

**2)  Position the new flashing** over the vent pipe and secure it with nails. Be sure to place the nails so the replacement shingles at the back and sides will cover the nail heads.

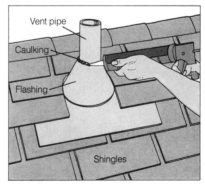

**3)  Replace the shingles** (pages 31–32), covering the nail heads and flashing joints thoroughly with roofing cement. Use a caulking gun to caulk the joint between the flashing and vent pipe.

# Gutters & Downspouts

A roof sheds water, but it's the gutter and downspout system that carries the water away from the house.

Most gutters and downspouts are made from galvanized steel, aluminum, or vinyl, though you may find some made from wood or copper. Usually, they can be painted to match the exterior of the house.

Gutters are attached to the eaves of the house with strap, bracket, or, most commonly, spike-and-ferrule hangers (see at right). Downspouts are attached to the exterior walls with straps.

In order to work efficiently, gutters and downspouts must be in good condition, must be sloped properly, and must be free of leaves and other debris.

**Gutter and downspout maintenance.** Regular inspection and maintenance are crucial for keeping your gutters and downspouts in good working order. Inspect them in the autumn and spring, and clean out accumulated leaves and other debris, as shown below. Then check the slope of the gutters by running water through them. If drainage is slow, reposition the gutters for the correct slope: they should be tight against the fascias and should slope toward the downspouts at a rate of 1 inch for every 20 feet. You can correct low spots by adjusting the hangers.

Test for weaknesses in gutters, downspouts, and fascia boards by probing with a thin screwdriver or knife. Also, look for flaking or peeling paint, rust spots, broken hangers, and holes or leaky joints.

**Repairing fascias, gutters, and downspouts.** If you find dry-rotted fascia boards, repair them first. Carve out bad spots and fill them with wood putty or replace the damaged section with a piece of well-seasoned lumber (apply a wood preservative first), then finish to match the existing boards.

Tighten any loose hangers and replace any that are broken. Check that the downspout straps are secured to the walls and that all elbow connections fit tightly.

Patch any leaky joints or holes in gutters (see facing page), taking care to clean them thoroughly first. Seal pinholes with a dab of roofing cement. If a section of your gutter system is badly damaged, replace it (for instructions, see the *Sunset* book *Do-It-Yourself Roofing & Siding*).

Repaint the inside of wood gutters as necessary with asphalt roof paint. Sand down rusted and corroded areas of metal gutters and apply asphalt aluminum paint to the inside, rust-preventative zinc-base primer outside. Then paint the outside of wood or metal gutters to match the house exterior (see page 42 for tip on preparing and painting exterior wood).

## A TYPICAL GUTTER SYSTEM

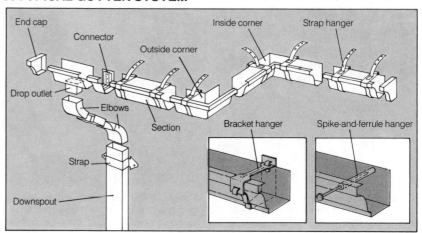

## UNCLOGGING GUTTERS & DOWNSPOUTS

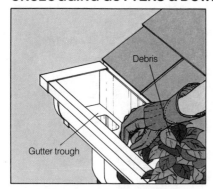

**Remove leaves,** twigs, and other debris from gutter troughs (protect your hands with gloves). Loosen dirt with a stiff brush; hose all debris out of the system.

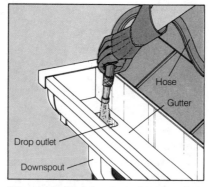

**Clean a blocked downspout** by spraying with a garden hose turned on full force. Or feed a snake into it and then flush all loosened debris out with a hose.

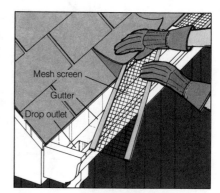

**Add mesh screens** to deflect leaves, twigs, and other debris over the edge of the gutter. A leaf strainer (not shown) will admit water and filter out debris.

## THREE GUTTER REPAIRS

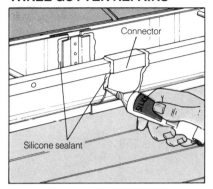

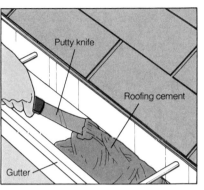

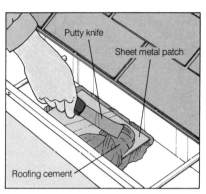

**Leaky joint.** Seal by applying silicone sealant or caulking around the seams between sections on the inside and outside of the gutter.

**Small hole.** Using a putty knife, patch with a thin coat of roofing cement, extending the cement beyond the hole in all directions.

**Hole larger than ½ inch.** Cover with roofing cement and embed a sheet metal patch in the cement. Apply another coat of cement over the patch.

## IMPROVING DOWNSPOUT DRAINAGE

Water that's allowed to flow from your downspouts directly into the ground may end up in your crawl space or basement and can erode the soil alongside the house, causing settling of the structure.

To divert water away from the house, you can use splashblocks, flexible plastic sleeves attached to the downspouts, or clay drainage pipes that carry water to a dry well located several yards from the house.

**Splashblocks.** Place a ready-made concrete or plastic splashblock below an elbow attached to the downspout. Tilt the splashblock slightly so the water flows away from the foundation.

**Sleeves.** An alternative to splashblocks is a plastic or fabric sleeve that you attach directly to the downspout. Some sleeves are perforated to disperse the water over a large area. Another type unrolls as the water comes down and carries the water several feet from the house; a spring inside the sleeve rolls it back up once the water has drained. Look for sleeves in home improvement centers.

### THREE DRAINAGE DEVICES

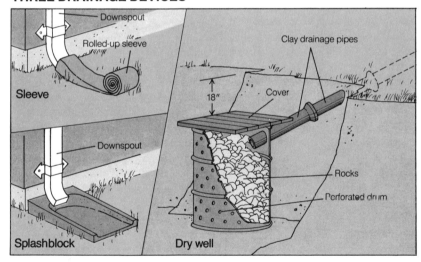

**Dry wells.** If you live in a wet climate, you may want to link your downspouts to a dry well (check your local building code before installing one).

Locate the dry well 10 or more feet from the foundation. The well itself can be simply a hole 2 to 4 feet wide and 3 feet deep; or you can bury a 55-gallon oil drum after puncturing it with holes and removing both ends.

Fill the well with rocks or broken concrete blocks; cover the top with wood slats or heavy roofing paper. The well's top should be at least 18 inches below ground level; the bottom should be above the water table.

Underground drainage pipes, sloped ½ inch per foot, carry water from the downspouts on the house to the dry well.

# Chimneys

Most chimneys are built of brick and lined with fireproof flue tiles. A cap of mortar seals the top against the weather.

A chimney that's used regularly must be cleaned and inspected at least once a year. Using a strong flashlight, check inside the chimney for soot buildup and any obstructions, such as birds' nests or leaves. Also check the flue tiles for cracks or missing mortar. On the chimney's exterior, look for crumbling mortar between bricks and at the cap, loose or missing bricks, or flashing that has corroded or pulled away from the chimney; all can cause chimney leaks.

To clean the chimney or make minor repairs, see below. If the chimney is leaning, if a number of bricks are missing, or if the flue needs repair, consult a professional.

**Cleaning a chimney.** Clean your chimney regularly, since built-up soot and creosote may cause a chimney fire and will restrict the draft, making your fireplace or wood stove inefficient.

You may want to hire a chimney sweep to do this messy job. If you do it yourself, first cover the fireplace opening with newspaper and protect nearby furniture, carpets, and draperies. Wear a dust mask and goggles.

Use a good steel chimney-sweeping brush to clean the chimney from up on the roof. Attach the brush to a rope at least the length of the flue and

## ANATOMY OF A CHIMNEY

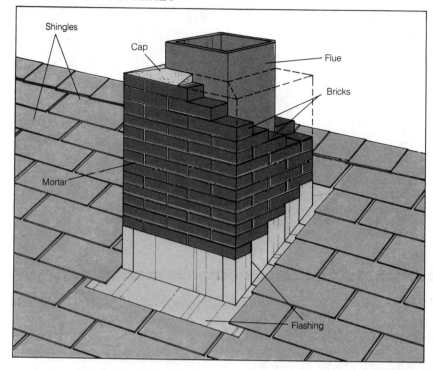

chimney, and attach weights to the end of the brush. Pass the brush repeatedly down to the flue bottom and up again until the brush no longer brings up large amounts of soot and creosote. Using a heavy-duty, not a household, vacuum, clean out the fireplace.

Brushes and weights are available from home improvement centers and wood stove dealers. You also can buy fiberglass rods that attach to the brush;

they're useful for cleaning long horizontal runs of stovepipe or for cleaning a chimney from below.

**Repairing a chimney.** To repair a cracked or crumbling cap, see the illustrations below. Replace mortar around chimney bricks as you would for brick veneer (page 47). For instructions on making repairs to chimney flashing, see page 35.

## REPAIRING A CHIMNEY CAP

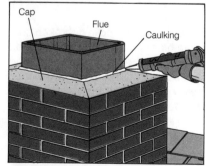

**Minor cracks.** Caulk all joints and any cracks in the cap; seal the joint between the flue and the cap with caulking.

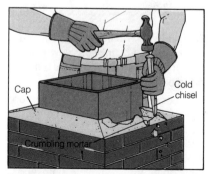

**Crumbling cap.** Chip out the old mortar and rebuild the cap with new mortar, sloping the cap away from the flue.

**PROFESSIONAL HINT**
MAKING CHIMNEY IMPROVEMENTS

You can install mesh spark arresters to prevent sparks and embers from flying out of the chimney and starting a fire, and to discourage birds from entering. Rain guards and draft deflectors deflect flying embers, rain, and drafts. Look for these at home improvement centers.

# CONTROLLING ICE & SNOW ON YOUR ROOF

Winter storms can wreak havoc on your roof. Ice dams that form at the eaves can result in leaks; snow can slide off the roof in a mini-avalanche, carrying roofing material and gutters with it. You can prevent most problems by keeping your gutters clean and by installing one of the devices described below.

## Ice dams

Ice dams (see illustration below) forming at the eaves can cause water from melting snow to back up under the shingles and leak into the house. Ice dams can result from alternate thawing and freezing of the snow on the roof due to a period of warm days and cold nights, or from heat loss through the roof of a poorly insulated and badly ventilated house, causing the snow to melt and then, in cold weather, freeze again in the colder eave area.

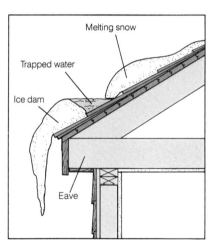

**Ice dams** form at the eaves, where repeated thawing and freezing occur.

**De-icing tapes.** Electrically heated cables installed along roof eaves and in gutters and downspouts, de-icing tapes (shown at top right) facilitate proper drainage of melting snow and ice, and help prevent ice dams.

These tapes, insulated for safety, are clipped to the shingles in a zigzag pattern (or run along gutters and downspouts) and are plugged into a weatherproof electrical outlet. When heated, they create miniature drainage channels for water that otherwise would back up behind an ice dam or freeze inside downspouts.

Look for de-icing tapes at home improvement centers or roofing supply companies. To install them, follow the manufacturer's instructions.

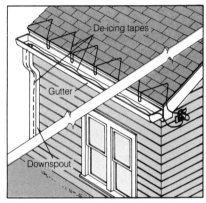

**De-icing tapes,** when heated, create drainage channels for water.

**Fans and soffit vents.** To prevent ice dams resulting from poor ventilation, install an attic fan (page 185) and soffit vents (see below). They vent warm attic air that might otherwise melt the snow on the roof. Soffit vents come in a variety of styles. Follow the manufacturer's instructions to install them.

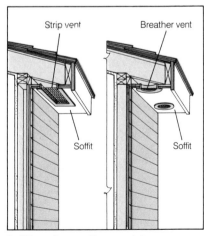

**Soffit vents** permit warm air to escape from the attic.

**Eave reinforcement.** For extra protection on a section of roof where ice dams often form, you can reinforce the eave area by installing a sheet of roll roofing or roofing felt under the shingles so it extends 12 inches inside the wall line. (This is best done when a new roof is being installed; if you're not reroofing, you'll have to remove and replace several courses of shingles.)

Each type of roofing requires a particular treatment; check your local building code for the material best suited to your roof.

## Snow buildup

Snow tends to slide off roofs like an avalanche, tearing gutters from their fastenings, ripping away roofing materials, and smashing plants or objects below.

To help hold snow in place, attach metal snow guards in staggered rows over the roof. You'll find several styles (see below for one type), including long, narrow ones for use over doorways.

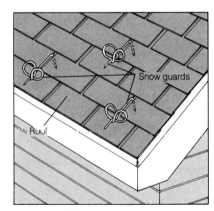

**Snow guards** keep snow on your roof, preventing avalanches.

The number of snow guards you install depends on your roof's slope. Generally, for every 100 square feet of roof, you'll need 50 guards on a roof with a 6 in 12 slope, 75 guards for an 8 in 12 slope, and 125 guards for a 12 in 12 slope.

# Siding

Whether it's made from wood, aluminum, vinyl, masonry, or stucco, the exterior wall covering on your house is called siding. In addition to its decorative role, siding gives strength to exterior walls and acts as a moisture barrier and insulator, protecting your house from the elements.

Siding may be plagued by a variety of ills—from obvious problems like peeling paint to less obvious insect infestation and dry rot. Many problems can be remedied if caught early on; regular inspection and maintenance (see facing page) are crucial. When the damage is already done, you can repair or replace siding; directions appear on pages 42–49.

## Understanding Siding

Siding comprises only one layer of the exterior wall of a house. It's important to understand the entire wall structure if you're repairing or replacing siding.

### Anatomy of a wall

Wood frame walls are usually constructed from 2 by 6 or 2 by 4 studs (see at right). Any insulation is placed between the studs, which are then covered with sheathing.

If the walls are to be finished with wood, aluminum, or vinyl siding, or with masonry veneer, the sheathing is covered with building paper. Then the siding is nailed on or, for masonry walls, a veneer of brick or stone is applied. Each course, or tier, of bricks or stones is attached to the underlayment with short metal strips called ties. The bricks or stones are mortared in place.

For stucco siding, wire mesh is nailed directly to sheathing covered with building paper, or the mesh is nailed to spacer strips as shown at right. The stucco is applied over the wire mesh in three layers.

### Types of siding

Residential siding falls into one of three categories: wood, masonry, or manufactured. Each has its own particular problems; repair and replacement methods depend on the type of siding you have. If you need to replace damaged siding, note the style, finish, and dimensions of the existing siding so you can find an exact match.

**Wood siding.** This category includes board siding as well as shingles and shakes. Board siding, available in

**ANATOMY OF A WALL**

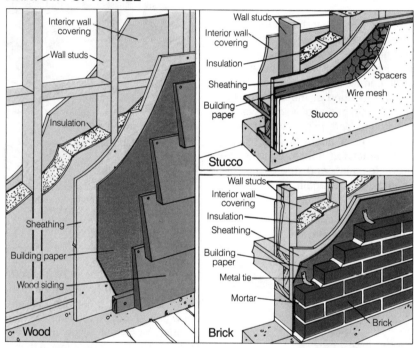

many types of wood and milled in a variety of patterns (page 44), can be installed vertically, horizontally, or even diagonally. Shingles and shakes are also available in a number of patterns. With regular maintenance, wood siding should last from 30 years to the life of the house.

**Masonry siding.** Grouped under masonry siding are stucco, brick, and stone.

Stucco is a cement-base plaster. You can either add pigment to the last coat or paint it when it's dry. The finish coat can be tooled in a number of textures.

Brick walls may be laid in one of several patterns; the bricks themselves come in a wide variety of sizes, colors, and textures. Stone veneer can also be laid in a variety of patterns. Mortar—a mixture of cement, sand, lime, and water—holds the bricks or stones together.

Masonry siding is practically impervious to weather and should last the life of the house.

**Manufactured siding.** Vinyl and aluminum siding panels are applied either horizontally or vertically; they usually come with trim pieces into which the panels are fitted. Vinyl siding is available in white and pastel colors; smooth and wood-grain textures are typical. Aluminum panels come in a wide range of factory-applied colors and textures. With regular maintenance, both will last from 40 years to the life of the house.

# Inspecting & Maintaining Siding

With routine maintenance, your siding should last for years. To keep your house looking its best, inspect your siding for damage in the spring and autumn, make any needed repairs promptly, and clean and repaint regularly.

**Inspecting your siding.** Look for obvious problems such as warped boards, missing or damaged shingles, holes in stucco, crumbling mortar, cracks, and defective paint. Don't ignore less obvious interior problems such as dry rot and termite damage; these can eventually destroy your house.

Begin with a visual inspection: the drawing at right indicates vulnerable areas. When you make your actual inspection, let the following list of problems and solutions guide you:

- **Deteriorated caulking.** Make a note of any caulking that has dried out and renew the seals (page 49). Check the seals around windows and doors, around protrusions, and where a deck or masonry fireplace adjoins the house. Caulk any cracks in board siding.

- **Defective paint.** Often, repainting the defective area is all that's needed. To treat minor paint problems, see page 42. If necessary, repaint all the siding.

- **Cracks.** Long, vertical cracks in masonry walls may indicate settling. Place tape over a crack and leave it in place for several months. If the tape twists or splits, consult a professional to determine if there's a serious structural problem; otherwise, repair the cracks (pages 46–47).

- **Mildew.** Combined heat and humidity may mildew wood and painted surfaces. To retard mildew, see the cleaning tips below.

- **Efflorescence.** Brick or stone veneer may become covered with a white powder called efflorescence, formed when water-soluble salts are washed to the surface. In an old wall,

## SIDING PROBLEM AREAS

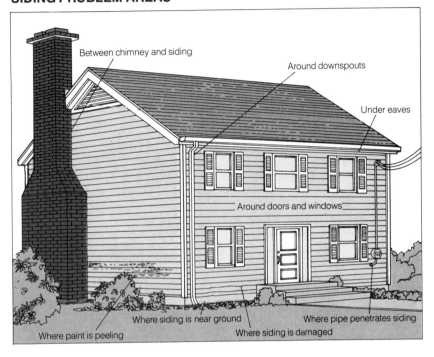

Between chimney and siding

Around downspouts

Under eaves

Around doors and windows

Where siding is near ground

Where pipe penetrates siding

Where paint is peeling

Where siding is damaged

this may indicate a leak that should be fixed. Cleaning the siding (see below) will remove efflorescence.

- **Dry rot and termite damage.** Dry rot is a fungus that causes wood to crumble; termites destroy wood by chewing out its interior. Both can work away at wood timbers and siding so inconspicuously that they can easily escape your notice.

To detect damage, probe the edges of wood siding with a knife and look for soft, spongy spots. Pay special attention to any part of the siding that's close to or in contact with the ground, even indirectly.

Check for visible evidence of termites; look for their translucent, ½-inch-long wings or the mud tubes they sometimes build (usually visible from under the house). If you find evidence of dry rot or termites, consult a licensed termite inspector or pest control professional.

**Cleaning your siding.** To keep siding in good shape, hose it down and, if

necessary, brush it with a carwash brush that attaches to a hose.

Hose down vinyl panels and sponge them with a mild liquid detergent.

If brick or stone veneer suffers from efflorescence, scrub the siding, one small area at a time, with a mild solution of muriatic acid (one part acid to ten parts water) and rinse the wall well with clear water.

You can retard the growth of mildew by washing the siding with a solution of ⅓ cup detergent, ⅔ cup trisodium phosphate, and 1 quart household bleach in 3 gallons of water. Brush or sponge the walls, then rinse.

CAUTION: When working with this solution or with muriatic acid, wear goggles and gloves, and cover your plants with a plastic tarp.

After cleaning the siding, repair any caulking (page 49) and paint or stain any areas that are chipped or peeling (page 42). Wood siding is especially vulnerable to rot when the finish deteriorates.

# SOLVING EXTERIOR PAINT PROBLEMS

Paint damage on exterior wood surfaces can result from any of a number of causes. Before you repaint, try to diagnose the cause of the problem so your repair will be lasting. Then you can prepare the surface, select an appropriate paint or stain, and apply the finish, as explained below.

**Diagnosing paint problems.** Typical causes of paint damage include improper surface preparation, careless painting, use of the wrong paint, and structural problems that trap moisture in the wood. Common paint problems and their causes are described below.

- **Blistering.** Blisters appear in paint when water or solvent vapor is trapped under the paint. Cut the blister open. If you find bare wood underneath, it's a water blister created by moisture escaping from damp wood. If you find paint, it's a solvent blister, often caused by painting in direct sunlight or on wet wood.

- **Peeling.** Paint peels and curls away from wood when it's applied over dirty, greasy, or wet wood, or over loose paint.

- **Alligatoring.** A checkered pattern of cracks resembling alligator skin results when the top coat is applied before the bottom coat is dry or when the paints in the bottom and top coats are incompatible.

- **Wrinkling.** Wrinkles in paint are the result of careless painting. If paint is applied too thickly, the top surface dries too rapidly and the paint underneath droops down.

- **Chalking.** High-quality exterior paint is designed to chalk so rain will clean dirt from the surface. But chalking that comes off when you rub up against the surface indicates that the surface was unprimed or finished with paint of poor quality.

**Preparing the surface.** Wood surfaces must be clean, dry, and in

## COMMON PAINT PROBLEMS

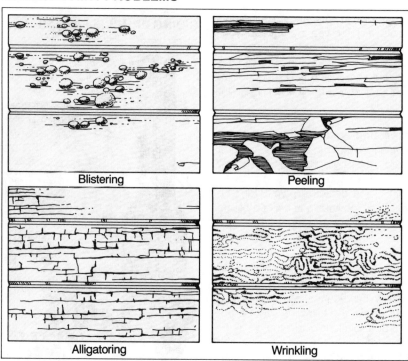

Blistering

Peeling

Alligatoring

Wrinkling

good condition before you repaint. Repair any damaged boards, trim, or shingles and fix any structural damage that allows water to penetrate.

Remove dirt and all loose, peeling, or blistering paint with a stiff wire brush or paint scraper. Where paint damage is severe, remove the paint down to the bare wood. Feather the edges of any remaining sound paint with medium-grade sandpaper, then sand again with fine-grade sandpaper. If the top coat didn't adhere to a previous coat, rough up the damaged paint with sandpaper.

Wash greasy or very dirty wood with a mild detergent, hose it off, and let the wood dry before painting.

If moisture is causing paint damage, apply a water repellent, prime with an oil-base prime coat, and cover with two coats of high-quality paint after you've prepared the surface.

**Applying the finish.** Apply a clear waterproofing sealer to the ends of all wood boards to prevent water pene-

tration. Brush a prime coat on bare or new wood. Where heat and humidity cause wood to deteriorate quickly, treat boards with a wood preservative before sealing.

With the exception of redwood, cedar, and southern red cypress (which should be sealed to help retard color changes), wood needs to be painted or stained to protect it from the elements. Use a finish that matches the existing one as closely as possible. A 2-inch brush for trim and a 4-inch brush for wider surfaces are usually best. For a larger area, you may want to use a 9-inch roller; choose a fine nap for smooth surfaces and a thick nap for textured surfaces.

Exterior painting is best done in fair, dry weather with temperatures between 50° and 90°F. Wait until the morning dew has evaporated and stop painting before evening dampness sets in. Don't paint when conditions are windy or dusty, particularly if you're using a slow-drying, solvent-base paint.

# Wood Siding

Whether it's in the form of boards, shingles, or shakes, wood siding is durable and, with annual maintenance, should last the lifetime of the house.

To prevent deterioration of wood board siding, repair simple surface problems—holes in the wood, split and warped wood, and damaged paint—as soon as they appear (see below and on facing page). Severely damaged board siding can't be effectively repaired; in this case, you'll need to replace the affected siding (follow the instructions on pages 44–45).

When shingles or shakes are damaged, it's usually best to replace them, since repairs to these materials are hard to conceal. Instructions for replacement appear on page 45.

Be sure to determine the cause of any serious damage before replacing siding. If moisture is causing the problem, find the source by checking for deteriorating roofing (page 29), leaking gutters or downspouts, and poor drainage (pages 36–37). Consult a professional if you can't locate the source of the leak. Once you pinpoint the problem, be sure to make the necessary repairs; new siding installed over problem areas will just deteriorate again after a short time.

If after removing damaged siding you see evidence of dry rot or insect infestation (page 41), call in a professional.

## Repairing Board Siding

Damage to wood board siding can often be repaired inconspicuously. Repairs usually involve filling holes, fixing split or warped boards, and repainting. Siding that's badly damaged should be replaced (pages 44–45).

**Repairing holes.** Small holes in wood board siding can be filled with wood putty, available at lumber and paint stores. The putty comes in a variety of shades for matching lightly stained wood.

To conceal a small hole, fill it with wood putty and allow the putty to dry completely. If the hole is fairly large, apply the putty in layers, letting each one dry completely before applying the next. When the final layer is dry, sand the surface smooth. Then finish the putty to match the surrounding siding (unless you've used putty in a shade that matches the exterior).

**Repairing split boards.** A clean split or crack can be repaired by prying the board apart and coating both edges with waterproof glue, as shown at right. Then either nail or screw the board back into position or, for a less visible repair, drive a row of temporary nails just under the lower edge of the board and bend them up over the edge to hold the board in place. Remove the nails once the glue has set.

**Repairing warped boards.** Warped or buckled boards usually show up where boards have been fitted too tightly during installation. If a board has nowhere to expand when it swells with moisture, it warps or buckles.

To straighten a warped or buckled board, first try to pull it into line by driving long screws through it and into the wall studs. Use a portable electric drill to drill pilot holes and countersinks for the screws (page 15), then insert the screws and tighten them. Cover the screw holes with wood putty; then sand and finish as you would after repairing holes in siding.

If that doesn't work, you'll have to shorten the board to give it more room. Pull out the nails within the warped area or cut them with a hacksaw blade. Continue removing nails to the nearest end of the board. Pull the end of the board outward; then file it with a rasp, sand with sandpaper, or use a block plane to remove wood on the end little by little until the board fits. Renail the board.

**Fixing paint problems.** Paint problems can result from a variety of causes: wrong paint, improper surface preparation before painting, careless painting, harsh sunlight over a long period of time, or improper wall ventilation. Except in the last case, the problem can be remedied with a proper paint job (see facing page).

Ventilation depends on your climate and the presence or absence of a vapor barrier. Increasing the amount of ventilation may involve adding vents to the roof, gables, and soffits (page 39) or installing a fan (page 185). Check your local building code for the recommended ventilation for your home.

### REPAIRING A SPLIT BOARD

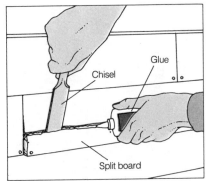

**1) Carefully pry the damaged board apart** at the crack and liberally coat the edges of both pieces with waterproof glue.

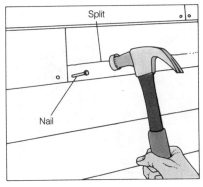

**2) Push the edges of the two pieces tightly together,** predrill holes, and secure both sections to the sheathing with nails or screws.

# ...Wood Siding

## Replacing Damaged Boards, Shingles & Shakes

Sometimes, a board is so badly damaged or decayed that your only choice is to replace it. Similarly, a shingle or shake that's damaged should be replaced rather than repaired.

### Replacing boards

The approach to replacing board siding depends on the milling of the boards (common types are shown below) and how they're nailed. Often, the trickiest part of the job is finding a replacement that matches the original.

No matter what type of siding you're replacing, you'll have to cut the damaged piece and remove the nails in order to pry it out. After repairing any damage to the building paper with roofing cement, you'll need to carefully measure and cut the new piece so it will fit correctly. For best results, cut out and replace a section that spans at least three studs. Use a carpenter's square when marking cutting lines to keep them at right angles. Pull nails out of the old siding with a nail claw or nail puller, or cut off nail heads with a hacksaw blade.

**Tongue-and-groove siding.** Because the boards are locked together by the tongues and grooves, the damaged piece must be split lengthwise as well as cut at the ends, as shown below, before it can be removed.

It's easiest to make the cuts with a circular saw; set the blade depth just shy of the thickness of the siding. Saw almost to each edge, holding the blade guard back and dipping the moving blade down into the wood to start each cut. Hold the saw firmly—it may kick back. Also, be careful not to cut into adjacent boards.

**Overlapping styles of siding.** Clapboard, bevel, Dolly Varden, shiplap, channel rustic, and other overlapping styles (bottom left) are face nailed to

### COMMON BOARD SIDINGS

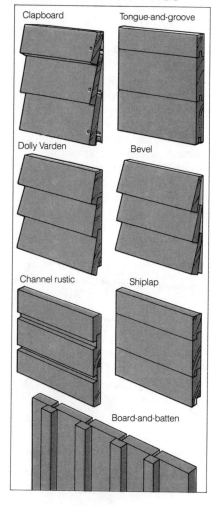

Clapboard

Tongue-and-groove

Dolly Varden

Bevel

Channel rustic

Shiplap

Board-and-batten

### REPLACING TONGUE-AND-GROOVE SIDING

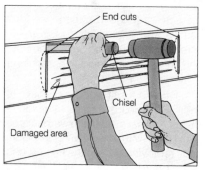

End cuts

Chisel

Damaged area

**1)  Pull out all exposed nails** in the area to be removed. Mark the end cut lines, then cut with a circular saw almost to the top and bottom of each mark and finish the end cuts with a chisel.

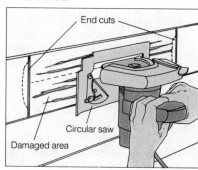

End cuts

Circular saw

Damaged area

**2)  Rip along the center** of the damaged section with the circular saw, cutting almost to the end cuts. Again, complete the cuts at both ends with a hammer and a chisel.

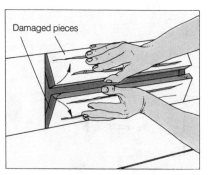

Damaged pieces

**3)  Cave in the board;** then pull out the loosened pieces. If you find any cuts or tears in the building paper, repair them with roofing cement before installing the new board.

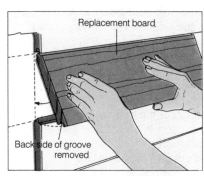

Replacement board

Back side of groove removed

**4)  Remove the back side** of the groove on the replacement board; slide it in place and face nail the board. Countersink the nail heads, caulk or putty the nail holes and ends, and finish.

studs or sheathing. Though the boards overlap, you can replace a damaged piece without removing other boards (you may need to pry up the board above the one you're replacing to free the last pieces of damaged board). To replace all types of overlapping siding, follow the directions for replacing clapboard siding illustrated below.

To provide a solid nailing base for the replacement board, center the end cuts over studs, if possible. You can use a back saw to cut clapboard, bevel, and Dolly Varden siding; make the cuts in shiplap and channel rustic siding with a circular saw, as described under ''Tongue-and-groove siding,'' facing page. If nails are in the way of your saw cuts, pull them out.

**Board-and-batten siding.** To remove board-and-batten siding, pry up the battens on either side of the damaged board far enough to raise the nail heads, then pull out the nails. Repeat this process until you're able to remove the damaged board.

Patch any cuts or tears in the building paper with roofing cement. Replace the damaged board and batten with identically sized new ones. Seal all joints with caulking compound; then stain or paint.

## Replacing shingles & shakes

When a shingle or shake splits, curls, warps, or breaks, you'll have to take it out and replace it. The replacement technique depends on whether the shingles or shakes are applied in single or double courses (rows).

In a single-course application, each course overlaps the one below by at least half a shingle or shake length. The nails are concealed under the shingles or shakes of the course above. Replacement procedures are the same as for a shingle or shake roof (page 32).

Double-coursing calls for two complete layers of shingles or shakes. Here, the nail heads are exposed. To replace a damaged shingle or shake, simply pull out the nails, remove the damaged piece, slide in a replacement, and nail.

## REPLACING CLAPBOARD SIDING

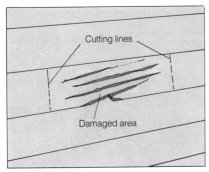

**1)  Mark cutting lines** on each side of the damaged area, centering the lines over wall studs. (If the damage is near a joint in the siding, you'll need to make only one cut.)

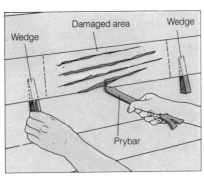

**2)  Pry up the bottom edge** of the damaged board with a prybar or stout chisel. Drive small wedges underneath the board at either end outside the cutting lines to keep it raised.

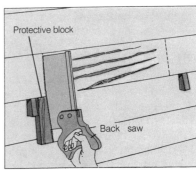

**3)  Cut through the board** along both cutting lines using a back saw; finish the cuts with a keyhole saw or a chisel. Break the damaged board out—in pieces, if necessary.

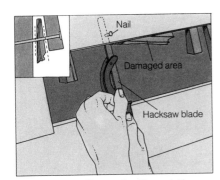

**4)  Cut any nails** passing through the board above with a hacksaw blade or pull them out to free the top of the damaged board. Repair any tears in the building paper with roofing cement.

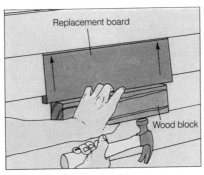

**5)  Trim the replacement board** to the right length (measure across at both top and bottom) and drive it into the exact position, hammering against a wood block placed along its lower edge.

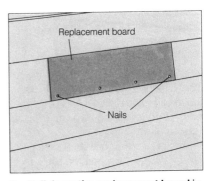

**6)  Nail down the replacement board** in the same way the surrounding siding was attached. Caulk or putty the nail holes and board ends; stain or paint the new board to match the existing siding.

# Stucco Siding

Stucco walls typically consist of three layers of stucco applied over wood spacers and wire mesh. The final coat is either pigmented or painted and can be textured in a variety of ways.

Cracks and holes in stucco can result from several causes, including poor-quality or poorly applied stucco and settling. To protect your house from moisture damage, repair damaged stucco right away.

The keys to a successful repair job are slow curing of the patched stucco and careful matching of the color and texture of the patch to the existing wall. To match color, you can either add pigment to the final coat of stucco or paint the patch later on. Texturing is done with floats, trowels, or brushes.

Following are directions for repairing cracks, small holes, and large holes.

**Cracks.** You can cover hairline and small cracks with a coat of latex paint or fill them with latex caulking compound and then paint with latex paint.

To fix larger cracks, use a cold chisel and ball peen hammer to undercut the edges of the crack in the form of an inverted V (use the same technique as for interior plastered walls, pages 90–91). Then brush away loose stucco and dust with a stiff brush and dampen the crack with a fine spray of water.

With a mason's trowel or putty knife, fill the crack with stucco patching compound (available at home improvement centers), packing it in tightly; texture to match the surrounding stucco (see text at right). Cure the stucco by dampening it once or twice a day for about 4 days.

**Small holes.** To repair a hole up to about 6 inches wide, first remove loose stucco with a cold chisel and ball peen hammer, undercutting the edges as for a crack, and blow out any dust. If the wire mesh is damaged, staple in a new piece. Dampen the patching site with a fine spray of water and pack the hole with stucco patching compound, using a mason's trowel or putty knife. To cure the stucco, keep it damp for about 4 days.

**Large holes.** Holes larger than about 6 inches wide should be repaired using the same methods as for applying new stucco. You'll need three coats of stucco—a "scratch" coat, a "brown" coat, and a final coat that you color and texture to match the original.

The first and second coats are made from one part Portland cement, three parts coarse sand, and ⅒ part hydrated lime, with enough water to make a fairly stiff paste. For the final coat, you use one part Portland cement, three parts coarse sand, and ¼ part hydrated lime (use *white* Portland cement and sand if you're adding pigment to the stucco).

To apply the stucco (see illustrations below), first prepare the surface by removing all the loose stucco, undercutting the edges, and adding new wire mesh if necessary. Be sure to press the first coat well into the mesh for a good bond. When this coat is firm, scratch it with a nail to provide grip for the second coat. Keep the first coat damp and let it cure for 2 days.

Dampen the area with a fine spray of water before applying the second coat and keep the second coat damp for 2 days.

The final coat, the one you color, if desired, and texture, should be flush with the surrounding wall. While it's wet, texture it to match (you'll have to experiment a bit). For a smooth texture, draw a metal float across the surface. For other textures, daub a sponge or brush on the surface, or splatter it with more stucco and smooth down the high spots. To cure the stucco, keep it damp for about 4 days. If you plan to paint it to match the surrounding area, wait a month after curing.

---

## PATCHING A LARGE HOLE IN STUCCO

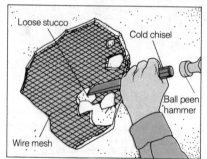

**1)  Remove loose stucco** from the hole with a cold chisel and ball peen hammer; blow out the dust. Staple new wire mesh over any damaged mesh. Spray with water.

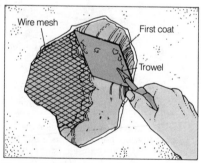

**2)  Apply the first coat** of stucco to within ¼ inch of the surface, using a mason's trowel or putty knife (stucco should ooze behind mesh). When firm, scratch with a nail. Cure for 2 days.

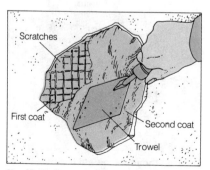

**3)  Apply the second coat** over the dampened first coat to within ⅛ inch of the surface, using a mason's trowel or putty knife. Smooth the stucco and let it cure for 2 days.

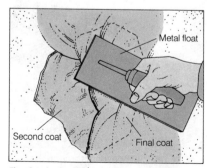

**4)  Apply the final coat** over the dampened second coat with a metal float or mason's trowel. Smooth it flush with the existing surface. Texture as desired; cure for 4 days.

# Brick Veneer

Brick veneer siding is usually applied to a wood frame wall over building paper; the mortared joints may be "tooled," or finished, in a number of ways, as shown at right. Properly tooled joints are essential to ensure strong, watertight walls.

**Problems with brick veneer.** Most problems develop at the mortar joints. Sometimes, the mortar shrinks, causing the joints to open; old-fashioned lime-base mortar often crumbles. Freeze-thaw cycles in cold-winter climates, excess moisture, and settling also result in mortar problems.

**Repointing mortar.** To repair cracked or crumbling mortar, you'll have to remove the old mortar and "repoint" the joints (fill them with new mortar), as shown below.

Though you can make your own mortar, it's easier to use dry ready-mixed mortar (use weather-resistant type N), available at building supply stores. Prepare the mortar according to package directions. When you're filling the joints, you may want to use a special tool called a hawk (illustrated below) to hold the mortar conveniently close to the job.

Using a jointer, steel rod, or trowel, tool the new joints to match the existing ones. Mortar joints should be tooled when they are "thumbprint hard" (neither so soft that they smear the wall nor so hard that a metal tool leaves black marks). Keep tooled joints damp for 4 days to cure the mortar.

CAUTION: When chipping out old mortar with a mallet or ball peen hammer and cold chisel, protect your eyes with goggles.

## TYPES OF MORTAR JOINTS

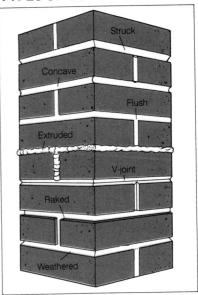

---

## REPOINTING DAMAGED MORTAR JOINTS

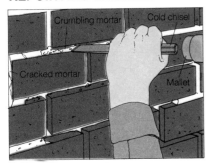

**1)   Chip out** cracked and crumbling mortar to a depth of at least ½ inch, using a cold chisel and mallet. Clean the joints with a wire brush and dampen them.

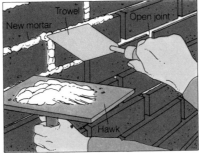

**2)   Pack mortar** into dampened (not wet) open joints, using a small trowel and a hawk. Tamp the mortar with a trowel or piece of wood.

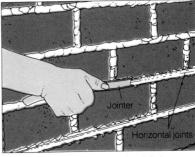

**3)   Finish the horizontal (bed) joints** when the mortar is thumbprint hard by pressing and drawing a jointer (or other appropriate tool) along each joint.

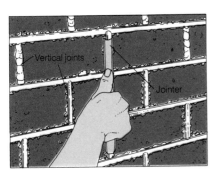

**4)   Finish the vertical (head) joints** in the same manner as the horizontal ones, pressing and drawing the tool along each joint to match the existing ones.

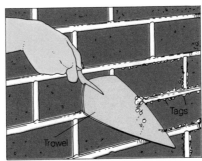

**5)   Cut off the tags** (excess mortar) by sliding the trowel along the wall. Finish the horizontal and vertical joints again (see Steps 3 and 4).

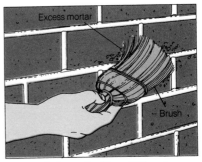

**6)   Brush the wall** with a stiff brush or broom once the mortar is well set. Keep the joints damp for 4 days to allow the mortar to cure.

# Aluminum & Vinyl Siding

Both aluminum and vinyl siding panels have interlocking flanges along both edges. The panels are nailed to the sheathing through slots along one flange; the other flange interlocks with the adjacent panel. Panels may be installed vertically or horizontally.

You can successfully repair minor dents, scratches, and corrosion in aluminum siding. More extensively damaged aluminum siding or damaged vinyl siding usually can't be repaired; instead, it must be replaced, as shown below.

**TYPICAL ALUMINUM OR VINYL PANELS**

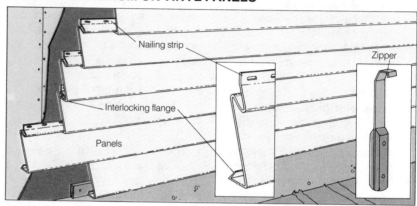

Nailing strip

Zipper

Interlocking flange

Panels

### Repairing aluminum siding

To remove a dent in aluminum siding, drill a hole in the center of the dent and screw in a self-tapping screw with two washers under the screw head (the screw cuts its own thread as it's driven in). Gently pull on the screw head with a pair of pliers. Remove the screw and fill the hole with plastic aluminum filler (follow directions on the tube). When dry, sand the filler smooth and touch up with matching paint.

Conceal scratches in aluminum siding by applying metal primer over the scratch. When the primer is dry, coat with latex house paint.

Repair corrosion by cleaning the rust off with fine steel wool. Prime the area with rust-resistant metal primer and cover with latex paint.

### Replacing aluminum siding

If a section of your aluminum siding is damaged beyond a simple surface repair, you can replace it by cutting out the damaged part of the panel, leaving the nailed portion in place (see below). Use tin snips to cut the new section of siding (it should overlap the existing siding by 3 inches on each side); then install it.

### Replacing vinyl siding

If vinyl siding is cracked or punctured, you must remove the entire damaged section before you can install a replacement piece. To do this, you'll need a special tool called a "zipper" to separate the interlocked panels. It's best to

do the work during warm weather, when the vinyl is pliable.

Using the zipper, unlock the panel adjacent to or above the damaged one and lift it up to expose the nails securing the damaged panel. Pry out the nails. Mark cutting lines on each side of the damaged area, using a carpenter's square and pencil. With tin snips or a back saw, cut the panel along the lines and remove the damaged section.

Cut a replacement piece 2 inches longer than the section you just removed to allow for a 1-inch overlap on each end. (Cut only 1 inch longer if the damaged section ends at a corner or joint.) Snap the top edge of the new section in place and nail it with aluminum box nails long enough to penetrate 1 inch into the sheathing. Using the zipper, snap in the other edge.

---

**REPLACING A DAMAGED SECTION OF ALUMINUM SIDING**

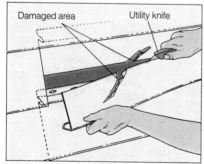

Damaged area　　Utility knife

**1)　Cut through the center of the panel** to just beyond both sides of the damaged area, using a utility knife. Make vertical cuts on both ends; remove the lower half of the damaged section.

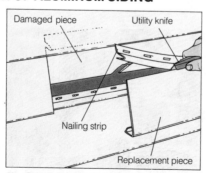

Damaged piece　　Utility knife

Nailing strip

Replacement piece

**2)　Cut the nailing strip** off the replacement with a utility knife (the new piece should be 6 inches longer than the damaged section, 3 inches if one end is at a joint or corner).

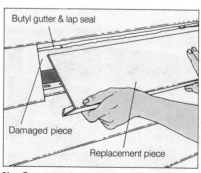

Butyl gutter & lap seal

Damaged piece

Replacement piece

**3)　Generously apply** butyl gutter and lap seal to the remaining portion of damaged panel. Press the new piece in place so each end overlaps the existing siding by 3 inches. Hold or prop until dry.

# Exterior Caulking

Caulking compound helps keep air, moisture, and insects out of your house and costly heated and cooled air inside. But caulking eventually dries out and requires renewal, so always check for cracked, loose, or missing caulking as part of your spring and autumn maintenance inspections.

The different types of caulking compound, the areas around your house that require caulking, and the application techniques are discussed below.

**Types of caulking.** The five basic types of exterior caulking are elastomers, butyl rubber, acrylic latex, non-acrylic latex, and oil base. The chart on page 25 lists the characteristics of each. When making your choice, weigh price against each compound's expected lifetime and consider the kinds of materials to which the caulking must adhere.

Caulking comes in four forms: as disposable cartridges for use with a half-barrel caulking gun, in a can for application with a full-barrel caulking gun or a putty knife, in a small squeeze tube, and as rope caulk. The half-barrel caulking gun fitted with a cartridge is the most popular dispenser, since it's the easiest to use for applying an even bead of compound. Use rope caulk as a temporary filler for very wide cracks or joints—it may not adhere for very long.

CAUTION: Before you buy any caulking, read the label: Some types won't work in cracks or joints less than ¼ inch wide; others work well only in narrow cracks. Take note of any precautions and follow the directions when you're using the product.

**Where to caulk.** Generally, you'll need to caulk in areas where different surfaces meet. Here are some of the places requiring caulking:

■ **On the roof** where one flashing meets another flashing, between flashing and a roof or dormer surface, and where a chimney, flue, plumbing or electrical pipe, attic fan, or skylight protrudes through the roof surface.

■ **On the siding** where the siding and trim meet at corners; around window and door frames; between badly fitting pieces of siding; where pipes, framing members, and other protrusions pass through the siding; and where the siding meets the foundation, patio or deck, or any other different part of the house.

It's also a good idea to examine interior window and door frames, especially between sliding door or window tracks and the sill or jamb.

**Applying caulking.** Before you can apply new caulking, you'll have to remove the old or damaged sections. First, dig out or chip off all of the old caulking with a putty knife, old screwdriver, or scraper. Then brush the area with a wire brush to remove debris and wipe the surface with a cloth soaked in the appropriate solvent for the type of caulking you're removing.

Before applying the new caulking, check the label to see if you need to prime the surface. Plan to caulk on a warm, dry day when the temperature is between 50° and 70°F. In hotter weather, refrigerate the caulking for an hour or two before use so the compound won't run.

Directions for using a half-barrel caulking gun appear below. It may take a bit of practice to get the bead of caulking to flow evenly. Start by holding the gun at a 45° angle to the surface; then, moving the gun across the surface, squeeze the trigger to keep the caulking flowing smoothly. Make sure the compound fills the crack completely and overlaps adjoining surfaces evenly. If the crack is deep, apply two beads.

If you're using rope caulk, simply unroll the amount you need and use your fingers to stuff it into the crack.

---

## USING A HALF-BARREL CAULKING GUN

**1)   To load the gun,** pull the plunger out (notches should face up). Insert the cartridge, bottom end first; push the plunger in and rotate it so that the notches face down, then pull the trigger.

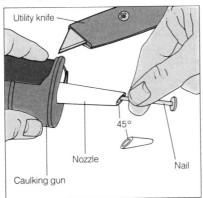

**2)   Cut off the end of the nozzle** at a 45° angle with a utility knife (for a narrow bead, cut close to the tip; cut farther away for a wide bead). Break the seal with a nail.

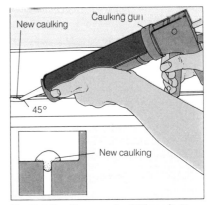

**3)   Holding the gun at a 45° angle** to the joint, slowly move the gun along the joint as you steadily squeeze the trigger. Make sure the bead overlaps both sides of the crack evenly (see inset).

# CONTROLLING MOISTURE IN A BASEMENT

The most common basement problem a homeowner faces is water. The problem can range in seriousness from damp walls and floors to water gushing out of a crack. The source may be simply humid air condensing on cool surfaces or ground water finding its way through your basement's walls or floor. Before you can correct the problem, you'll need to determine the source of the water.

**Where's the water coming from?** If you can see water flowing out of a crack in a wall or floor, you know that the source is ground water. In the absence of such obvious evidence, you'll have to make a test to determine whether the dampness in your basement is caused by condensation or water from the ground.

Cut two 12-inch squares of plastic sheeting or aluminum foil. Tape one to the inside of an outside wall and one to the basement floor (make sure the surfaces are thoroughly dry). After two or three days, remove the plastic or foil and examine the surface that was next to the wall or floor. If it's dry, the culprit is condensation; if it's wet, it's a sign that ground water is seeping through the wall or floor.

## Reducing condensation

When the basement air is humid, the moisture in the air may condense on cool surfaces, such as cold water pipes, concrete or masonry walls, or a concrete floor.

Though you can apply a coating (see facing page) to reduce condensation, it's best to lower the air's humidity, using these suggestions:

- **Improve ventilation** by opening basement windows or installing an exhaust fan (page 185) in the basement.

- **Raise the temperature** in the basement.

- **Vent moist air** from a clothes dryer to the outside.

**COMMON CAUSES OF A WET BASEMENT**

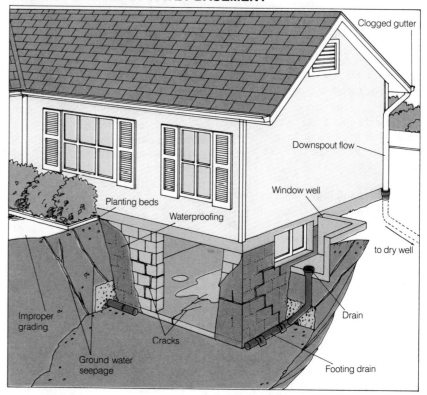

Clogged gutter

Downspout flow

Window well

to dry well

Drain

Footing drain

Cracks

Ground water seepage

Improper grading

Waterproofing

Planting beds

- **Install a dehumidifier** in the basement area.

- **Insulate cold water pipes** and basement walls.

## Controlling ground water

When water collects next to a foundation wall or when the water table (the water level under your property) is higher than your basement floor, hydrostatic pressure can force water through joints, cracks, and porous areas in concrete walls and floors and through cracked or crumbling mortar joints in masonry walls. Poor construction practices—clogged or nonexistent footing drains, poorly applied or nonexistent waterproofing on the foundation, through-the-wall cracks, and improper grading—often are the cause.

Correcting any of these problems is a major job that requires digging

out the foundation to the bottom of the footings. Though this may well be the most permanent repair, first try the remedies that follow. If they don't work, then you'll have to contact a foundation engineer or contractor for a more lasting solution.

CAUTION: If you see horizontal cracks in a wall that's bowing inward, long, vertical cracks wider than ¼ inch, or a crack that's getting wider (measure it periodically), you have a structural problem. Contact a soils or foundation engineer at once.

**Exterior remedies.** Roof and surface water collecting next to the foundation may be causing the dampness in your basement. Make a careful inspection outside, using the following checklist, and correct any problems you find.

- **Gutters and downspouts** should be clear and should direct water away from the foundation. To clean gutters and improve drainage at downspouts, see pages 36–37.

- **Proper grading around the house**—the ground should drop 1 inch per foot for the first 10 feet away from the foundation walls—is essential to ensure good surface drainage.

- **Planting beds** next to the foundation should not allow water to collect or pool there.

- **Window wells around basement windows** should be free of debris, have good drainage, and be properly sealed at the wall.

**Interior remedies.** These simple interior repairs may alleviate or cure your water problems:

- **Apply a coating to the wall.** Most coatings are painted on, though some are plastered on with a trowel. Except for epoxy coatings, all are cement-base products with various additives. Epoxy does the best job. Look for coatings at home improvement or masonry supply centers.

- **Patch cracks** in walls and floors with Portland or hydraulic cement patching compound. Hydraulic cement expands and dries quickly, even in wet conditions. Cracks wider than ⅛ inch should be undercut— chiseled out so the bottom of the crack is wider than the top (see illustration at top left). This will prevent water pressure from popping out the patch.

- **Chisel out a groove along the wall** if water is entering through a floor/wall joint. Fill the groove with hydraulic or epoxy cement and cove (form in a concave shape) as shown below.

- **Chisel out cracked mortar joints** in masonry walls and fill them with hydraulic or epoxy cement.

Water that comes through cracks in a concrete floor or through the joint between the floor and wall is caused by hydrostatic pressure. In addition to those described above, remedies include installing drains under the floor, adding a sump pump, or laying a new floor over a waterproof membrane placed on the old floor—all jobs for professionals.

## PATCHING A CRACK

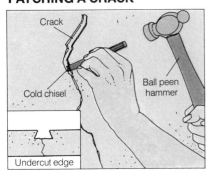

**1)  Chisel out any crack** wider than ⅛ inch, undercutting it (see inset) and beveling the edges.Clean out the crack.

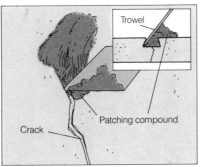

**2)  Apply patching compound** with the tip of a trowel. Force it well into the crack so the bottom is completely filled.

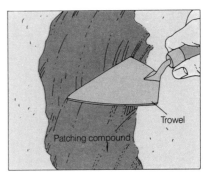

**3)  Smooth the patching compound** with a wet trowel after it has set so it's flush with the rest of the wall.

## PATCHING A FLOOR/FOUNDATION JOINT

**1)  Chip out the joint** with a hammer and cold chisel (wear goggles) to make a groove 1 to 2 inches deep; undercut the edges.

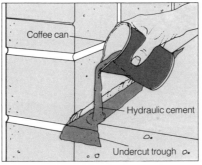

**2)  Pour a soupy mixture** of hydraulic (or epoxy) cement from a bent coffee can to within ½ inch of the top of the groove.

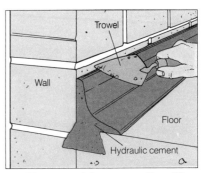

**3)  Fill the rest of the groove** with a stiffer mixture of the cement,  coving it several inches up the wall and along the floor.

# Windows & Doors

Double-hung window

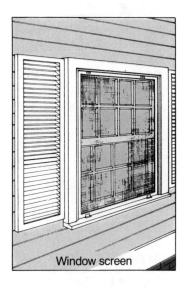

Window screen

Windows and doors open up your house to allow movement of light, air, and people; at the same time, they shield you from the elements—rain, snow, and wind. Shown below are some of the common types of windows and doors discussed in this chapter. Such jobs as repairing a sagging door, a binding window, and a torn window screen are also covered in full detail.

Exterior door

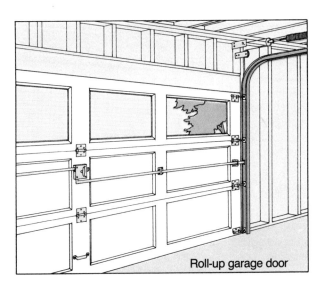

Roll-up garage door

Sliding patio door

# Double-hung Windows

A double-hung window consists of two sashes: an upper, outside sash that moves down and a lower, inside one that moves up. A pulley and weight system or balances located in the jambs control the movement of the sashes. Double-hung windows may be made from wood, aluminum, or vinyl.

As a wood window sash ages, it may begin to misfit its frame, or the system controlling sash movement may break down. Some common window problems and their solutions are discussed below. Instructions for removing wood sashes and replacing a window's balance system appear on pages 56–57.

Metal and vinyl windows seldom require repairs. To keep them operating smoothly, occasionally clean the channels with very fine steel wool and coat them with silicone spray.

### Correcting ill-fitting sashes

Wood double-hung window sashes that don't fit or don't move correctly are annoying. Often, a simple sash or stop repair can restore the window to good working order. If none of the simple repairs described below works, you'll need to remove and reposition the stops (see facing page).

**Freeing a stuck sash.** If a sash is temporarily stuck because moisture has swelled the wood, a change of weather may correct it. For a sash that's paint-bound, use one of the methods shown on the facing page.

**Freeing a tight sash.** If a sash moves reluctantly, the sash channels may need to be cleaned and lubricated or even widened (see facing page). If the sash itself is too wide, you may need to sand it down or, in severe cases, plane it (pages 70–71).

**Correcting a loose sash.** A sash that rattles and lets in unwanted air is too loose. Often, installing spring-type weatherstripping can correct the problem (page 64).

If the gap isn't too wide and the stop is nailed rather than screwed, you

can move the stop slightly without actually removing it. Score the paint between the stop and jamb and place a cardboard shim between the stop and sash. Holding a block of wood against the stop to protect it, hammer toward the sash along the length of the stop until the paint breaks and the stop rests against the shim. Secure the stop with finishing nails.

If you need to remove and reposition the stop to correct a wide gap, see the instructions on the facing page.

**Tightening sash joints.** If a sash's joints are loose, you'll have to remove the sash from the frame (page 56).

Clean the joints; then repair the frame as shown on page 62.

### Repairing window balance systems

If a sash refuses to remain open or closed, or if it jams in one position, repair or replace the balance system.

Your windows may have a traditional weight and pulley balance system like that shown above, or a more modern spiral-lift, tension-spring, or cord balance system (page 57). Instructions for repairing and replacing balances appear on pages 56–57.

## A DOUBLE-HUNG WINDOW

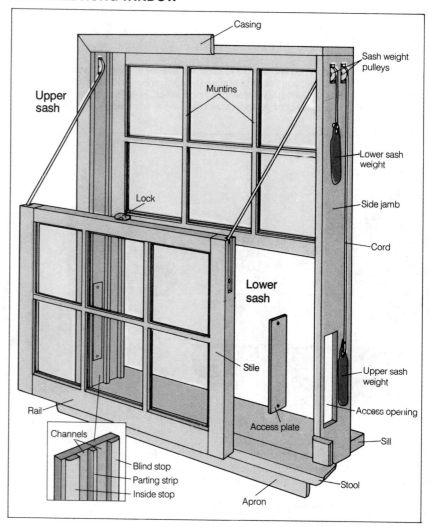

Casing · Sash weight pulleys · Muntins · Upper sash · Lower sash weight · Side jamb · Lock · Cord · Lower sash · Stile · Upper sash weight · Access opening · Access plate · Sill · Rail · Channels · Blind stop · Parting strip · Inside stop · Apron · Stool

## THREE WAYS TO FREE A PAINT-BOUND SASH

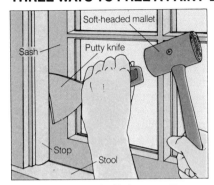

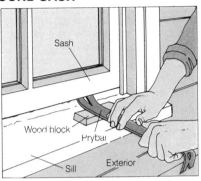

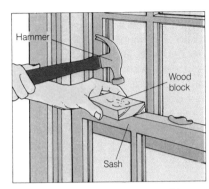

**Work a wide putty knife** between the sash and frame after scoring the paint along the edges with a utility knife. Tap to break the paint seal.

**From outside, wedge a prybar** between the sill and sash; work alternately at each end so the sash moves up evenly. Protect the sill with a wood block.

**If the window is stuck open** too wide to be pried, place a wood block on the sash at one side; tap with a hammer. Continue tapping, alternating sides, until sash is freed.

## THREE WAYS TO LOOSEN A TIGHT SASH

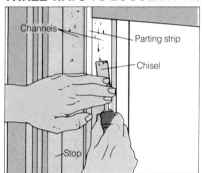

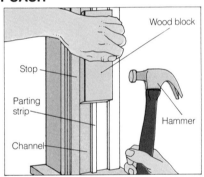

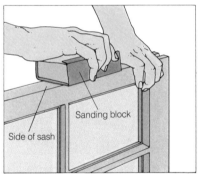

**Chisel any dirt** or large globs of paint from the channels; then sand them smooth. Coat all surfaces with paraffin so the sash moves easily.

**To widen the channel** where stops are nailed, place a wood block wider than the channel at the point that binds. Tap the block against the stop until the sash moves.

**If the sash is too wide,** remove it (page 56) and lightly sand each side. Check constantly for fit: sanding too much can result in a loose sash.

## REPOSITIONING THE STOPS

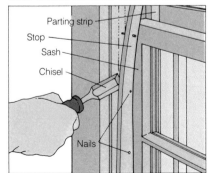

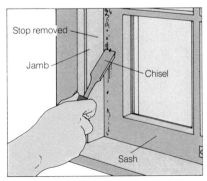

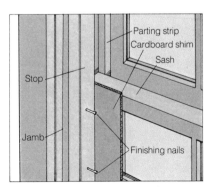

**1)   Pry off the stops** and the nails with them after scoring the paint between the jambs and stops (remove screws first if stops are screwed).

**2)   Chisel any built-up paint** off the edges of the sash, stops, and parting strip. Sand the edges smooth and apply paraffin to them.

**3)   Nail the stops back on** the jambs, using a thin cardboard shim between the stop and sash as a spacing guide. Then remove the shim.

# ... Double-hung Windows

## Broken Balance Systems

When a window's balance system is broken, the window will not remain open or closed. The repair depends on the type of system—pulley and weight, spiral-lift, tension-spring, or cord—used in the window.

To repair or replace a balance system, you'll have to remove one or both sashes (see below). If just the lower sash is affected, remove only that one.

If the repair involves the upper sash, remove both. Be sure to take off any interlocking weatherstripping before removing the sash.

### Pulley & weight system

Pulleys and weights traditionally operate double-hung windows. The weights are suspended on cords or chains located behind the side jambs.

If you're replacing a broken cord, it's a good idea to replace all the cords in the window at the same time, preferably with long-lasting chains, as shown below. To replace a defective chain, follow the instructions for cords. Before detaching the old chain, be sure to immobilize the weights on each side by

---

**REMOVING WOOD SASHES & REPLACING CORDS**

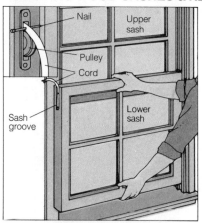

**1)** **Angle the lower sash** out after removing the inside stops (page 55). Untie and slip each cord out of the groove (nail keeps cord from slipping through pulley).

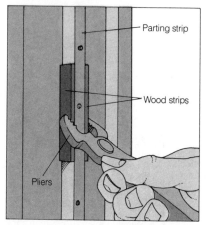

**2)** **Pull out each parting strip** with pliers (use wood strips to protect wood). Angle the upper sash out of the frame; disconnect the cords (see Step 1).

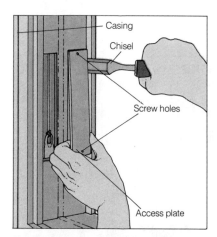

**3)** **Remove the screws** holding each access plate and pry the plates off to get at the sash weights. (If there are no plates, carefully remove the window's casings.)

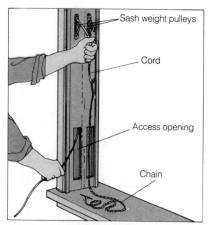

**4)** **Tape an end** of each new chain to an end of each cord; slip a nail through each chain's other end. Untie the weights; pull the cords out of the openings.

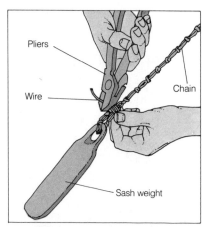

**5)** **Loop each chain** through the hole in each weight; secure the chains with wire. Clear the access openings of any debris and replace the weights.

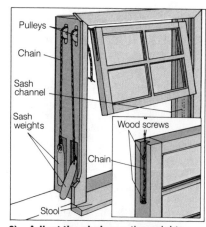

**6)** **Adjust the chains** so the weights will be 2 inches above the stool when the sash is up. Secure the chains to the sash channels; replace the access plates.

drawing up the chains until the weights touch the pulleys. Slide a nail through a link at each pulley to hold the chains in place; then detach the chains from the sash.

Once the new chains are in place, replace the upper sash, parting strips, access plates, bottom sash, and stops, in that order, checking the operation of each sash as you go.

## Spiral-lift system

In a spiral-lift balance system, a spring-loaded spiral rod encased in a tube rests in a channel in the side of the stile. The top of the tube is screwed to the side jamb; the rod is attached to a mounting bracket on the bottom of the sash (see illustration below). Each sash has two such units.

**Adjusting the tension.** With a spiral-lift balance, adjusting the spring tension may be all that's needed to make the window operate properly. If the sash tends to creep up, loosen the spring by detaching the tube from the sash channel and letting the spring unwind a bit. If the sash keeps sliding down, turn the rod clockwise a few times to tighten the spring. If this doesn't help, you'll need to replace the unit.

**Replacing the unit.** To remove a broken balance, pry off the stop on the affected side (page 55) and unscrew the tube where it's fastened to the top of the side jamb. Let the spring unwind; then raise the sash 6 to 8 inches and angle it out of the frame. If the rod is attached to the bottom of the sash with a detachable hook, unhook it; support the sash in a raised position with a wood block, and unscrew and remove the mounting bracket.

Position a new tube in the channel and screw it into the top of the side jamb. Pull the spiral rod down as far as it will go and turn it clockwise about four complete turns to tighten the spring. Let the rod retract into the tube far enough so you can fasten the mounting bracket to the bottom of the sash. Replace the sash.

Check the movement of the sash by sliding it up and down, and adjust the tension as described at left. Once the window is operating properly, reposition the stop (page 55).

## Tension-spring & cord systems

In a tension-spring balance system, each sash is operated by two balance units with spring-loaded drums inside; the units fit into the side jamb near the top. A flexible metal tape hooks onto a bracket screwed into a groove in the sash.

A cord balance system, not shown here, is a variation of the tension-spring system. Two spring-loaded reel units fit into each corner of the top jamb. Nylon cords connect the units to each sash; plastic top and side jamb liners conceal the working parts.

**Replacing the unit.** If any part of a tension-spring or cord balance system breaks, you'll have to remove the unit and install a new one.

To remove a tension-spring unit, remove the stop on the affected side (page 55) and ease out the sash. Unhook the tape from the bracket and let it wind back on the drum. Remove the screws from the drum plate and pry the unit out of the jamb pocket.

Insert the new balance into the jamb pocket and secure it with wood screws. Using needlenose pliers, pull the tape down and hook the end to the bracket on the sash. Replace the sash, check its operation, and reposition the stop (page 55).

A cord balance unit is replaced in the same way as a tension-spring unit. You'll need to remove the jamb liners in order to remove the sash and then pry out the balance unit from the top jamb.

---

## REPLACING A SPIRAL-LIFT UNIT

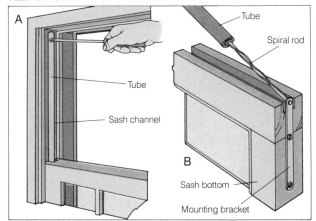

**To remove the unit,** unfasten the tube from the jamb (A) and remove the mounting bracket from the sash bottom (B). To install a new unit, attach the new tube to the jamb, tighten the spring, and fasten the new mounting bracket to the sash.

## REPLACING A TENSION-SPRING UNIT

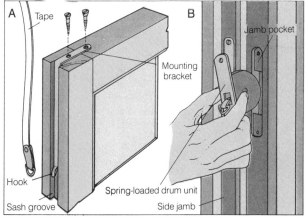

**To remove the unit,** unhook the tape from the sash (A) and let it wind back on the drum. Unscrew and remove the drum unit from the side jamb (B). Insert the new unit into the jamb pocket and screw it on. Pull down the tape and hook it to the sash.

# Casement Windows

A casement window, whether made from wood or metal, has a sash hinged at the side and is operated either by a sliding rod (usually found in older windows) or by a crank and gear mechanism. A window made from metal seldom experiences problems if the hinges, latch, and window operator are lubricated regularly. Problems that can develop include a faulty window operator and, with a window made from wood, a binding or warped sash.

## Repairing a faulty window operator

You can prevent most window operator problems with a simple maintenance routine. Occasionally clean the mechanism and lubricate with paraffin, a few drops of light penetrating oil, or silicone spray. If a casement window resists opening or closing, use one of the methods below to get it in working order again.

**Sliding rod mechanism.** Look for hardened grease or paint on the sliding rod. Cleaning and lubricating the rod, channel (if any), and pivot points, as shown below, usually solves the problem.

**Crank and gear mechanism.** First try cleaning and lubricating the extension-arm track (see below).

If the window still doesn't operate properly, check the gear assembly in the crank mechanism. To do this, you'll have to unfasten and remove the operator. Open the window partially and remove the screws that hold the operator to the frame. Slide the extension arm toward you along the track until it slips free. Then pull the extension arm in through the window frame.

Inspect the gears; if the teeth are worn, replace the unit with an exact duplicate that cranks in the same direction as the old one.

If the gear teeth are still sharp but are clogged with dirt, remove any dirt or grease with a piece of stiff wire or clean the assembly with a solvent, such as kerosene. Let it dry. Lubricate metal gears with graphite powder, silicone, or petroleum jelly; then turn the crank several times to spread the lubricant. Use silicone spray on nylon gears. If the gears still malfunction, replace the entire assembly with a duplicate.

## Correcting a binding sash

If a sash sags or sticks, adjust the hinges as for a door (page 69).

To fix a paint-bound sash, scrape away any excess paint and sand the surface smooth. If a wood sash has swollen, sand the part that's rubbing. If the stop has swollen, remove it, sand as necessary, and reposition it (page 55).

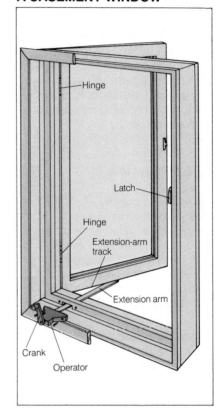

### A CASEMENT WINDOW

Hinge
Latch
Hinge
Extension-arm track
Extension arm
Crank
Operator

Seal and refinish any bare wood after sanding.

A mild warp in a sash made from wood can be compensated for by adjusting the stops (page 55) or by adding weatherstripping (page 64).

---

## CLEANING THREE TYPES OF WINDOW OPERATORS

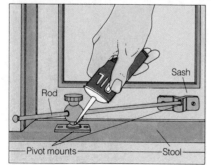

Rod
Sash
Pivot mounts
Stool

**Rod that slides through a pivot mount.** With steel wool, remove any dirt or paint from the rod; lubricate it with paraffin. Oil all pivot points and tighten the screws holding the mounts to the sash and stool.

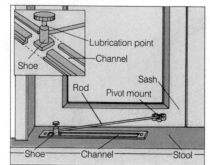

Lubrication point
Channel
Shoe
Rod
Sash
Pivot mount
Shoe
Channel
Stool

**Rod with a sliding shoe.** Unscrew the channel and clean both the channel and stool. Lubricate the channel with paraffin and replace it. Tighten all the screws; oil all pivot points.

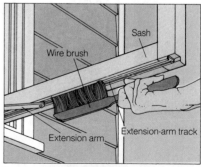

Sash
Wire brush
Extension arm
Extension-arm track

**Crank and gear mechanism.** Open the window and clean the track. Lubricate the inside of the track with petroleum jelly or silicone spray, removing any excess. Lubricate the operator.

# Sliding Windows

Sliding window sashes move along metal, wood, or vinyl tracks fitted into the window frame at the top and bottom. To ease their movement, large sashes often have plastic rollers attached to the top and bottom, or to the bottom only.

Paint sealing the sash to the frame, a dirty or bent track, or sticking rollers can cause the sash to stick or bind. The window can jam or not close properly if its catch is bent, loose, or damaged.

**Freeing a paint-bound sash.** If a sash is clogged with paint, score the edges with a sharp utility knife, then rock the sash from side to side to loosen it. Clean any dirt from the sides of the sash and the frame, and lubricate both with paraffin.

**Cleaning and repairing a track**
Use a wire brush to clean dirt from the track; for stubborn particles, use the blade of a screwdriver. Lubricate the track with paraffin to keep the sash movement smooth.

Repair a bent track using the method shown below. You may need to remove the sash from the track before making the repair.

If the rollers are sticking, lubricate them with graphite powder or silicone spray until they move freely. If they're broken, you'll need to remove the sash (see below) and have a glazier replace the rollers.

## A SLIDING WINDOW

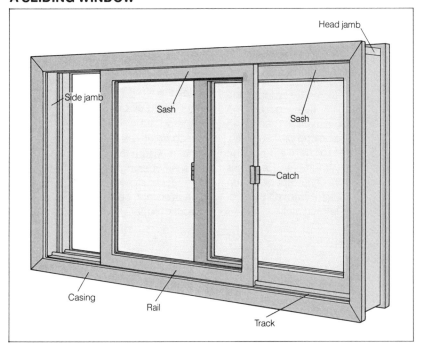

**Repairing a catch.**   Sliding windows are secured with a variety of catches; the type used depends on the manufacturer and whether the windows are made from metal or wood. If the catch doesn't work properly, you may need to remove the sash from the frame (see below) to fix it.

You may be able to reshape a bent catch. First note how much it will have to be reshaped. Then remove the catch and clamp it in a vise. Using pliers or a hammer, bend the catch to the proper angle. Replace it and check the latch operation—it should click as the window closes, and it should have to be depressed fully for the window to open.

Usually, the best solution is to replace a malfunctioning catch or one that is worn or broken with an exact duplicate.

## STRAIGHTENING A BENT TRACK

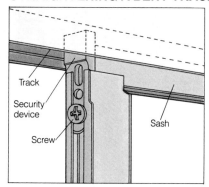

**1)   To remove the sash,** first look for any security devices at the top; loosen the screws holding them in place and remove the devices.

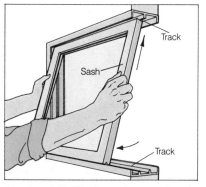

**2)   Carefully lift the sash up** to clear the track and angle the bottom edge out of the frame. Align the top rollers with the key notches, if any.

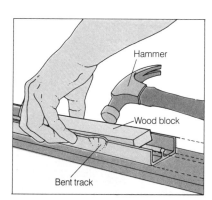

**3) Place a wood block** in the track; using a hammer, tap the block against the bent metal until the side of the track is flat. Replace the sash.

# Window Glass

Replacing a pane—especially a small one—in a window sash isn't difficult. After carefully removing the old glass and measuring the opening, you can either cut new glass to size yourself or have it done. Install it in the same way the original glass was installed.

CAUTION: Take care when working with glass. Wear heavy gloves and safety goggles if you're removing shards. Before removing broken glass, tape newspaper to the inside of the sash to catch any fragments. Pad glass with several layers of newspaper when you're transporting it and dispose of glass fragments immediately.

**Wood sashes.** In wood sashes, tiny metal glazier's points and glazing putty on the outside of the window hold the glass in the sash.

The steps in reglazing a wood sash are shown below. After you've removed the glass, you'll need to chisel out all the old putty. If it's hard, soak it with linseed oil or gently heat it with a propane torch.

To determine the size for the new pane, measure the width and height of the sash opening and subtract ⅛ inch from each dimension. Measure the sash at several points to allow for its being out of square.

NOTE: Since wood sashes are re-puttied from the outside, you may have to remove an upper-story window or get up on a ladder to reglaze it.

**Metal sashes.** In windows with metal sashes, glass may be held in place in several ways. Metal casement windows (page 58) may use putty or a combination of putty and metal spring clips. Glass in these windows is replaced in much the same way as for wood sashes. In other windows, the glass is secured with rubber seals, a rubber gasket, or beveled metal or plastic snap-out moldings.

---

## REGLAZING A WOOD SASH

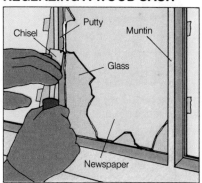

**1)  After removing large glass shards** with gloved hands, chisel out remaining bits of glass and putty. Remove glazier's points with pliers. Clean and sand the wood; coat it with wood sealer.

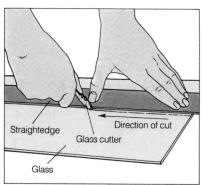

**2)  If the glass isn't precut,** measure the window opening and plan to cut the glass ⅛ inch smaller in each dimension. Score the glass deeply with a glass cutter (dip wheel in kerosene first).

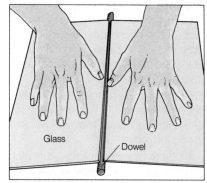

**3)  Place the score** over a small dowel and press down on both sides (or tap the underside of the score with the ball end of the cutter). Using the notches on the cutter, nibble off any uneven pieces.

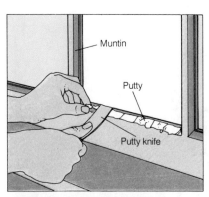

**4)  Working from outside the window,** use a putty knife and your fingers to press a rope of glazing putty about ¼ inch thick around the edges of the opening to make a bed for the replacement glass.

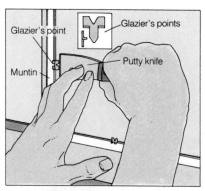

**5)  Press the pane** into place; remove excess putty. Push glazier's points into the frame with a putty knife (use two points on each side for small panes and a point every 4 to 6 inches for larger ones).

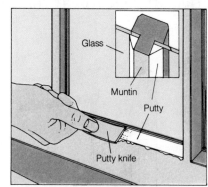

**6)  Roll more putty** into a rope about ¼ inch thick; apply it around the outside edges. With a putty knife, smooth and bevel the putty to form a neat seal. When dry, paint to match the wood.

# Window Sills

Window sills bear the brunt of snow, rain, and sun. Though they're designed to be tough, it's no wonder they show signs of wear. Annual maintenance—filling cracks with putty, caulking the edges, and repainting sills regularly—can prolong their life.

To restore a sill that's not badly damaged, clean out cracked or rotted wood with a chisel and screwdriver. Then soak the sill with wood preservative. When dry (about 24 hours), coat it with linseed oil and let it dry. Then fill in any cracks or holes with wood or epoxy putty. If a crack or hole is very deep, build up the putty in layers, letting each layer dry completely. Prime and repaint the sill (for painting tips, see page 42).

A sill can also be patched with fiberglass patching material, which is pliable and waterproof. This material conceals holes and cracks but doesn't fill them, so you may first want to build up deep cracks with putty. Check at a paint or hardware store for fiberglass patching material and the tools and instructions needed to apply it.

If you're not fussy about looks, you can cover a badly damaged sill with a sheet of aluminum painted to match the wood. First, build up the sill with putty. Cut a paper template that fits the sill top and wraps underneath it; use the template to cut out the aluminum. Caulk the edges of the sill; then butt one edge of the aluminum up to the stool and nail it to the sill. Move a block of wood over the surface, tapping it with a hammer to shape the aluminum around and under the sill. Nail the aluminum to the sill's underside; seal any gaps with caulking. Clean the aluminum and paint it.

Below are directions for replacing a severely damaged sill. Have a new one milled to match at a lumberyard or cut one yourself. Buy lumber that's pressure-treated with a preservative compatible with the paint or stain you plan to use.

## REPLACING A WINDOW SILL

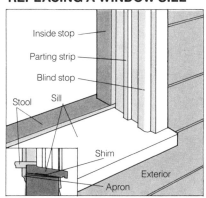

**1) Carefully pry off** the interior casings and inside stops (page 55). Remove the sash (page 56) and pry off the apron. Remove any nails from the stool and take it out in one piece.

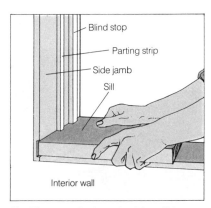

**2) Measure the length** of the sill between the jambs. Saw the sill into three pieces; remove the center piece, then the end pieces. Cut off any nails with the blade of a hacksaw.

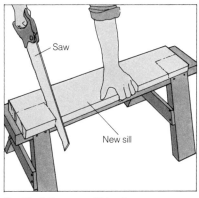

**3) Mark the new sill** for the correct length, allowing for any grooves in the jambs (use the old sill's end pieces as templates). Cut the new sill, beveling the ends slightly for an easier fit.

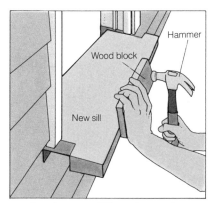

**4) Tap the new sill** into place, using a wood block to protect the edge. Don't force the sill; if it sticks, remove it and sand it lightly. Then try again.

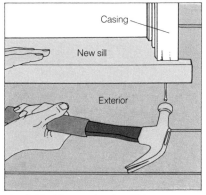

**5) Add shims** under the sill for a snug fit, if needed. Nail the sill to the side jambs from underneath and toenail it through the inside edge.

**6) Sink any exposed nail heads,** fill the holes, and seal the wood. Caulk the sill's edges and finish (page 42). Replace the stool, apron, sash, stops, and casings.

# Window Screens & Storm Windows

The window screens and storms in your home may be the kind you can remove, or they may be aluminum-frame combination storm and screen windows you can leave in place year-round. The frames may be wood or metal, the screening metal or fiberglass.

With regular maintenance, your storms and screens should last for years. Clean screening periodically with a stiff bristle brush; apply thinned screen enamel, paint, or varnish to galvanized metal screening. Paint wood storm and screen frames when necessary to protect them from weathering. Clean aluminum frames with aluminum polish or steel wool and coat them with paste wax.

**Mending a frame.** If a frame begins to separate at the corners, you can mend and reinforce the corners with glue or with metal reinforcing angles, corrugated fasteners, wood screws, or glued-in wood dowels (see below).

Lay the screen or storm on a flat surface and clean out the gap in the joint. If the frame is in good condition and the joint is clean, simply pour waterproof glue into the joint. Clamp it until the glue dries.

If the frame is still loose, attach metal reinforcing angles or corrugated fasteners at the corners, or fasten with wood screws.

To reinforce the corners with glue-coated dowels, clamp together opposite frame rails, using a long bar clamp. Tap the dowel into a predrilled hole, as shown below.

**Repairing or replacing screening.** If the screening has a small hole or tear, patch it (see below) before the flaw gets any bigger. You can fix a small hole in fiberglass screening by gluing a patch in place.

If the hole or tear is very large, or if the screening is old and worn, it's best to replace it (see facing page). To replace fiberglass screening in a wood frame, follow the instructions for replacing metal screening, but cut the screening with a razor blade and turn the edges under 1½ inches to form a hem. If you are replacing fiberglass screening in an aluminum frame, use a screen-spline roller to roll both the screening and the spline into the channel in one operation.

**Replacing storm window glass.** Glass in storm windows is replaced in the same way as glass in permanent windows (page 60).

## THREE WAYS TO REPAIR A WOOD FRAME

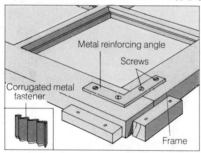

**Glue the frame at the corner** and hold it in place with two wood blocks nailed to the work surface. Screw in a reinforcing angle or hammer in a corrugated metal fastener.

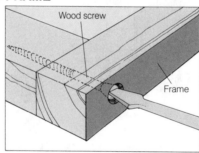

**Glue the frame at the corner;** then countersink a long wood screw through the corner joint. Cover the screw head with wood putty; sand, then paint over it to match the frame.

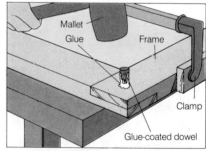

**Drill a hole** centered in the frame's corner (make it 5/16 inch in diameter and ¼ inch shorter than the frame's thickness). Tap in a 5/16-inch-diameter glue-coated dowel; trim, sand, and paint.

## THREE WAYS TO PATCH A SCREEN

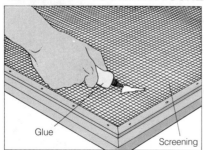

**Repair a very small tear** in metal or fiberglass screening with epoxy or acetone-type glue. Layer the glue on until the tear is filled.

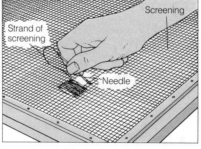

**Repair a small hole** by weaving or darning strands of scrap screening into the tear. Weave the strands into sound fabric to close the hole.

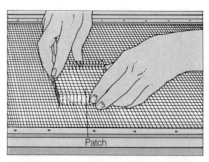

**For a large tear,** cut a patch larger than the tear. Unravel each side, bend the end wires, and push them through. Bend the ends back to hold the patch.

## REPLACING METAL SCREENING IN A WOOD FRAME

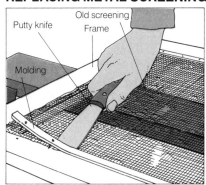

**1) Carefully pry off the molding** with a putty knife or chisel, working from the ends toward the center; set it aside. Remove and discard the old screening (or save for making patches).

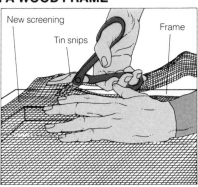

**2) Using tin snips,** cut a new piece of screening 2 inches larger than the opening on all sides. Staple the screening to one end of the frame so the staples will be under the molding.

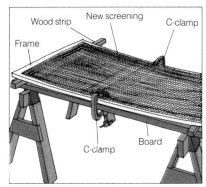

**3) To bow the frame,** place it on boards over sawhorses and put ¾-inch-thick strips under the ends; clamp the middle. Staple the other end of the screening; remove the clamps and the supports.

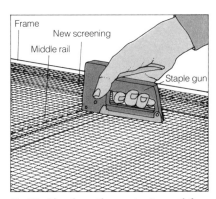

**4) Working from the center toward the ends,** staple each side of the screening, pulling it tight. Staple the middle rail last.

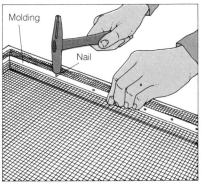

**5) Nail on the molding.** Countersink the nail heads and fill in any holes. (Refinish any new molding to match the frame.)

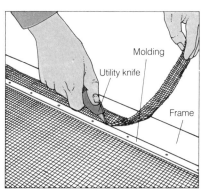

**6) With a utility knife,** carefully cut away the excess screening around the frame, using the molding as a guide.

## REPLACING METAL SCREENING IN AN ALUMINUM FRAME

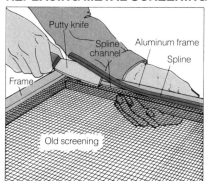

**1) Pry off the splines.** Cut new screening the same size as the frame's outer dimensions, squaring the corners. Place the screening flush with the channel's outer edges on one end and side.

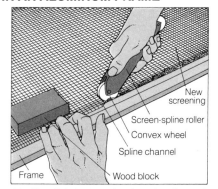

**2) Bend the screening** into the channel at the end of the frame, using the convex wheel of a screen-spline roller or a putty knife. Use a wood block or brick to weight down the screening.

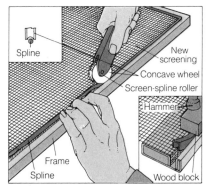

**3) Push the spline** back into the channel, using the concave wheel of the roller or a wood block and hammer. Holding the screening edges tight, insert splines in the other end and sides. Trim any excess.

# WEATHERSTRIPPING WINDOWS

Most windows manufactured now are weatherstripped at the factory. If your windows aren't weatherstripped, you can seal them yourself with weatherstripping. The three types generally available are spring type, pliable gasket, and compressible felt strips. Look for weatherstripping in a building supply store or home improvement center.

Spring-type weatherstripping made from bronze, aluminum, or stainless steel is either bent in the shape of a V (cushion-metal strips) or slightly angled (spring-metal strips); made from plastic, it's shaped like a V. You fasten it with nails to the window frame, except at the bottom where you nail it to the bottom of the sash.

Pliable-gasket weatherstripping is made from resilient material, such as vinyl, vinyl-and-foam, felt, or sponge. This type of weatherstripping is either backed with adhesive or attached with nails; it should fit on the window stop so the sash presses lightly against it. Though not visible from the inside, the strips may be very noticeable from the outside.

Compressible felt strips are the least effective and durable type of weatherstripping, but they're useful in some situations (see below). Some strips fasten with nails or glue; others are backed with adhesive.

**Double-hung windows.** Spring-type weatherstripping is best for a double-hung window (page 54). Though it's more difficult to install than pliable gasket, it's more durable and less visible. Install the weatherstripping in the channels, on the top of the upper sash top rail, on the bottom of the lower sash bottom rail, and on the side of the upper sash bottom rail where the sashes meet.

**Casement windows.** Pliable-gasket weatherstripping works well on wood casement (page 58) and other hinged windows. Cushion-metal weatherstripping can also be used on wood casement windows. Some metal casement windows can be weatherstripped with a special spring-metal strip or vinyl gasket (these must be special ordered).

You can attach compressible felt strips to the frame of a metal or wood casement window where the sash meets the stop and frame. Though the strips wear out quickly, they're good for a warped window that doesn't close tight.

**Sliding windows.** For sliding windows with wood sashes (page 59), install pliable-gasket weatherstripping along the outside top and bottom of the frame. If only one sash moves, use pliable-gasket weatherstripping along the side of the fixed sash and spring-type weatherstripping in the channel where the movable sash closes against the frame.

If both sashes move, install pliable-gasket weatherstripping where each sash fits against the side of the frame and between the two sashes so it forms a seal where they meet.

## THREE TYPES OF WINDOW WEATHERSTRIPPING

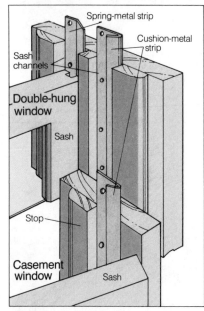

**Spring-type weatherstripping** fastens with small nails to the frame of a double-hung or casement window. After installation, the flange is pried up for a tight fit.

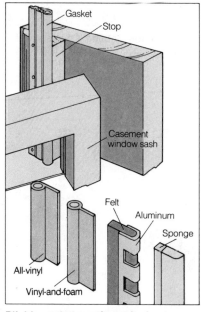

**Pliable-gasket weatherstripping** is adhesive-backed or attached with small nails. Fasten it to the stops so the sash presses lightly against it.

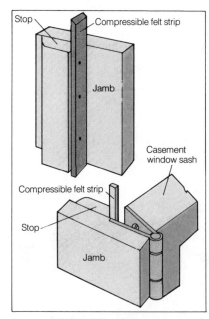

**A compressible felt strip** (used on metal or wood casement windows) is nailed or glued to the stop. On the hinge side, it's glued to the frame.

# Window Coverings

## Rollers & Shades

A window shade is attached to a roller, which is held in place by two brackets on the window frame. A blade at one end of the roller fits into one bracket; a stationary pin fits into the other. A spring inside the roller controls the shade tension. A pawl at one end of the roller engages a ratchet tooth to lock the shade in place.

The usual failures of rollers are bent or loose brackets, too much or too little spring tension, or a dirt-clogged part in the spring-and-lock assembly. Fortunately, these problems are usually not difficult to correct. Basic window shade repairs are described in the chart below.

**Replacing a roller and/or shade.** If a problem cannot be corrected, you may need to replace the roller and/or the shade with new ones cut to size.

If the old roller and shade fit well, measure the old roller's width; then unroll the shade completely and measure its length.

An alternate method is to measure the window opening (a typical window is shown on page 54). For mounting inside the frame, measure the distance between the brackets on the side jambs to determine the roller width. Measure from the top jamb to the stool and add 8 inches to determine the shade length.

For mounting outside the frame, measure the distance between the brackets for the roller width. Then measure from the middle of the top casing to the stool and add 8 inches for the shade length.

To cut a replacement roller to size, remove the cloth; then remove the barrel and stationary pin. Make the cut with a saw (be careful not to cut the spring). Replace the barrel and pin in the exact center of the end of the roller.

To cut a shade to size, unroll it completely. Square the corners, then measure the shade's new width at several points and mark it with a straightedge. Cut the shade to size with a pair of scissors, shorten the bottom slat as needed, and drill a new hole for the pull cord. Align the top edge of the shade with the roller guideline and staple it in place.

### ANATOMY OF A ROLLER

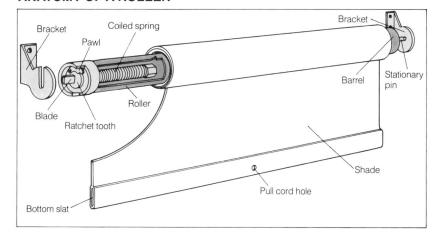

Labels: Bracket, Coiled spring, Pawl, Bracket, Blade, Ratchet tooth, Roller, Barrel, Stationary pin, Bottom slat, Pull cord hole, Shade

### SOLVING WINDOW SHADE PROBLEMS

| Problem | Possible Cause | Remedies |
| --- | --- | --- |
| **Shade winds up too quickly** | Tight spring tension | Roll up shade, remove roller from bracket, then partially unroll shade; replace roller and test; if not fixed, try again or replace |
| **Shade winds up too slowly** | Loose spring tension | Pull shade down about 24 inches, letting ratchet tooth catch; then remove roller from brackets, reroll shade about 6 or 8 inches, replace roller, and test; if not fixed, try again or replace |
| **Shade binds** | Brackets too close together | Hammer brackets out, bend out, or reposition; if shade is mounted inside window frame, trim stationary pin with a hacksaw or heavy-duty cutting pliers |
| **Shade wobbles** | Bent stationary pin | Straighten pin with pliers or replace |
| **Shade falls from its brackets** | Brackets too far apart | Move brackets in slightly; if shade is mounted inside window frame, shim out one or both brackets |
| **Shade doesn't catch** | Pawl not catching | Brush dirt off pawl and ratchet tooth; lubricate with graphite |

# ...Window Coverings

## Venetian Blinds

With their many moving parts, venetian blinds often need adjusting. The blinds are operated by a series of cords and a tube. A tilt cord or rod attaches to a pulley and worm gear, which in turn operates the tilt tube. Attached to the tube are ladder tapes, which adjust the slant of the slats. The blind is raised and lowered by the lift cord; it's threaded through the slats and lift cord pulleys.

If a blind rises unevenly, loosen the equalizer catch, adjust the cords so they're even, and reset the catch. If the operation is balky or stops altogether, check for worn or broken cords and tapes or dirt-clogged gears. Clean any dirt from the worm gear and lubricate it with light oil.

To replace worn or broken cords and tapes, see below. Be sure the new tapes have the same slat width and number of rungs as the old ones.

### ANATOMY OF A VENETIAN BLIND

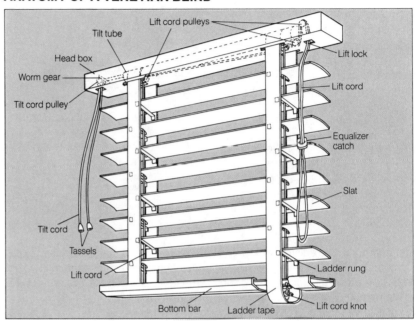

### REPLACING CORDS & LADDER TAPES

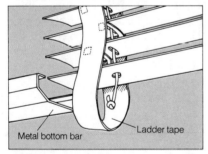

**1)  Take down the blinds;** slide off the metal bottom bar to free the ladder tapes.

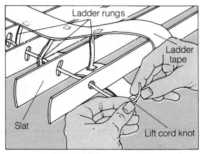

**2)  Untie the lift cord knots;** pull the cord up through the slats, off the pulleys.

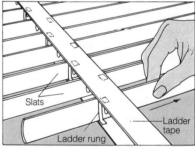

**3)  Remove the slats** to replace the tapes. Unclip the tapes from the tilt tube.

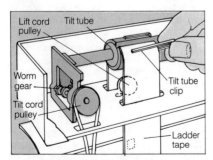

**4)  Clip the new tapes** in the tilt tube, slip them under the bottom slat, and replace the slats. Knot one end of the new lift cord; feed it up through the first slat.

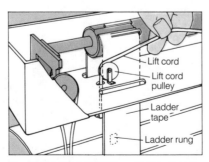

**5)  Thread the cord** through the slats (on alternate sides of ladder rungs), over both lift cord pulleys, and down through the other side; knot. Replace the bottom bar.

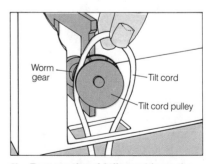

**6)  Remove the old tilt cord** (save the tassels). Simply loop the new tilt cord over the tilt cord pulley and replace the tassels.

# Traverse Rods

With a traverse rod, you can open and close your draperies by pulling on a cord which moves a series of slides along a track (the draperies are hooked onto the slides). A two-way traverse rod allows two drapery panels to overlap in the center and open to each side. A one-way traverse rod moves a single panel to one side. Both types are mounted on adjustable brackets.

If your draperies don't draw properly, check first for loose or misaligned brackets, obstructions in the track, or broken slides. Then look for worn cords or poor cord tension. If two-way draperies draw unevenly, the problem may be a slipped cord.

**Adjusting the brackets.** If the brackets are loose, replace any nails with screws and any loose screws with longer ones. Fill any stripped screw holes with glue-coated dowels (page 69) or install wall anchors; then reset the screws.

If the rod isn't parallel to the wall, adjust the setscrews so the bracket ends are all equidistant from the wall.

**Checking the track and cord.** Remove any obstructions on the track with a wire hook. You'll have to open the end gate, as shown below, to get past the slides.

## TWO TYPES OF TRAVERSE RODS

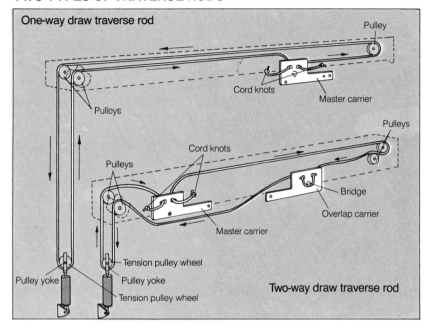

One-way draw traverse rod

Pulley · Cord knots · Master carrier · Pulleys

Pulleys · Cord knots · Pulleys · Bridge · Overlap carrier · Master carrier

Tension pulley wheel · Pulley yoke · Pulley yoke · Tension pulley wheel

Two-way draw traverse rod

To adjust a slipped cord or the cord tension, see below.

NOTE: It's easiest to take down the draperies and remove the rod from the brackets before working on it.

**Replacing a cord.** A badly worn or frayed cord should be replaced. The illustration above shows how cords are threaded. After knotting the end, thread the new cord through the master carrier, around the pulleys, under the bridge on the overlap carrier (for a two-way draw), and through the tension pulley wheel. Continue around the last pulley and through the master carrier again. Adjust the tension as shown below; knot the other end.

## THREE TRAVERSE ROD ADJUSTMENTS

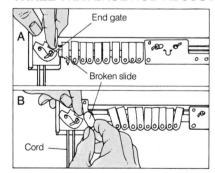

**To remove a broken slide,** push down on the end gate (A). Slip the slide (you may need to remove several slides to get at the broken one) out of the track (B). Replace the slide with an exact duplicate and return the gate to its original position.

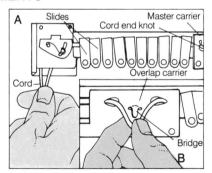

**If draperies don't draw evenly** (two-way rod), pull the cord to bring the master carrier to the end of the rod. Hold the cord taut (A). Push the overlap carrier to the other end of the rod and hook the cord under the bridge (B).

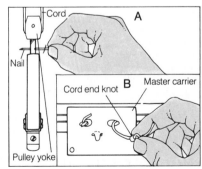

**To adjust poor cord tension** (one or two-way rod), pull the pulley yoke up and hold it in place with a nail (A). Retie the cord end knot in the master carrier to take up the excess (B). Remove the nail from the pulley yoke.

# Hinged Doors

All hinged doors have the same basic framework, sometimes hidden under a solid veneer. The framework consists of two stiles, which run vertically, and two or more rails, which run horizontally. The hinges are on one stile; the latch and lock are on the other.

The two types of wood doors are panelled and flush. A panelled door has a visible frame of stiles and rails that supports two or more panels. If multi-panelled, as shown here, the door has mullions and extra rails.

A flush door is faced with hardboard or wood veneer covering the frame. A flush door for exterior use should have a solid core made from several layers of hardwood or particle board; an interior flush door usually has a hollow core formed from a frame surrounding a grill-like structure.

The door is hinged to a frame, consisting of jambs, casing, stops, sill, and threshold. The jambs form the sides and head of the frame; the casing acts as trim and as support for the jambs. The stops are wood strips the door fits against when closed. In exterior doors, a sill fits between the jambs, forming the frame bottom. The threshold, or saddle, is fastened to the sill.

## Repairing a door

Age and continual use can cause even a well-fitted door to loosen, bind, or warp. Often, the latch no longer works properly. Fortunately, correcting these problems is usually fairly simple. But a door that's badly warped will have to be replaced (pages 72–73).

**Loose doors.** If a door is too small for its frame, an easy solution is to install weatherstripping (pages 80–81). If a loose door is causing latch problems, you may be able to adjust the latch (page 72).

**Binding doors.** Binding or sticking results from a number of causes, from a buildup of dirt and paint to a door that sags and no longer fits in its frame. Adjusting the fit of the door usually solves the problem (see facing page).

### A TYPICAL HINGED DOOR & FRAME

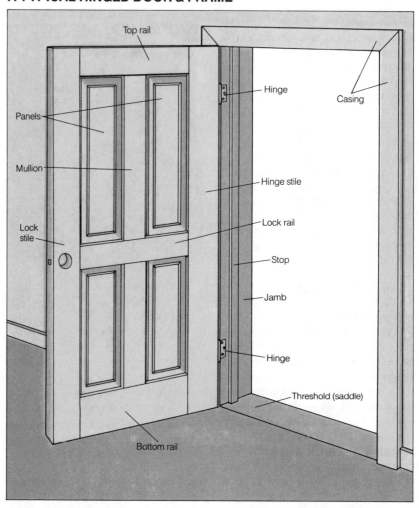

Top rail

Hinge

Casing

Panels

Mullion

Hinge stile

Lock stile

Lock rail

Stop

Jamb

Hinge

Threshold (saddle)

Bottom rail

**Warped doors.** If the warp is minor, you may be able to adjust the stop or hinges to compensate for it. See page 70 for more information.

**Latch problems.** When a latch refuses to work, the trouble may be either with the fit of the door or with the lockset (pages 77–79).

## Removing a door

If you're working on just one hinge at a time or on the top of a door, you need only open the door partially and drive a wedge underneath the latch side to hold the door steady. But for other repairs, such as sanding or planing the side or bottom of a door, you'll need to remove it from its hinges.

To remove the hinge pins, close the door securely (place a wedge under it or have a helper hold the door). Using a hammer and a nail or nailset, gently tap on the bottom of the lowest pin or on the underside of its head to drive it up and out of the hinge barrel. Remove the middle pin, if any, then remove the top pin. Lift the door off its hinges.

When you reinstall the door, replace the top pin first, then the middle and bottom ones. Drive the pins home only after the hinges are correctly aligned. Leave the pins a little loose so they'll be easier to remove for future repairs.

# Binding Doors

A common and annoying problem is a door that sticks or binds, making it difficult to open and close it easily. Binding can result from a buildup of paint or dirt, or from a misaligned or sagging door. The cure is usually to adjust improperly set or loose hinges and/or sand or plane the door edges (pages 70–71).

First, identify the spots that bind by inserting a thin strip of cardboard or wood between the door and jambs. Look for a buildup of dirt and paint on the door edges or jambs. Chisel off any large globs of paint and sand the sur-

face. Coat the door edges and the jambs with paraffin.

Often, simply tightening loose hinges gets a sagging door back in alignment. First, clean off any dirt and repair or replace any bent hinges. Tighten any loose hinge screws. If they can't be tightened, repair the screw holes as shown below and replace the screws.

If the door binds badly or isn't square in its frame, you can diagnose the problem (see below) to determine which repairs are needed. The hinges

may have to be shimmed or set in deeper mortises (page 70). Deepen the mortises as a last resort; getting the right depth can be tricky.

If you must remove excess wood from the door edges, sand with coarse, followed by finer, sandpaper. Keep the sanding as even as possible. Plane only if necessary. When sanding or planing the stiles, concentrate on the hinge side; the lock side is usually beveled to allow for a tight fit. (For information on using a plane, see pages 70–71.)

## TWO WAYS TO REPAIR STRIPPED SCREW HOLES

Glue-coated wood dowels

Screw hole

**Drive glue-coated wood dowels** or pegs into the holes. Let the glue dry; trim off excess wood. Redrill the holes.

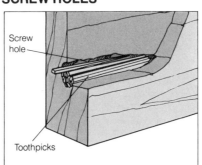

Screw hole

Toothpicks

**Pack the holes** with toothpicks or matchsticks as a quick fix for lightweight doors. Replace the screws with longer ones.

### QUICK FIX-UP
QUIETING SQUEAKY HINGES

Silence a noisy hinge by coating it with silicone spray or light penetrating oil. If the squeak persists, remove the pin and thoroughly clean the pin, barrel, and hinge leaves with steel wool. Coat them lightly with silicone spray or light penetrating oil and replace the pin.

## DIAGNOSING & ADJUSTING A BINDING DOOR

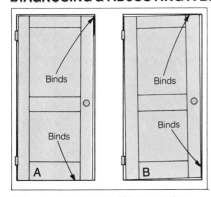

**If the door binds as in (A),** reseat the upper hinge (repair the screw holes and tighten the screws or deepen the mortise) and/or shim out the lower hinge. If the door binds as in (B), reverse the procedure.

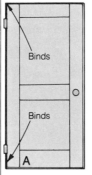

**If the door binds on the hinge side (A),** shim out both hinges, or remove the door and sand or plane the hinge side. If it binds on the lock side (B), sand or plane the hinge side and, if necessary, deepen the mortises for the hinges.

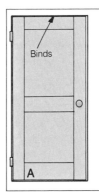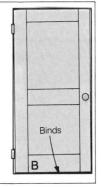

**If the door binds along the top (A),** wedge it open and sand or plane the wood along the top. If it binds along the bottom (B), remove the door and sand or plane the wood along the bottom. Take care not to remove too much wood.

# ...Hinged Doors

## Adjusting a Warped Door

The best insurance against warping is to seal the door on all surfaces to prevent moisture from swelling the wood. You may be able to compensate for a slightly warped door by repositioning the stop, partially shimming the hinges, or adding a hinge. It's best to replace a door that's badly warped (pages 72–73).

Where there's a slight bow on the hinge side, centering a third hinge between the top and bottom ones often pulls the door back into alignment.

If the bow is near the lock side and the door latches only when slammed, first try adjusting the latch (page 72). If this doesn't help, remove and reposition the stop as for a window (page 55) and, if necessary, adjust the strike plate alignment (page 72).

If the top or bottom of the door doesn't meet the stop on the lock side,

you can try to compensate for this type of warp by repositioning the stop and the strike plate. You may also have to shim the hinges (see below for instructions on making shims) to change the angle of the door's swing. Place a half-

shim, as shown below, under each hinge leaf either on the side of the leaf that's closest to the pin or on the opposite side (depending on the warp). Usually, the other hinge is shimmed in the opposite way.

### TWO WAYS TO ADJUST A WARPED DOOR

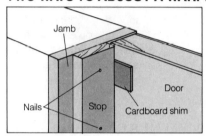

Reposition the stop (page 55), spacing with a cardboard shim; nail the stop in place.

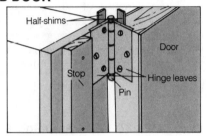

Place a half-shim of cardboard or thin wood under each hinge leaf to adjust the angle of a door that's slightly warped.

## Techniques for Working on Doors

Techniques for repairing a door include planing the edges, cutting or deepening hinge mortises, and making shims for hinges. To make these repairs, you may have to remove the hinge pins (page 68), take down the door, and support it on edge while you work.

**Supporting a door.** One way to support a door while you're working on it is to set it on edge and wedge one end into a corner of the room.

A better method is to build two door jacks (see facing page) and set the door on edge into the jacks, with the jacks near each end. The weight of the door will bend the plywood strips and press the 2 by 4 wood blocks against the door like a vise.

**Planing a door.** Don't be in a hurry to start planing. When only a small amount of wood must be removed, sandpaper wrapped around a wood block (page 20) is the best choice.

When you must plane, use a plane that's long enough to ensure flat cuts; the blade should be wider than the thickness of the door so the cuts will

be level. Though a jack plane (14 to 15 inches long) is preferable, a 9 to 10-inch-long smoothing plane will do the job.

To avoid gouging the wood, plane with the grain. Adjust the blade (page 19) to make paper-thin cuts so you don't remove too much wood (see facing page for planing tips).

If you're working on a binding door (page 69), plane the top or bottom rail if the door is binding there, or the hinge stile if the door binds on the hinge side. It's best to avoid planing a binding lock stile, since it involves maintaining the beveled edge along that side and, in some cases, repositioning the lockset. Instead, plane the hinge stile whenever possible to correct the problem.

You'll need to remove the hinge leaves before planing. Use a utility knife to cut through any paint around the leaves; then unscrew and remove the hinges. After you plane, deepen the hinge mortises, as explained below. If you must plane near the top or bottom of the lock stile, be sure to re-form the bevel after planing.

**Cutting hinge mortises.** Hinge mortises are recesses into which hinge leaves are fitted so they sit flush with the door or jamb surface. You'll need to cut hinge mortises (see facing page) if you're adding a middle hinge to straighten a warped door or if you're hanging a new door. If you're adjusting the position of the door in a jamb or you've planed the hinge stile, you'll have to deepen the mortises. To deepen a mortise, mark the new depth on the edge of the door or jamb; then go to Step 3 (see facing page, bottom right).

**Making shims.** To move a door closer to the lock side of the jamb, you can insert a shim under the hinge leaves. Use thin sheet brass (available in several thicknesses) or dense, hard-surfaced cardboard (such as that used in file folders).

Using a hinge leaf as a pattern, cut a shim and make the screw holes. (The shim should be minutely smaller in each dimension than the hinge.) Don't glue the shim in place—you may want to remove it later on.

**PROFESSIONAL HINT**
USING A PLANE

Use two hands when operating a plane, gripping the rear handle with one hand, the front knob or one edge with the other. At the beginning of the cut, apply slightly more pressure on the plane's toe; even out pressure as you continue the stroke, then near the end gradually switch pressure to the heel.

## SUPPORTING A DOOR

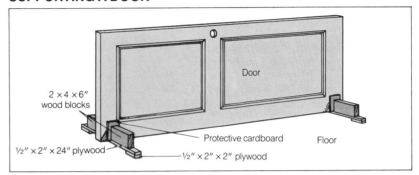

**To make a jack, nail 2 by 4 wood blocks** to strips of plywood. The clearance between the blocks should just accommodate the door and the protective cardboard.

## TIPS FOR PLANING DOOR EDGES

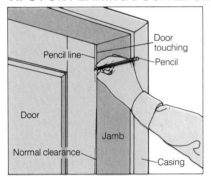

**Carefully mark the area** to be planed on both faces of the door before removing it from the hinges. Keep a close eye on your marks as you plane.

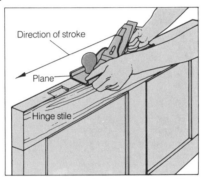

**Plane the stile,** using long strokes with the plane parallel to the stile; cut with the grain. If you're planing the lock side, be sure to re-form the bevel.

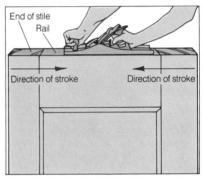

**Plane the top or bottom of the door** by cutting from the ends toward the center. This will avoid splitting the ends of the stiles.

## CUTTING A HINGE MORTISE

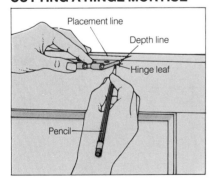

**1)  Using the hinge leaf as a template,** mark placement and depth lines for a new hinge or a depth line for a deeper mortise; then score with a hammer and chisel blade. If you're simply deepening a mortise, go to Step 3.

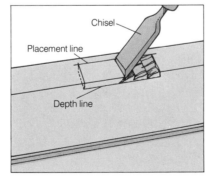

**2)  Make shallow, parallel cuts** to the desired depth, using a hammer and chisel held almost vertically. Then lower the chisel to a 30° angle, bevel side down, and without a hammer, chip out the wood to the desired depth.

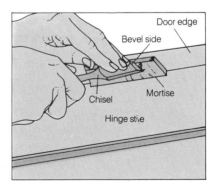

**3)  Make the final smoothing cuts** from the side, holding the chisel, bevel side up, almost flat. Position the hinge leaf and, for a new mortise, check that it's flush with the surface of the door or jamb. Mark and drill screw holes.

# ... Hinged Doors

## Adjusting Balky Latches

If a door latch doesn't catch or won't operate smoothly, the latch bolt on the door may not be lined up properly with the strike plate on the door jamb. Repairs range from minor latch adjustments to repositioning the door itself.

If the latch's operation isn't smooth, lubricate the latch with graphite. If it doesn't catch, close the door slowly to watch how the latch bolt meets the strike plate. The bolt may be positioned above, below, or to one side of the strike plate. (Often, scars on the surface of the strike plate will give you a precise clue to the degree and direction of misalignment.) The problem also could be that the door has shrunk and the latch no longer reaches the strike plate.

Once you've determined the adjustment needed, use one of the methods illustrated below to remedy the situation. Or, if the door has warped slightly, adjust the angle. To do this, you can either insert half-shims on the side of each hinge leaf that's closest to the pin, angling the door inward, or reposition the stop so the latch can engage the strike plate (see repairs for warped doors, page 70).

If the lock is causing the problem, turn to pages 77–79 for information on lock repairs.

### THREE WAYS TO ADJUST A STRIKE PLATE

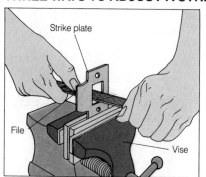

**For less than a ⅛-inch misalignment** of latch bolt and strike plate, remove the strike plate and file its inside edge to enlarge the opening. (You may need to extend the bolt mortise.)

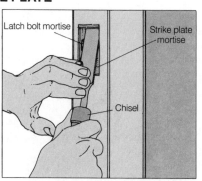

**For more than a ⅛-inch misalignment,** remove the strike plate and extend the mortise higher or lower as needed. Replace the plate, fill the gap at top or bottom with wood putty, and refinish.

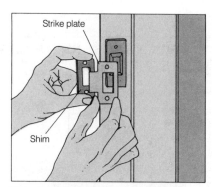

**If the latch doesn't reach** the strike plate, shim out the plate or add another strike plate. If the latch still won't reach, shim out the door's hinges. Replace the door with a wider one, if necessary.

## Replacing a Door

Hanging a replacement door (see facing page) takes patience. Following the steps in order and using the tips listed below will make the work go faster.

You can fit a new door to a pre-existing frame (see facing page) or buy an easy-to-install prehung unit that comes with frame, door, and hardware, all fitted and ready to install. Both types of doors are available at building supply stores and lumberyards.

Before purchasing a replacement door, remove the old door and measure the opening from top to bottom on both sides. Then measure across the opening at two or more points; check the upper corners with a steel square. Doors, particularly hollow-core ones, have only a ½-inch trim margin, so be sure the replacement door you purchase will fit your opening.

CAUTION: Be sure to double check all measurements before cutting.

Here are a few points to keep in mind when hanging a door:

- **Sand or plane** any excess wood up to ¹⁄₁₆ inch on the door's top and bottom, up to ¼ inch on the sides. Saw off any excess that's greater; sand.

- **Leave a ¹⁄₁₆-inch clearance** around the door on the top and sides. Bottom clearance should be at least ½ inch—more if you need to clear a rug.

- **Bevel the lock side** of the door ⅛ inch so the door will clear the jamb as it opens and closes. If the door is already beveled, install it so the beveled edge is on the lock side.

- **When installing a hinge** on the door, leave at least a ⅜-inch margin between the door edge and the hinge leaf edge.

- **If you're hanging a new door in an existing frame** (see facing page), use the existing hinges if possible. If you can't use them or must reposition them, follow Steps 6 and 7 and the instructions for making a hinge mortise on page 71.

- **Place the top hinge** about 7 inches below the top of the door, the other one 11 inches above the bottom of the door. If you're installing a third hinge, center it between the two.

## HANGING A REPLACEMENT DOOR

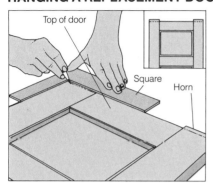

**1)  Mark the horns** on the replacement door to be cut off flush. If the opening isn't square, mark the door itself to fit, being careful not to exceed the door's trim margin (usually ½ inch).

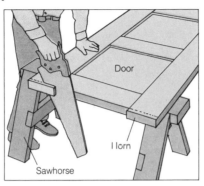

**2)  Rough-trim the new door.** Prop the door in the opening to check the fit. If the opening isn't standard size, make any additional cuts on the door that are necessary for fit.

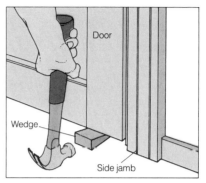

**3)  Place the door in the opening** and shim at the top for a ¹⁄₁₆-inch clearance; insert wedges under the door to hold it in place. Mark and cut the bottom, leaving a minimum ½-inch clearance.

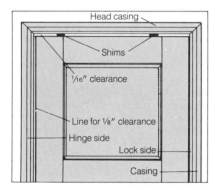

**4)  Wedge the door snugly** against the lock side, maintaining the ¹⁄₁₆-inch top clearance. Mark a trim line for a ⅛-inch clearance on the hinge side; trim. Bevel the lock side if necessary.

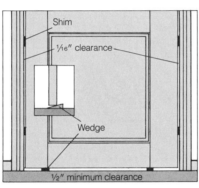

**5)  Hold the door** in position with shims and wedges and double check the clearances—¹⁄₁₆ inch on the top and sides and a minimum of ½ inch on the bottom. Lightly sand where needed.

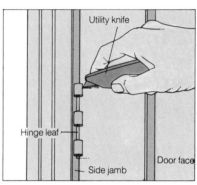

**6)  Remove the hinge-side shims** and push the door tight against the hinge jamb. Mark the hinge locations on the door with a utility knife, using the hinge leaves on the jamb as guides.

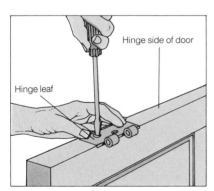

**7)  Outline the hinges,** using the marks made on the door. Cut the mortises with a hammer and chisel (page 71). Position the hinge leaves in the mortises, drill pilot holes, and insert the screws.

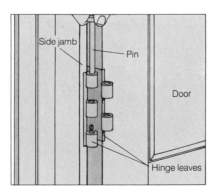

**8)  Start the top pin** through the barrel and position the door. Insert the middle and bottom pins. Wiggle the door until the pins slip in. Check for fit, trimming if necessary.

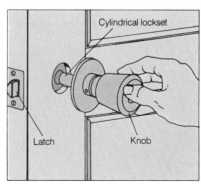

**9)  Install the new lockset** (pages 77–79). Take the door down and seal all surfaces with a sealer or primer to prevent swelling and warping. Finish the door and replace.

# Door Thresholds & Sills

The thresholds inside your house and the sills and thresholds in exterior doorways are the hardest-working parts of your doors. Because they're exposed to continual foot traffic and, in the case of exterior doorways, the elements, both may eventually need to be replaced.

The sill forms the bottom of the frame of an exterior doorway and serves the same function as a window sill—it diverts water away from the door and house. The sill fits snugly under the casing and against or under the jambs.

Fastened to the sill is a threshold, which helps seal the air space under a door. Thresholds are often used inside as well to make a neat transition between different flooring materials.

Thresholds, also called saddles, are available in either hardwood or metal (usually aluminum). You can also get special thresholds that act as weatherstripping (pages 80–81).

**Removing a threshold or sill.** Remove a damaged threshold or sill very carefully so you don't damage the door frame or, in the case of a sill, any flashing underneath. If necessary, you can cut them out, as shown for window sills on page 61. Unscrew and remove a metal threshold. Be sure your replacement is long enough and measure carefully before making any cuts.

**Installing a new threshold or sill.** Check that the clearance between the bottom of the door and the new threshold is about 1/8 inch. If it's less, mark the bottom of the door using the new threshold as a guide, and sand or trim the door to fit. For installation instructions, see at right.

If you're adding weatherstripping along the door bottom (page 80), follow the manufacturer's recommendations for clearance.

Once a wood threshold is in place, sink the nail heads and fill them. Sand the threshold smooth and coat an interior one with clear varnish or sealer. Fasten a metal threshold with screws.

Be sure to finish a sill and threshold in an exterior doorway to protect the wood against the elements.

## REPLACING A WOOD THRESHOLD

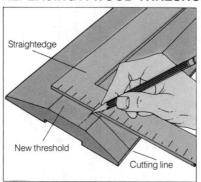

**1)   Mark the new threshold** to fit between the jambs; cut, notching the ends to fit around the stops. Sand all cut edges. Caulk the underside and ends; center it under the door.

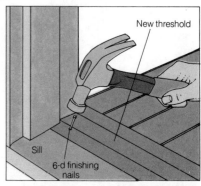

**2)   Nail the threshold** to the sill with 6-penny finishing nails (predrill the holes). Countersink the nail heads and fill the holes with wood putty. Finish the threshold as desired.

## REPLACING A SILL

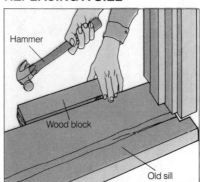

**1)   Drive out the old sill** (or saw it into three pieces and remove the center, then the ends) after removing any nails. Take care not to damage any flashing underneath.

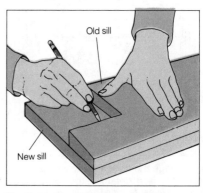

**2)   Using the old sill** as a template, mark and cut the new sill to fit (if the old sill isn't in one piece, fit it together and make very accurate measurements before cutting).

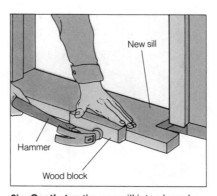

**3)   Gently tap** the new sill into place, being careful not to force it. (A wood block protects the sill.) Sand or trim the sill for a snug fit.

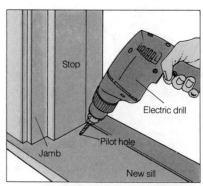

**4)   Drill pilot holes** for nails or screws after shimming the sill for fit, if necessary. Secure the sill, sink the nail or screw heads, and fill the holes with putty. Finish.

# Sliding Doors

All sliding doors operate in basically the same way, though the variety of their hardware is almost unlimited. Some lightweight sliding doors, such as closet doors and pocket doors (which slide into walls), and extremely heavy garage doors are hung from the top rail. Moderately heavy doors, such as patio doors, usually rest on the bottom rail.

Nearly all sliding doors glide on rollers which can be adjusted to make the door ride higher or lower. Plastic guides at the top or bottom keep the doors vertical and aligned with their tracks.

Removing a sliding door for maintenance or repair is simple (see below), but keep in mind that the door can be very heavy, especially when made from glass.

All tracks, especially the one that supports the rollers, must be kept free of foreign objects and dirt. Occasional application of a little graphite or paraffin to the track and a drop of oil to each roller bearing helps keep the operation smooth and quiet.

Inspect all hardware periodically. Tighten any loosened screws in the frame or track and replace any part that's worn, broken, or missing.

If a door jumps off its track, check for a dirty track, a section that's bent, or a guide that's out of alignment (see below). A door tilted in its frame usually needs roller adjustment (there should be a 3/8-inch clearance between the bottom of the door and the floor or rug).

Compensate for a minor warp in a door by adjusting the rollers. If a door is badly warped, you'll need to replace it.

## REMOVING THREE TYPES OF SLIDING DOORS

**Lift a bottom-supported door** straight up to clear the track; to remove it, sharply angle the lower part of the door outward. You may need a helper to hold the door, since it can be heavy.

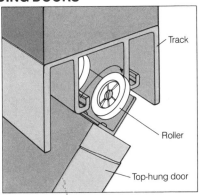

**Lift a top-hung door** straight up and angle it to lift the rollers out of the track. (Some top-hung doors have notches on the track that you must align with the rollers before you can lift the door out.)

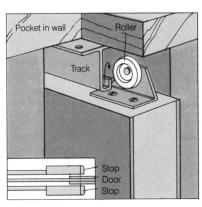

**On a pocket door,** remove both stops from the head jamb and one side jamb stop to allow the door to swing out. To remove the door, angle the bottom out, then lift it up.

## THREE SLIDING DOOR ADJUSTMENTS

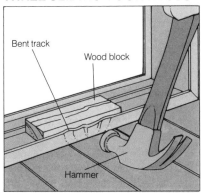

**Use a hammer and wood block** to straighten a bent metal track. Replace a badly bent or broken track.

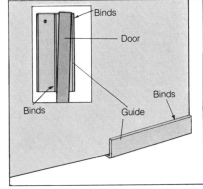

**Check the alignment** of the guide if the door binds. Reposition the guide so the door doesn't catch on it.

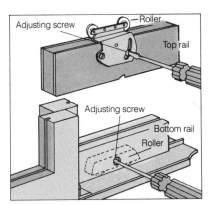

**Adjust the roller height** at both ends of a tilting or dragging door until the door is correctly aligned.

# Storm & Screen Doors

Storm and screen doors are hung outside your home's exterior doors. Storm doors have an upper panel of glass and a lower metal or glass panel; a crossbar divides the panels. The frame is usually made from aluminum or steel. Screen doors may have an aluminum or wood frame with metal or fiberglass screens. Popular now are combination doors—screens are fitted into the door for summer use and are replaced with glass panels in winter.

All storm and screen doors should have a door closer—either a simple chain-linked snubber or a pneumatic or hydraulic type (see at right). The closer ensures that the door closes smoothly and protects the door from being opened too wide or with too much force.

Like storm and screen windows, doors are subject to problems with their frames, glass, and screens. Door closers may also require adjustment, as described below.

**Maintenance and repair.** Maintain and repair your screen doors in the same way as window screens (page 62). Keep the hinges of both screen and storm doors oiled and tight, and lubricate the door closers once a year. Check that the latches work well.

Replace hardware, glass (page 60), and screens as necessary. In addition, replace the clips holding the screens and glass in place if they become bent, broken, or lost.

Replacement parts are usually available at building supply centers and hardware stores. Because each manufacturer's hardware may be slightly different, be sure the replacement part will fit your particular door.

**Adjusting door closers.** The simplest type of closer is a snubber; it attaches to the head jamb and the top rail of the door. You can adjust the length of the chain if the door opens too wide or not wide enough.

A pneumatic closer attaches to the door and the hinge jamb. The closing speed of this type can be adjusted by turning the adjustment screw in the end cap. A hold-open washer can be posi-

## THREE COMMON DOOR CLOSERS

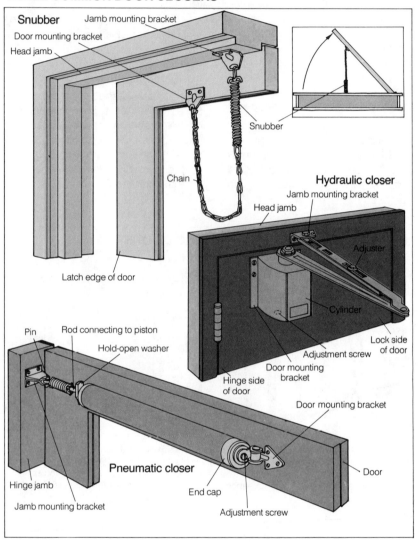

Snubber — Jamb mounting bracket — Door mounting bracket — Head jamb — Snubber — Chain — Latch edge of door

Hydraulic closer — Jamb mounting bracket — Head jamb — Adjuster — Cylinder — Lock side of door — Adjustment screw — Door mounting bracket — Hinge side of door

Pin — Rod connecting to piston — Hold-open washer — Door mounting bracket — Door — Pneumatic closer — End cap — Adjustment screw — Hinge jamb — Jamb mounting bracket

tioned on the rod to prop the door open.

A less common type of door closer is the hydraulic closer. Some types fit only a right-handed or a left-handed door; others can be adjusted for either type of door by inserting a screwdriver in the adjustment screw, pushing in, and turning the screw 180°. A slight adjustment to the same screw changes the door's closing speed.

**Installing a door closer.** Installing a closer is fairly simple. Before you begin, check that the door operation is smooth and that the door hardware is in good working order.

If you're installing a snubber, fasten the door mounting bracket to the door's top rail and the jamb mounting bracket to the head jamb. Adjust the length of the chain as necessary.

For a pneumatic closer, install the door mounting bracket on the door's top rail, mount the closer in the bracket, and fasten the jamb mounting bracket to the hinge jamb; adjust the closing speed.

To install a hydraulic closer, attach the door mounting bracket and the cylinder to the top rail. Then fasten the jamb mounting bracket to the head or side jamb and adjust the closing speed.

# Door Locksets

Most locksets for doors fall into two categories, depending on the way they're installed. One type, encompassing both cylindrical and tubular locksets, fits into a hole bored in the door's face; the other type, a mortise lockset, fits into a large recess cut into the edge of the door.

Most exterior doors have a cylindrical or mortise lockset operated with a key. Interior doors have either a cylindrical lockset operated with a push button or a tubular lockset, similar to a cylindrical one but simpler and less rugged. An older home may have keyless interior mortise locks. (For examples of cylindrical and mortise locks, see pages 78–79.)

Though locksets require immediate attention when they fail, many lockset problems tend to develop gradually and can be corrected before they become serious. If a lockset needs to be replaced, it's easiest to replace it with one of the same type. To change the type of lockset, see page 78.

**Troubleshooting a lockset.** Problems with locksets generally affect either the latch assembly or the lock mechanism. A latch problem may be the result of a poorly fitting door (page 68). A lock mechanism problem may be caused by a dirty or dry lock (though locksets are lubricated during assembly, the grease can get gummed up or dried out). Often, you can solve the problem simply by applying a lubricant. A more complicated lock problem may call for a locksmith or for a replacement lock.

Solutions to a range of common problems appear in the chart below. If your problems require professional help, keep in mind that removing the lock and taking it to a locksmith is far less expensive than having the locksmith come to you.

**Replacing a lock.** Often, it's simpler and less costly to replace the entire lockset, as shown on pages 78–79, than to try to fix it. You can buy mortise locksets for exterior doors and cylindrical and tubular locksets at building supply centers, hardware stores, and from some locksmiths. Mortise locksets for interior doors are less widely available. You may find a kit that converts a mortise lockset to a cylindrical or tubular one or you can try to order a replacement from the manufacturer.

If possible, take the old lockset with you when you're buying a new one. If you can't, you should have the following information:

- **Type of lock**—cylindrical, tubular, or mortise
- **Diameter** of the cylinder and latch holes or the size of the mortise
- **Backset measurement** (distance from the edge of the door to the center of the doorknob)
- **Thickness** of the door (most locks are designed for standard doors)
- **Direction** the door opens

## SOLVING LOCKSET PROBLEMS

| Problem | Possible Causes | Remedies |
|---|---|---|
| **Latch sticks or responds slowly** | Gummed up or dirty lock mechanism | Blow a pinch of graphite into lock mechanism or keyway; or inject light penetrating oil or silicone spray into lock mechanism |
| **Key doesn't insert smoothly** | Dirty keyway and tumbler area | Blow a pinch of graphite or spray silicone spray into keyway (do not use oil) |
| | Foreign object in keyway | Attempt to dislodge object with thin, stiff wire |
| **Lock is frozen** | Accumulated moisture frozen solid | Chip ice from opening; carefully heat key with a match; then insert key in lock and work it gently until ice melts |
| **Key is broken in lock** | Improperly inserted key, ill-fitting replacement key, or wrong key forced into lock | Remove broken key with thin, stiff hooked wire or with blade of a coping saw; if this doesn't work, remove lock cylinder and push key fragment out from other side with thin, stiff wire |
| **Latch bolt doesn't engage or disengage easily** | Door loose on hinges or otherwise misaligned | Correct door problem and make any adjustments required to align latch bolt and strike plate (pages 69–72) |
| **Latch bolt doesn't extend fully into strike plate** | Shrunken wood in door | Shim out hinges (page 70) or strike plate (page 72), or both |
| | Shallow mortise or misaligned strike plate | Deepen mortise (page 71) or reposition strike plate (page 72) |
| **Key won't turn in lock** | Cylinder turned in face plate | Move cylinder to proper position (pages 78–79) |
| | Poorly duplicated key | Check key against original; replace if necessary |
| | Damaged tumblers | Replace cylinder or entire lockset (pages 78–79) |
| **Key turns but doesn't operate locking mechanism** | Broken lock mechanism | Repair; or replace lockset (pages 78–79) |

# ... Door Locksets

## —— Cylindrical & Tubular Locksets ——

Cylindrical locksets, commonly found in houses built since about 1960, are operated by a key inserted into the exterior knob; the interior knob is operated either by a small push or turn button on the knob or by a key inserted into it.

Tubular locksets are similar in construction to cylindrical ones. The major differences between them are that tubular locksets are simpler and have smaller locking mechanisms.

Removing a faulty cylindrical lockset and replacing it with a duplicate, as shown at right, is a job you can do yourself. (You remove and replace a tubular lockset in the same way.) See page 77 for information on buying a replacement.

When you're installing a new lockset, be sure the new face plate and strike plate are flush with the door edge and door jamb surfaces. If they aren't, you'll need to adjust the mortises by chiseling out a shallow mortise (page 72) or by building up a deep one with wood putty.

**Changing types of locksets.** Though it's easiest to replace an old lockset with a new one of the same type, sometimes you may want to replace a cylindrical lockset on an exterior door with a more secure mortise lockset or exchange an old mortise lockset on an interior door for a cylindrical or tubular one.

Such a change is a project requiring some skill in working with wood. To replace a cylindrical lockset with a mortise one, you'll first need to patch any holes in the face of the door and refinish the door; then you have to cut a deep mortise for the lock body and drill new holes for the other lock parts (see facing page).

If you're replacing a mortise lockset with a cylindrical or tubular one, you'll need to fill in the mortise as well as patch the door face, then refinish the door and cut a new hole for the cylinder. You may be able to find a kit that converts a mortise lockset to a cylindrical or tubular one.

### PARTS OF A CYLINDRICAL LOCKSET

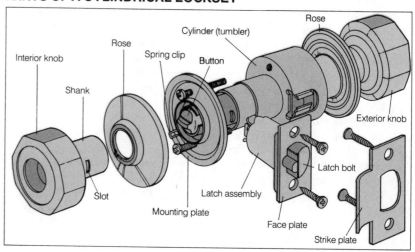

Interior knob · Shank · Slot · Rose · Spring clip · Button · Cylinder (tumbler) · Rose · Exterior knob · Latch bolt · Latch assembly · Mounting plate · Face plate · Strike plate

### REPLACING A CYLINDRICAL LOCKSET

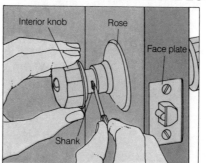

Interior knob · Rose · Face plate · Shank

**1) Push a screwdriver** into the slot on the shank (or insert a nail into the hole), or push the shank button, to release the interior knob. Snap off the rose.

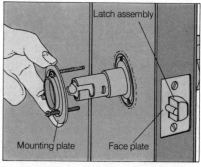

Latch assembly · Mounting plate · Face plate

**2) Unscrew and remove** the mounting plate; slip out the exterior knob and cylinder. Unscrew and remove the face plate, latch assembly, and strike plate.

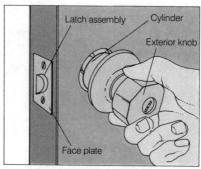

Latch assembly · Cylinder · Exterior knob · Face plate

**3) Insert and screw on** the new latch assembly and face plate. Holding the exterior knob and cylinder, slide the cylinder in and engage it with the latch assembly.

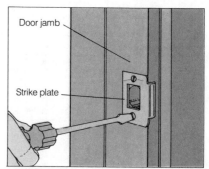

Door jamb · Strike plate

**4) Attach the mounting plate;** snap on the interior rose and knob. Screw on the new strike plate and check that the latch engages in the strike plate.

# Mortise Locksets

The one-piece body of a mortise lockset is set into a large, rectangular recess in the edge of the door. The lockset has one or two lock buttons in the face plate and usually a deadbolt that double-locks the door, as well as a spring-loaded thumb latch on the exterior handle.

When a mortise lockset fails, you can replace it either with another mortise lockset that will fit the recess or with a cylindrical lockset. Replacement mortise locksets are available at some hardware stores or from the manufacturer. Though more readily available, a cylindrical lockset doesn't provide the same security as a modern mortise lockset.

In older homes, the mortise locksets often found on interior doors are known as "iron-key" mortise locksets because of the old-fashioned iron keys used to operate the locking mechanism. When they fail, these locksets can be replaced with tubular ones.

Replacing a mortise lockset with a different type requires some woodworking skill. See the facing page for information on the steps involved.

---

**QUICK FIX-UP**
TIGHTENING A LOOSE DOORKNOB

Often, the doorknobs of old-fashioned mortise locksets become loose. To tighten, loosen the screw on the knob's shank. Hold the knob on the other side of the door tight and turn the loose one clockwise until it fits snugly against the rose. Then tighten the screw until you feel it resting against a flat side of the spindle. The knob should turn freely.

If this doesn't help, remove the knob and check the spindle; if it's worn, replace it.

---

## PARTS OF A MORTISE LOCKSET

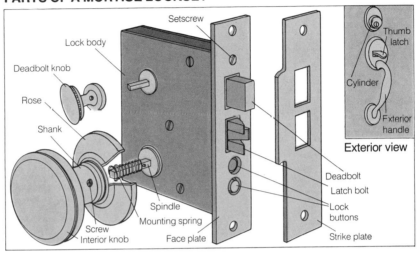

## REPLACING A MORTISE LOCKSET

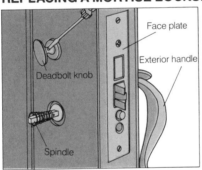

**1)   Remove the interior knob,** deadbolt knob, exterior handle, and any trim. Remove the spindle (a two-piece type will have to be unhooked in the middle).

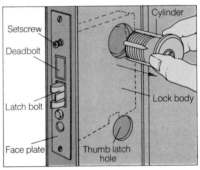

**2)   On the face plate, loosen the setscrew** opposite the cylinder. Unscrew and remove the cylinder by hand. Unscrew the face plate and remove the lock body.

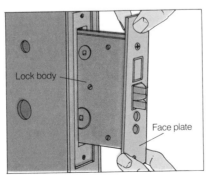

**3)   Slip the new lock body** into the mortise and fasten the face plate flush with the door edge. Install the cylinder; then mount the exterior handle, deadbolt knob, and interior knob.

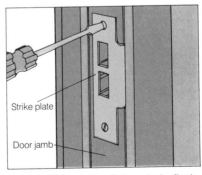

**4)   Install the strike plate** so it sits flush with the jamb edge. Check that the latch bolt and deadbolt engage the strike plate correctly; make any necessary adjustments. Install any decorative trim.

# WEATHERSTRIPPING DOORS

Drafts and moisture can penetrate easily through the cracks around an unsealed door. You can shut them out by applying weatherstripping to the door bottom and jambs. On these pages are a few of the types available.

Before installing weatherstripping, be sure to correct any fit problems on the door itself (pages 68–71).

**Types of weatherstripping.** For sealing the bottom of a door, you can use a rain drip, door sweep, automatic sweep, or door shoe (see below). Rain drips merely shed rain; other types block both drafts and moisture. Also available are special thresholds that

act as weatherstripping. Each comes in standard door widths but can usually be trimmed to fit.

For weatherstripping a door jamb, select spring-metal or cushion-metal, gasket, felt, or interlocking weatherstripping (see facing page). Spring-metal and cushion-metal types provide an efficient seal and are unobtrusive, but they tend to make a door difficult to open and close. Gasket weatherstripping, which includes felt, may be pliable or rigid; both types are efficient, though very visible.

Interlocking weatherstripping for both door bottoms and jambs can be either surface mounted or recessed in

the door. Both installations require precise fitting. The recessed type (not shown here) fits into grooves routed in both the door and frame; unless you're handy with tools, it's best to let a professional install it.

**Adjusting existing weatherstripping.** If your weatherstripping is ineffective, try these simple repairs. Bend cushion-metal or spring-metal weatherstripping to increase the pressure on the door. If threshold weatherstripping has elongated screw holes, adjust the height for a better fit. The vinyl insert in a vinyl-gasket threshold is replaceable.

## SIX KINDS OF THRESHOLD WEATHERSTRIPPING

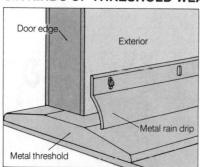

**A metal rain drip** sheds rain from the bottom of a door; you'll need additional weatherstripping with this type. To install the rain drip, cut it to size and screw it onto the lower outside edge of the door.

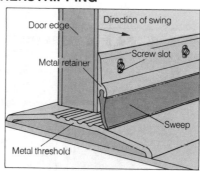

**A door sweep** screws onto the door's bottom face; elongated screw slots allow for height adjustment. Place the sweep on the exterior side of an outward-swinging door, the interior of an inward-swinging one.

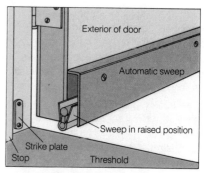

**An automatic sweep** has a sweep spring loaded inside a metal frame. The sweep retracts to clear the floor when the door is opened. (When trimming the sweep to fit, take care not to cut the springs.)

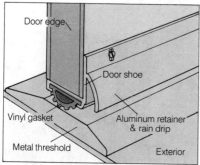

**A door shoe** has an aluminum retainer holding a rounded vinyl gasket that presses lightly against the threshold when the door is closed. Notch the rain drip at both ends to clear the stops.

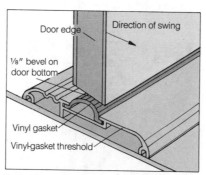

**A vinyl-gasket threshold** replaces a standard one. The door should press lightly against the gasket when closed. Bevel the door bottom ⅛ inch, tapering down in the direction of the swing.

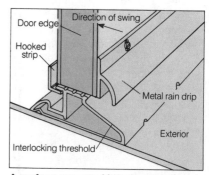

**A surface-mounted interlocking threshold** consists of a special threshold plus a hooked strip that's mounted on the door. Allow a ⅛-inch clearance between the threshold and the door bottom.

## FOUR TYPES OF JAMB WEATHERSTRIPPING

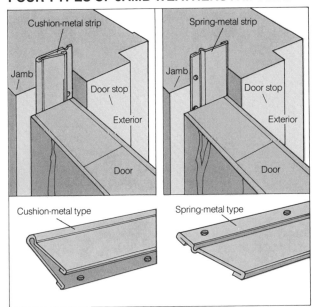

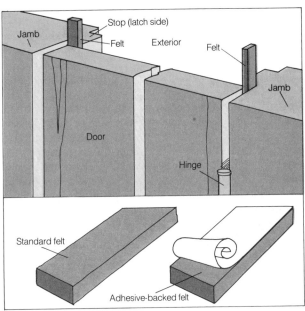

**Cushion-metal and spring-metal weatherstripping** are nailed to the jambs around the door, beginning on the hinge side. Cushion-metal strips butt against the stops; spring-metal strips don't quite touch them. Miter the top corners; cut the lock side strip to fit around the strike plate.

**Felt weatherstripping** attaches to the jamb on the hinge side and to the stops on the latch side and top. Adhesive-backed types are pressed into place; others are nailed with either rust-resistant carpet tacks or small nails. Clean the jamb and stop surfaces and lightly sand any rough spots before installation.

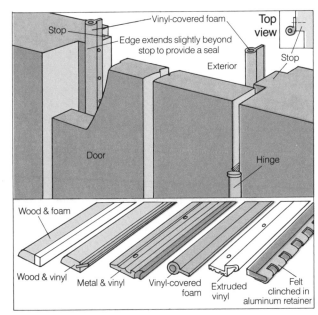

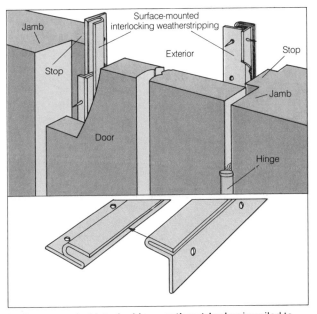

**Gasket weatherstripping** is nailed or screwed to the face of the stops and head jamb. Attach the top piece so it's flush with the side stops; the side pieces should butt against the top piece (you may need to notch the top end of the side strips so they fit tightly). The seal should be light. Be careful not to kink the strips as you attach them.

**Surface-mounted interlocking weatherstripping** is nailed to both the door and the stops (follow the manufacturer's directions). Fit the top strips first, then attach the side strips to the jambs and the door edges, using small nails. Precise fitting is essential—the channels must align exactly in order for weatherstripping to be effective.

# Garage Doors

Most garage doors fall into two categories—roll-up, or sectional, doors and swing-up, or one-piece, doors. Both get their lifting power from coiled metal springs and require only minimal human or motorized effort for their operation.

**Repairing a garage door.** A garage door may bind or drag because of poor roller and track alignment, broken rollers, or loose hinges. If the door won't stay up or down, an adjustment of the tension may be necessary.

CAUTION: Adjusting or replacing the tension spring on a roll-up door or the springs of a swing-up door is a dangerous job best left to a professional, but you can adjust the wire cable (see facing page).

A one-piece door is susceptible to sagging, especially if it's left in the open position for long periods of time. To minimize the warp, see "Quick Fix-up" on the facing page.

**Maintaining a garage door.** Regular maintenance will head off many garage door problems. Periodically clean the tracks and lubricate them with penetrating oil or silicone spray. Tighten the screws on the hardware, and clean and lubricate the hinges and rollers. Use graphite on the lock. Keep the door itself sealed and painted, especially along the bottom edge, to prevent moisture damage.

Inspect the springs regularly and have any that are developing bulges or are unevenly spaced replaced. Have safety cables installed in the springs for one-piece doors if they're not already in place.

Garage doors, especially those that enclose a heated space, should be weatherstripped. Weatherstripping is usually nailed to the outside of a roll-up door on both the sides and the bottom, and to the face of the overhead jamb. On a swing-up door, only the bottom is weatherstripped. You may be able to find sweeps and shoes made specially for garage doors at building supply stores or garage door companies.

**Automatic door openers.** Automatic openers can be used with all types of overhead doors, provided the unit selected is suited to the particular door. The opener should have an automatic return switch so it will reverse automatically when it meets an obstacle.

If you're having problems with a door that has an automatic opener, try one of the adjustments shown on the facing page; make sure also that the track is correctly aligned. Each door opener is different, so refer to the owner's manual when making repairs.

## TWO TYPES OF OVERHEAD GARAGE DOORS

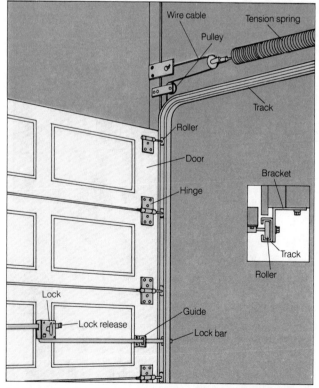

A roll-up door has either two tension springs, one at each side of the door, as shown above, or a single spring that extends across the top of the garage door opening.

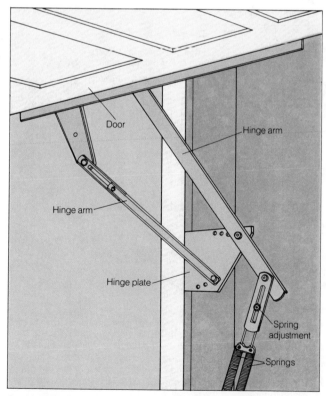

A swing-up door, also called a one-piece door, pivots on hinges and usually has springs on each side to adjust the balance (only one side is shown in this drawing).

## THREE ADJUSTMENTS FOR AN AUTOMATIC DOOR OPENER

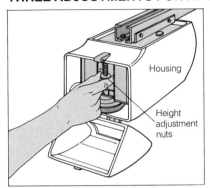

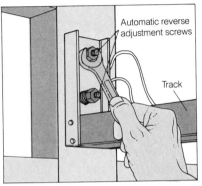

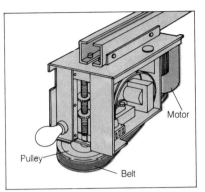

**If the door doesn't open or close completely,** tighten the height adjustment nuts located inside the housing, testing the door until it operates correctly.

**If the door will not reverse upon encountering an obstacle,** try adjusting the automatic reverse adjustment screws, using an open-end wrench.

**If the drive unit works but the door won't open,** tighten the belt connecting the pulley with the motor (*do not overtighten*).

## FIVE GARAGE DOOR REPAIRS

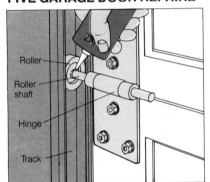

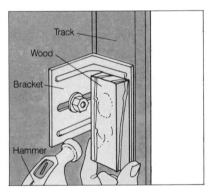

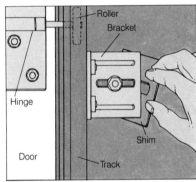

**If the rollers bind,** the cause could be bent or loose hinges or broken rollers. Tighten loose hinges, repair bent ones. Replace broken rollers and lubricate them with penetrating oil.

**If the door drags,** the tracks may be out of alignment. Loosen the brackets and tap the track with a hammer and wood block or a mallet until it's aligned, then tighten the brackets.

**If the door binds** due to rollers improperly positioned or set too deep, adjust the placement of the brackets. In some cases, the brackets may need to be shimmed out.

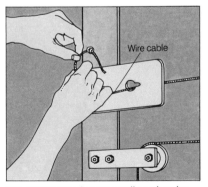

**If the lock bar doesn't catch,** loosen the screws in the guide and move it up or down until the lock bar catches. Tighten the screws.

**Adjust the tension** on a roll-up door by pulling on the wire cable to take up slack (door should be in open position). Knot the end of the cable to secure it in the slot.

### QUICK FIX-UP
SAGGING GARAGE DOORS

If a one-piece door sags in the middle, attach metal reinforcing rods or strips along the top and bottom of the door, using spacers between the rods and door at the midpoint of each rod. Set the door with a ½-inch outward warp, adjusting the rods by turning the nuts located at each end of the rods.

# Walls, Floors & Stairs

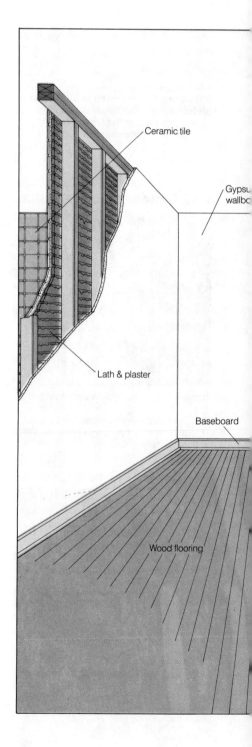

Ceramic tile

Gypsu wallbc

Lath & plaster

Baseboard

Wood flooring

Revealed below are structures usually hidden from view inside walls and under floors and stairs. You'll notice, too, a variety of popular surface materials: tile, gypsum wallboard, and wood paneling, as well as wood and resilient flooring. In this chapter, you'll learn how to repair them all, in addition to remedies for such hazards as a loose banister or floor board.

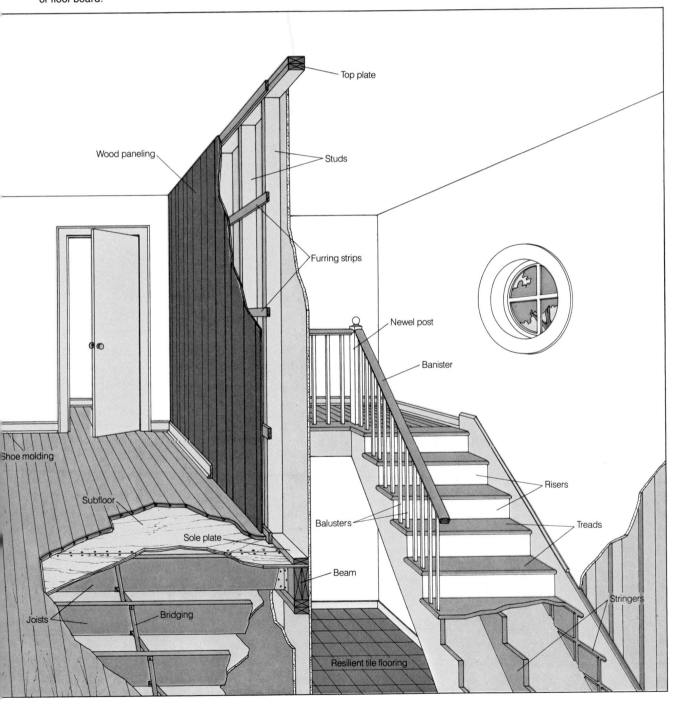

Top plate

Wood paneling

Studs

Furring strips

Newel post

Banister

Shoe molding

Subfloor

Risers

Sole plate

Balusters

Treads

Beam

Joists

Bridging

Stringers

Resilient tile flooring

# Gypsum Wallboard

Gypsum wallboard is used as a backing for many wall treatments—wallpaper, fabric, tile, and even some paneling. Standard wallboard is composed of a fire-resistant gypsum core sandwiched between two layers of paper. Some wallboard is water-resistant for use in bathrooms and other damp areas. Though panels are usually 4 by 8 feet and ½ inch thick, dimensions can vary.

Wallboard panels may be fastened to wall studs or furring strips (see drawing on page 85) and attached with wallboard nails, annular-ring nails, or adhesive. Usually, joints between panels are covered with wallboard tape and several layers of joint compound.

Wallboard repairs range from fixing minor dents to replacing an entire panel (page 88). When the work is done, the repaired area should blend with the surrounding surface.

### Making minor repairs

Wallboard can be plagued with a variety of minor ills, among them dents, small nail or screw holes, and popped nails. These problems can usually be repaired as shown below with simple techniques and tools—spackling compound, patching plaster, or joint compound, and a putty knife, a claw hammer, and sandpaper. After fixing the damage, you'll need to sand and prime the area, and finish it to match the rest of the wall.

### Repairing a large hole

To repair a large hole, the damaged section of wallboard must be cut out and replaced with a new piece of the same thickness (see facing page). After taping and sanding the joints to smooth them, you'll have to finish the surface to blend closely with the adjacent area.

**Cutting and nailing.** To remove the damaged wallboard, first locate the wall studs (page 89). Use a keyhole saw and utility knife to cut out the section, centering side cuts over studs.

CAUTION: To avoid danger from electrical wires behind the walls, shut off the power to the circuit (page 153) and run a light from another circuit.

Cut the replacement piece and smooth rough edges with a perforated rasp; then nail the new piece in place (see page 89 for nailing techniques).

**Taping and sanding.** This step, the key to blending the repair with the surrounding surface, is done in stages over a period of days. The tools and supplies you'll need include ready-mixed all-purpose joint compound; 2-inch perforated or mesh wallboard tape;

4, 6, and 10-inch taping knives; and No. 600 grit silicon carbide sandpaper. NOTE: To finish water-resistant wallboard, use water-resistant joint compound (follow the package directions).

Apply tape and layers of joint compound, following the steps on the facing page (see page 89 for finishing corners). To apply compound, dip the edge of a clean blade into the compound, loading about half the blade. Apply the compound across the joint; then, holding the knife at a 45° angle to the wall, draw the blade along the joint. Using increasingly wider knives for each layer makes the joint smoother.

Let each layer dry for at least 24 hours. When dry, wet-sand the compound to remove minor imperfections by wetting the compound with a sponge and sanding along the joints with sandpaper wrapped around a sanding block. Never sand the wallboard itself—the scratches may show through the finish.

CAUTION: When sanding, wear goggles and a painter's mask.

**Finishing.** Wipe the wallboard with a damp sponge to remove sanding residue. If you want to paint, apply a primer or base coat. For wallpaper, seal the wallboard with shellac or varnish. If you need to match a textured wall surface, use one of the techniques described on page 90.

---

## THREE MINOR REPAIRS

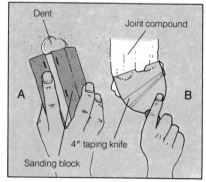

**Dent.** Sand the dent site (A) and fill it with one or more layers of all-purpose joint compound (B); allow each layer to dry before applying the next. When dry, sand and prime.

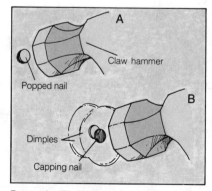

**Popped nail.** Hammer in and dimple the nail (A); drive and dimple another nail just below to hold it in (B). Cover the dimples with joint compound. When dry, sand and prime.

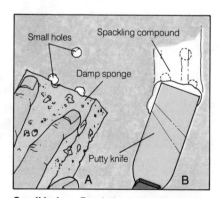

**Small holes.** Brush the holes clean and dampen them (A). Use a flexible, narrow-bladed putty knife to fill the holes with spackling compound (or use patching plaster) (B). When dry, sand and prime.

## REPAIRING A LARGE HOLE IN WALLBOARD

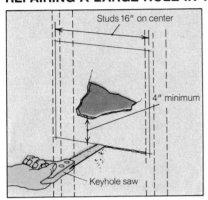

**1)    With a keyhole saw,** cut the damaged wallboard between the studs; cut the sides and corners with a utility knife. Remove the piece with a prybar; pull out remaining nails.

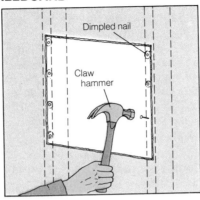

**2)    Nail a piece of new wallboard**—the same thickness as the original, and measured and cut to match the damaged section—to the studs. (See special cutting and nailing instructions on page 89.)

**3)    After applying a large daub** of joint compound across a joint with a 4-inch taping knife, draw the knife along the joint at a 45° angle to the wall. Repeat on all sides.

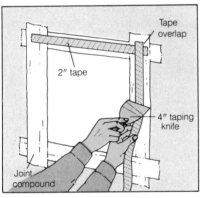

**4)    Center tape over each joint;** press down. Remove excess compound with a knife, feathering the edges. Thinly apply compound over the tape. When dry, wet-sand the compound (see facing page).

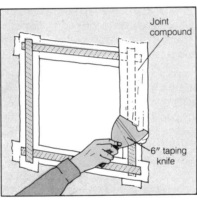

**5)    Apply a second coat** of compound, using a 6-inch taping knife; feather the edges. When the compound is dry, wet-sand the edges to remove minor imperfections.

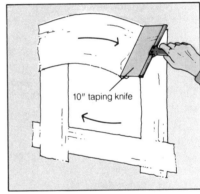

**6)    Apply a third coat** of compound, using a 10-inch taping knife held at a 45° angle to the wall. (Use only as much compound as necessary to cover the previous layer.)

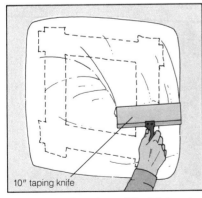

**7)    Feather the edges** of the third coat 12 to 18 inches out, using a 10-inch taping knife. Try to remove any ridges in the compound. Allow the compound to dry before doing the final sanding.

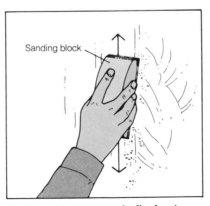

**8)    Give the compound a final wet-sanding** to remove imperfections, wetting it with a sponge and sanding it with sandpaper on a sanding block (see Steps 4 and 5).

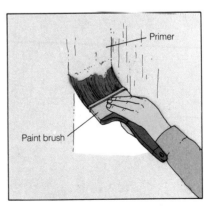

**9)    Wipe off** sanding residue with a damp sponge; let the compound dry. Then apply a primer or base coat of paint, or, for wallpaper, seal with shellac or varnish. For a textured wall, see page 90.

# ...Gypsum Wallboard

## Replacing a Wallboard Panel

When wallboard is water damaged or has large holes or cracks that run the length or width of a panel, you may need to remove the entire panel and replace it with a new one cut to fit the opening.

CAUTION: When sanding wallboard, wear goggles and a painter's mask.

### Removing a damaged panel

No matter how your wallboard is attached to the studs—with nails or with adhesive—the removal procedure is the same.

Use a utility knife to slit through the taped joints. Then punch through the center of the panel with a hammer or prybar and pull off pieces, using both hands. Working from the center, use a broad-bladed prybar to pry the panel edges off the studs. (If the panel is nailed to the studs, some of the nails will probably come off with it.)

When the entire panel is removed, pull out any remaining nails with a claw hammer. If the wallboard is attached with adhesive, you can leave the backing paper on the studs.

### Installing a new panel

After measuring the size of the opening, you cut the panel to fit, if necessary. Then you'll hang it, and tape and finish the joints with ready-mixed all-purpose joint compound. Because wallboard is bulky to handle, you may need a helper.

**Cutting the panel.** To make a straight cut, follow the directions on the facing page. To fit wallboard around doors, windows, electrical receptacles and switches, or other openings, you'll need to measure and mark the panel. Measure from the vertical edges of the opening to the edge of the nearest panel or to a corner; measure from the horizontal edges to the ceiling. Transfer your measurements to the wallboard and cut the panel, using a keyhole saw.

**Hanging the panel.** Mark stud locations on the floor and ceiling. Position the panel over the opening, supporting it with a 1 by 4 and a prybar, and nail the edges to the studs with wallboard nails (see below). Also nail the panel to the top and sole plates, and to the studs behind the panel ("in the field"). Nails

should be 8 inches apart and ⅜ to ½ inch from the panel edges. Panels can also be double nailed for extra holding power. Add a second nail 2 inches from each initial nail; space pairs 12 inches apart in the field.

Drive all nails so the last blow dimples the panel surface (see special nailing techniques on facing page).

**Taping the joints.** If your wallboard is a backing for paneling, you may not have to tape the joints (consult your local building code). But if it will be covered with paint, wallpaper, a textured finish, or tile, you'll have to tape all joints and cover all nail heads with joint compound.

Follow Steps 3 to 9 on page 87 to tape the joints and apply compound. To tape corners, see the facing page.

You'll also have to cover the nail heads with joint compound. Do this when you apply the tape. Using a 4-inch putty knife, cover the nail heads and fill the dimples with compound. When it's dry, apply one more coat over the nail heads. Let it dry, then sand as you would the joints. Wipe away any sanding residue with a damp cloth and prime if you plan to paint.

## HANGING A REPLACEMENT PANEL

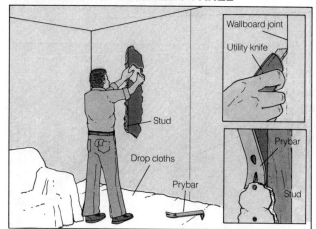

**1) Slit through taped joints** between the damaged panel and adjacent panels, using a utility knife. Punch through the center with a hammer or prybar and pull off pieces. Working from the center, pry the panel edges off the studs with a prybar.

**2) Position the replacement panel** over the opening (you may need a helper). Support the panel with a 1 by 4 and a prybar. Drive wallboard nails into each stud near the top of the panel first to hold it; then finish nailing, spacing nails 8 inches apart.

# Techniques for Working with Wallboard

Working with wallboard involves using special techniques when you're cutting it, nailing it, or working with corners.

When cutting wallboard, get a helper to hold the panel while you mark, score, and break it. When you nail wallboard, it's important to dimple the surface without puncturing the face paper or crushing the core. It takes practice—the secret is to hammer the nail heads squarely.

To tape corners, you'll need a corner tool and precreased tape for inside corners, metal cornerbead for outside corners. As with other joints, you feather the compound edges with 6 and 10-inch taping knives.

## CUTTING WALLBOARD

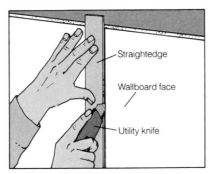

**1)   While a helper supports the panel** on edge, mark the cutting line on the panel's face, using a pencil and straightedge; use a utility knife and straightedge to deeply score the panel's face.

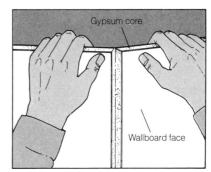

**2)   Break the gypsum core** by snapping the shorter section of panel away from you. Then tilt the short section back slightly while your helper cuts the back paper with a utility knife.

---

**PROFESSIONAL TIP**
LOCATING STUDS

If you can't locate a stud in your wall using a magnetic stud finder, try probing into the wall in an inconspicuous place about 2 inches above the floor with a nail or drill. When you find a stud, measure 16 or 24 inches from that point to find the center of the next stud.

## NAILING WALLBOARD

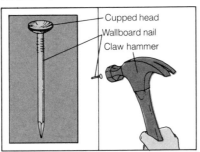

**1)   Use a claw hammer** to drive wallboard nails into the wallboard. Space the nails 8 inches apart, 3/8 to 1/2 inch from the edges of the panels.

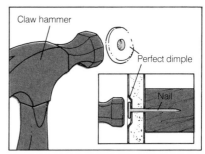

**2)   Drive nails in squarely** until the heads are flush. Dimple the board with another blow; don't puncture the surface or crush the core.

---

## TAPING WALLBOARD CORNERS

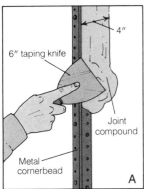 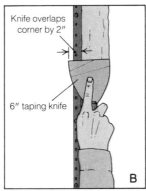

**On an outside corner,** nail up metal cornerbead. Using a 6-inch taping knife, apply a daub of joint compound across one side (A) and smooth it vertically (B); repeat on the other side.

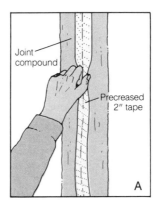 

**On an inside corner,** apply joint compound and cover with tape (A). Using a corner tool, press the tape into the compound and smooth a thin layer of compound over the tape (B).

# Plastered Walls

Plastered walls are composed of three layers: a base coat, a thick coat of plaster for strength, and a finishing coat for appearance. These may be applied over wood lath, metal mesh, special gypsum wallboard, or masonry.

On these pages, you'll find instructions for patching cracks and holes in plaster with or without a lath base, as well as tips on finishing the patched area to match the surrounding surface. If a large area is damaged or the base needs repair, you may want to consult a professional.

**Patching cracks and holes.** Fine cracks, nail holes, and small gouges in plaster can be repaired with spackling compound. You can also fill cracks with a special crack patcher.

To patch wide cracks and holes, apply two layers of patching plaster plus a layer of fine-textured finishing plaster. The first layer should fill a little more than half the depth, leaving enough space for the next two layers. Let each layer dry completely before adding the next.

To fill a hole without a base (for example, where an electrical box has been removed or where damage has affected the base), you'll have to install metal mesh (see facing page).

**Finishing the patch.** Matching an existing texture requires skillful treatment of the still-wet finishing plaster. You'll have to experiment to achieve a good match.

For a smooth surface, pull a metal float or wide putty knife dipped in water across the plaster. When dry, sand to remove minor imperfections; prime before painting.

For a textured surface, use a paint brush, stippling brush, household sponge, sponge float, whisk broom, or wire brush—whatever will give you the desired finish. Daub or swirl the plaster in a uniform, random, or overlapping pattern. To create peaks in the plaster, use a brush or a tool with bristles; when the peaks start to stiffen, gently draw a clean metal float over the surface to smooth them. Let the plaster dry; then prime and paint.

## PATCHING FINE CRACKS

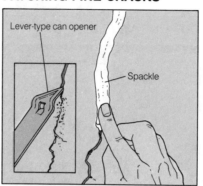

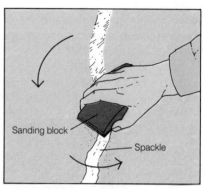

**1) Widen the crack** to about ⅛ inch with the tip of a lever-type can opener; blow out dust and debris. With your finger or a putty knife, fill the crack with spackle.

**2) Sand the spackle when dry,** using a block wrapped with fine-grade sandpaper; sand in a circular motion. Prime the patch with sealer before painting.

## PATCHING WIDE CRACKS

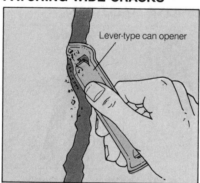

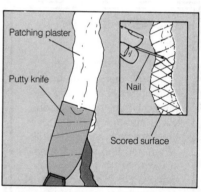

**1) Undercut the crack** with a lever-type can opener or a putty knife to help bond the new plaster; blow out dust and debris. Dampen the crack with a wet paint brush or sponge.

**2) Use a putty knife** to fill just over half the depth of the crack with patching plaster. Score the plaster with a nail when firm but not hard to provide "bite" for the next layer.

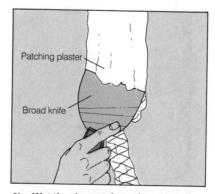

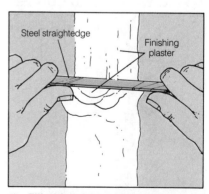

**3) Wet the dry patch again;** use a broad knife to apply the next layer to within ⅛ to ¼ inch of the surface. Let the patch dry before applying the finish coat.

**4) Fill with finishing plaster** and screed with a straightedge to remove excess plaster. To finish, see "Finishing the patch," at left. When dry, prime and paint.

## PATCHING A HOLE WITH A BASE

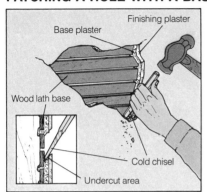

**1)  Remove cracked plaster** from the edges with a cold chisel and hammer. Undercut the edges to ensure a good bond; blow away debris. Dampen the edges with a sponge.

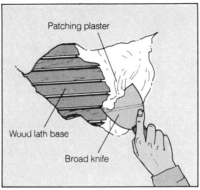

**2)  Using a broad knife,** fill a little more than half the hole's depth with patching plaster; force it through gaps in the lath. Score the plaster with a nail when firm. Let the plaster dry.

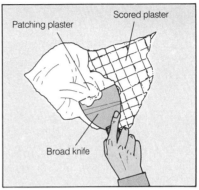

**3)  Wet the patch again;** use a broad knife to apply a second layer of plaster to within ⅛ to ¼ inch of the surface. Score the plaster with a nail to provide "bite" for the next layer; let the plaster dry.

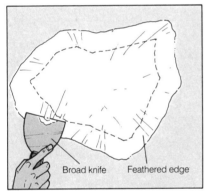

**4)  Use a broad knife** (or, for a large hole, a wallboard taping knife) to apply finishing plaster; feather the edges an inch or more beyond the edges of the patch.

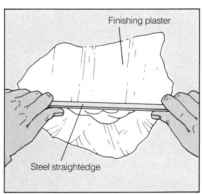

**5)  Screed the wet finishing plaster** with a straightedge to remove excess plaster. For a textured surface, see "Finishing the patch," facing page.

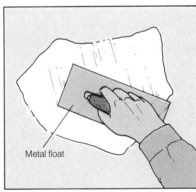

**6)  For a smooth finish,** dip a metal float in water and, holding the float at a slight angle to the wall, draw it down from top to bottom. When dry, sand and prime.

## PATCHING A HOLE WITHOUT A BASE

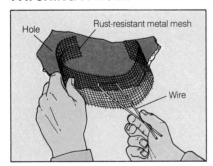

**1)  After removing loose plaster** from around the hole with a cold chisel and hammer, loop a wire through a piece of rust-resistant metal mesh. Roll the edges, insert into the hole, and flatten.

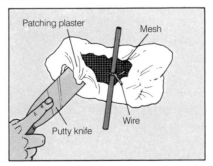

**2)  Tightly wind the wire** around a stick. Dampen the hole's edges with a sponge. Using a putty knife, fill just over half the hole's depth with patching plaster, forcing it through the mesh.

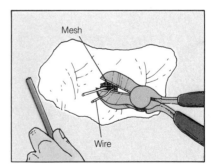

**3)  Unwind the wire** and remove both the wire and stick. When the plaster is firm, score it with a nail to provide "bite" for the next layer. Finish the patch as shown in Steps 3 to 6, above.

# Paneled Walls

## Repairing Solid Board Paneling

Solid board paneling is made up of ¼ to ¾-inch-thick hardwood or softwood boards ranging from 3 to 12 inches wide. Boards may have square edges, but most often are milled to overlap or interlock. Milling may be tongue-and-groove (shown below) or shiplap. The paneling may be attached to studs, furring strips (page 85), or wallboard.

Damaged board paneling responds well to a variety of techniques for repairing minor scratches and gouges, dents, and even deep gouges. But if you can't repair the damaged paneling to your satisfaction or if the damage is more serious, you may want to replace one or more boards (see directions below). Be sure to carefully match any new paneling and its finish with adjacent surfaces.

**Minor scratches and gouges.** One of the most common ways to conceal shallow scratches and gouges is to fill them with a putty stick, then wipe away any excess putty with a clean cloth. Choose a color that matches the finish of your paneling. You can also conceal minor scratches on paneling as for furniture—with furniture polish or an almond stick, a compressed-fabric stick impregnated with oil.

**Dents and deep gouges.** You can try to restore dented wood fibers by removing all the finish from the dent site, then placing a damp cloth and hot iron over the dent until the wood fibers rise to the level of the surrounding surface. Let the wood dry thoroughly before sanding it smooth and refinishing the area to match.

To repair a deep gouge or a nail hole, fill it with a matching wood putty, using a flexible putty knife to apply the putty. Let it dry; then sand the patch smooth with fine-grade sandpaper wrapped around a sanding block. Finish it to match the surrounding area.

## REPLACING A DAMAGED TONGUE-AND-GROOVE BOARD

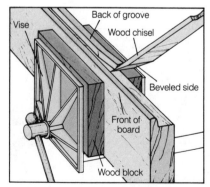

**1) Remove the baseboard** (see facing page). Adjust the blade depth of a circular saw to the board's thickness (test with a drill). Saw up the board's center; split the ends with a chisel.

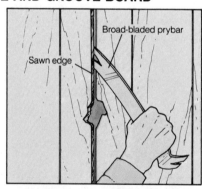

**2) Wedge a broad-bladed prybar** or wide chisel between the sawn edges. Pry the sections away from the wall, one at a time. (The tongue section may be blind nailed.)

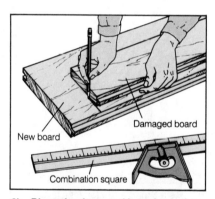

**3) Place the damaged board** over the new board; mark the correct length with a pencil and combination square. Use a crosscut saw to cut the replacement board to length.

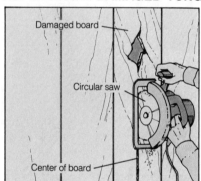

**4) Remove the back of the new board's groove** with a wood chisel (beveled side down) and a mallet, holding the board in a vise and using wood blocks to protect the board.

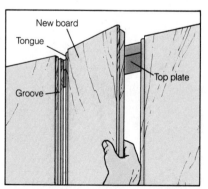

**5) Align the replacement board** with the adjacent one, starting at the ceiling. Fit the tongue of the new board into the groove of the adjacent board and slip it into place.

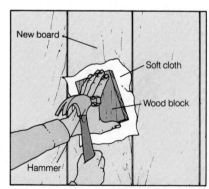

**6) Tap the board in place,** using a padded block. Face nail with finishing nails at top and bottom. Sink the nail heads with a nailset, fill the holes with wood putty, and finish. Replace the baseboard.

# Repairing Wood Veneer Sheet Paneling

Sheet paneling may have a veneer of wood, simulated wood, or even fabric or vinyl. Of these, wood veneer responds best to repair, though even your most careful efforts may show.

Panels usually measure 4 by 8 feet and are fastened to wall studs or furring strips (see illustration on page 85) with adhesive or nails. Following are directions for concealing minor scratches and nicks and for filling gouges and cracks in finished wood veneer paneling. If you can't conceal the damage to your satisfaction or if the paneling has holes, you may want to replace an entire panel (see below).

**Minor scratches and nicks.** The simplest way to conceal these flaws is to use a putty stick to "draw" over the mar; wipe away any excess putty with a clean cloth. (Putty sticks come in a variety of colors to match finished wood paneling.) You can also hide scratches and nicks with shoe polish (test first), floor wax, or an almond stick.

A more thorough method involves sanding, staining, and refinishing the veneer. Lightly rub the damaged area with fine steel wool or fine-grade sandpaper, applying less pressure toward the edges; wipe away any residue. Apply wood stain with a cotton swab.

After the stain is dry, lightly buff the area again with a fine abrasive and wipe away the sanding residue. Spray a light coat of varnish on the area and let it dry; then lightly buff with a fine abrasive and wipe. If the original panels were waxed, wax the entire panel and buff to a sheen with a clean cloth.

**Deep gouges and cracks.** Use a putty knife to fill deep gouges and cracks with wood putty. When the putty is dry, sand it smooth. Use a small brush to stain or paint the putty so it matches the finish of the panel or use colored putty that matches the finish.

## REPLACING A DAMAGED WOOD VENEER PANEL

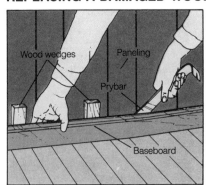

**1)  Insert a prybar** between the baseboard and paneling, placing wood wedges in the gap. Pry off the baseboard and remove the remaining nails with pliers or a claw hammer.

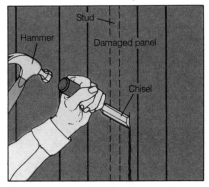

**2)  Split the panel** near one edge (not on a stud), using a hammer and chisel. (The split should be large enough to allow space for inserting a prybar to pry the panel off the studs.)

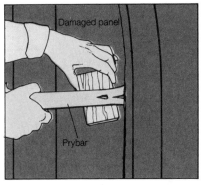

**3)  Pry the panel** off the studs with a prybar, being careful not to damage adjacent panels. Wedge a prybar between the panel and studs to break any adhesive bond.

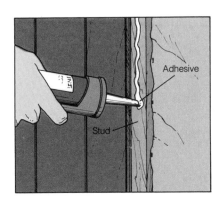

**4)  Apply a bead of adhesive** along the length of the studs to hold the new panel, after pulling off the old paneling and scraping off any adhesive (or removing nails).

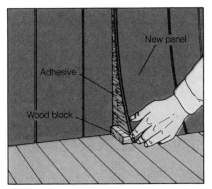

**5)  Position the new panel;** drive 4 finishing nails near the top of the panel to secure it. Then pull it out at the bottom, holding it with a wood block until the adhesive is tacky.

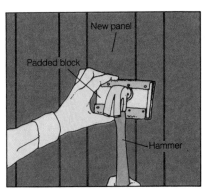

**6)  Remove the block** and press the panel firmly in place. Using a padded block, hammer along the edges and over the studs. Remove the finishing nails if not needed and replace the baseboard.

# Tiled Walls

When ceramic tiles get cracked or chipped or work loose from the wall, it's time to replace them. Before you re-fasten any loose tiles, check underneath—a common cause of loosening is moisture under the tiles. Be sure to correct the problem—such as a leaking pipe or roof—and check that the substructure is in good condition.

The directions below for replacing ceramic tiles apply to floors and counter-tops as well as walls. But note that they apply only to tiles installed in a thin-set mastic or mortar-type adhesive, not the thick mortar bed professionals use.

When you replace tiles, be sure to choose the appropriate mastic for the area you're tiling. If you're using water-resistant mastic, work in a well-ventilated area. In addition to mastic, you'll need patching plaster to create a base for the new tiles, latex primer, and grout for filling the spaces between tiles.

If you don't have spare tiles to re-place chipped or broken ones, take a sample to a tile dealer, manufacturer, or contractor. They may have "bone piles" of old and discontinued tiles where you can find a match.

CAUTION: When chipping out old tiles, be sure to wear goggles to protect your eyes from flying tile fragments.

## REPLACING DAMAGED CERAMIC TILE

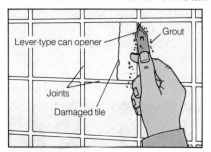

**1) Remove grout from the joints** around a damaged tile with a lever-type can opener, unless the joints are wider than ⅛ inch—then chip them out at Step 4.

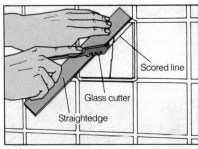

**2) Using a glass cutter** and a steel straightedge, heavily score an X across the face of the tile from corners to corners through the center.

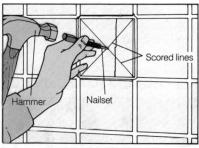

**3) Punch a hole** through the center of the damaged tile with a hammer and nail-set. Be careful not to damage the backing as you work.

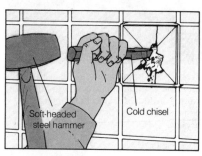

**4) Chip out the tile** from the center with a soft-headed steel hammer and cold chisel using light, rapid blows.

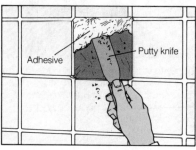

**5) Clean the area behind the tile,** re-moving all old adhesive and grout. Use sandpaper to smooth rough spots; dust.

**6) Fill the backing** with patching plaster if necessary to level the backing. When dry, paint with latex primer.

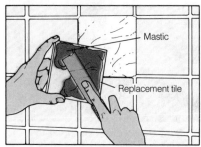

**7) Apply mastic** to the back of the tile with a putty knife when the primer is dry. Keep the mastic ½ inch from the edges.

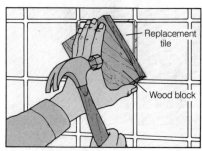

**8) Center the tile** and, using a hammer and wood block, gently tap it flush with the surface. Wait 24 hours before grouting.

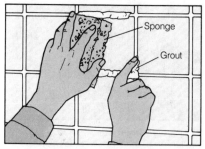

**9) Fill the joints with grout,** using a damp sponge or cloth. Smooth the joints with a wet finger. Sponge off excess grout.

# ATTACHING SPECIAL WALL FASTENERS

Ordinary nails or screws often won't anchor firmly in plaster, gypsum wallboard, paneling, or masonry walls. To hang objects from these walls, you may need special fasteners.

**Plaster, gypsum wallboard, and paneled walls.** You can usually use conventional nails to hang lightweight objects from these walls. You may want to drill a pilot hole for the nail to avoid cracking the wall material.

To secure shelf brackets and other heavy items, use wood screws attached to the studs (see page 89 for tips on locating studs). Where you can't drive into a stud, choose anchors or toggle bolts; once through the hole, they expand to distribute weight more widely than a screw. Be sure to buy the proper size fastener for the thickness of the wall and the weight of the object you're hanging.

To install anchors, drill a hole, install the anchor, and insert the screw; then tighten it to spread the anchor.

With a toggle bolt, slide the bolt through the hook or object to be mounted *before* inserting the toggle in a hole drilled into the wall; if you remove the bolt when the fastener is in place, you'll lose the toggle. Don't fasten the bolt or screw too tightly; this pulls the anchor or toggle into the wall material and weakens its grip.

**Masonry walls.** For these walls, hang lightweight objects from special tempered-steel masonry nails; use anchors that have a resilient sleeve that expands to hold a screw or bolt in place for heavier objects. Drive in nails with a claw hammer (be sure to wear safety goggles).

The key to successful installation of masonry anchors is proper drilling of the hole to receive the sleeve and screw. Use an electric drill with a carbide masonry bit (page 16) to drill the hole. Then push in the sleeve, insert the screw through whatever you are fastening, and drive it into the sleeve.

## MASONRY WALL FASTENERS

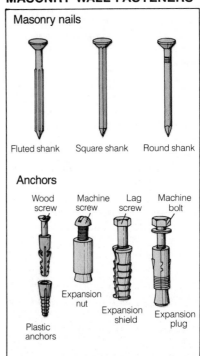

Masonry nails

Fluted shank · Square shank · Round shank

Anchors

Wood screw · Machine screw · Lag screw · Machine bolt

Plastic anchors · Expansion nut · Expansion shield · Expansion plug

---

## PLASTER, WALLBOARD & PANELING WALL FASTENERS

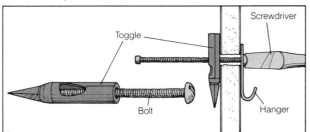

**Nailable toggle bolt.** Use a hammer to drive in the fastener; the toggle will flip into position. Screw on the bolt.

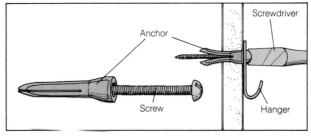

**Plastic anchor.** Drill a pilot hole slightly smaller than the anchor. Tap the anchor into the hole; insert and tighten the screw.

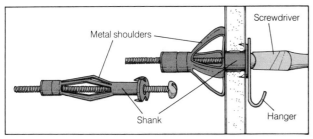

**Spreading anchor.** Drill a hole; insert the anchor. Tighten the bolt until you feel resistance. Remove the bolt, add the hanger, reinsert and tighten the bolt.

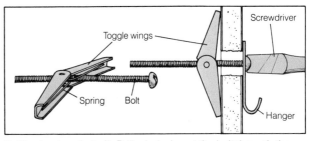

**Split-wing toggle bolt.** Drill a hole; insert the bolt through the hanger and toggle. Pinch the toggle wings together, insert the bolt with the toggle, and pull it toward you; tighten the bolt.

# Wallpaper

As wallpaper ages, it's subject to loosened edges, tears, bubbles, and other damage—all of which you can easily repair. When making a repair, use lap-and-seam adhesive to hold the wallpaper in place. A seam roller helps you press the wallpaper smoothly to the wall.

**Repairing loose edges and tears.** To reglue an edge or fix a tear, follow the directions at right. Don't use too much adhesive—it can soak through and stain the wallpaper.

**Patching damaged paper.** Some damage, such as stains, scuff marks, or wallpaper completely torn off, requires patching with a matching piece of wallpaper if one is available. Cut a square or rectangular replacement piece slightly larger than the damaged area, taking care to match patterns. Apply the patch as illustrated at right.

**Repairing bubbles.** Use a clean, damp cloth to moisten the area with the bubble. Using a utility knife or sharp razor blade, slit the bubble. Avoid making a straight cut—a V-shaped slit or one that follows the wallpaper's pattern will conceal the cut and make gluing easier.

With a narrow putty knife, force glue through the slit. Use a damp sponge to spread the glue so it completely fills the area beneath the bubble; press the wallpaper smoothly to the wall.

---

**PROFESSIONAL TIP**
CLEANING WASHABLE WALLPAPER

To remove dirt, grease, and stains from washable wallpaper, thoroughly sponge the soiled area with a solution of mild soap and cold water. Rinse with clear, cold water; wipe dry with a clean, absorbent cloth. NOTE: Test wallpaper before washing it.

---

## REPAIRING LOOSE EDGES & TEARS

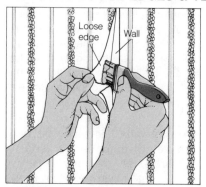

**1)** **Moisten the damaged area** and carefully lift the wallpaper away from the wall. Apply a thin, even layer of adhesive to the back of the paper.

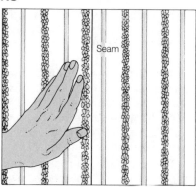

**2)** **Press the wallpaper** back in place. Sponge off any excess adhesive, taking care not to soak the paper so much that the adhesive loosens behind the paper.

---

## PATCHING DAMAGED WALLPAPER

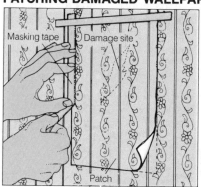

**1)** **Align the replacement patch** so the pattern exactly matches the pattern on the damaged section. Attach the patch to the wall with masking tape or tacks.

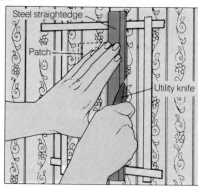

**2)** **Cut through** both the patch and the wallpaper underneath simultaneously, using a utility knife and steel straightedge. Remove the patch and set it aside.

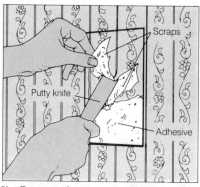

**3)** **Dampen the scored wallpaper** with a wet sponge and peel it off. Scrape off scraps and adhesive with a putty knife. Clean the wall and let it dry.

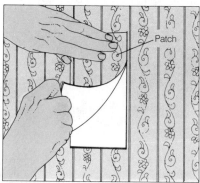

**4)** **Apply a thin layer** of adhesive to the back of the patch. Position the patch carefully; smooth it with a clean, damp cloth or a seam roller. Wipe off excess adhesive.

# Ceiling Tiles

Prefabricated ceiling tiles are attached either to an existing ceiling or to furring strips. Staples or nails, either with or without adhesive, or adhesive alone secures the tiles.

Often, ceiling tiles show the effect of water damage. To conceal stains or streaks in tiles, apply a primer or clear sealer. When the tiles are dry, you can paint them with latex paint.

Another problem you may encounter is dents or chips in tiles. Illustrated at right are the steps in removing and replacing a dented tile with tongue-and-groove edges. You cut through all four joints and pry the tile off its backing; pry out the cut-off tongues from the grooves in the adjacent tiles. Use pliers to remove remaining staples or nails; scrape off adhesive.

After cutting the tongue off one side of the replacement tile, apply adhesive to the back of the tile or to the ceiling (follow the tile manufacturer's directions). Position the tile over the opening, slip the remaining tongue into the groove of an adjacent tile, and press in place until the adhesive holds; or use a floor-to-ceiling brace to hold the tile until the adhesive is dry.

## REPLACING A DAMAGED CEILING TILE

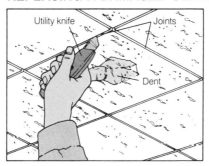

**1)** **Cut through all four joints** of the damaged tile; use a prybar to remove it.

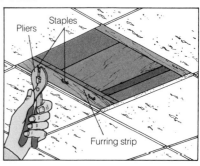

**2)** **Remove remaining staples or nails;** scrape off adhesive with a putty knife.

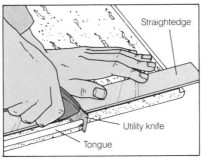

**3)** **Cut the tongue** from one edge of the new tile using a utility knife and straightedge.

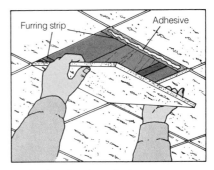

**4)** **Apply adhesive;** slip the tongue into an adjacent tile's groove, and brace until dry.

---

## PAINTING OVER WALL REPAIRS

A fresh coat of paint is a fast and effective way to conceal wall repairs. Depending on the size of the repair and the availability of matching paint, you can paint just the repaired area, the whole wall, or the entire room. Here are some guidelines to help you get ready for the job.

**Selecting paint and tools.** The type of surface you're covering determines the kind of paint required. If you have paint left over from the original job, you're in luck. If not, refer to the chart at right for the appropriate paint.

Choosing the correct brush is important, too. The type of bristle should suit the paint or stain you're using; the brush size must fit the job. Select a natural-bristle brush to apply oil-base paint, polyurethane, varnish, or shellac. Use brushes with synthetic bristles to apply water-base (latex) paint. For wood stains, use either type of brush. Choose a 1-inch brush for hard-to-reach areas, a 2 to 3-inch brush for medium-size surfaces, and a 3½ to 4-inch brush or 9-inch roller for large areas, such as entire walls. Use a thick-napped roller for textured walls.

**Preparing the surface.** Before you can apply the paint, you may need to sand and wash the surface. In most cases, you will at least have to apply a primer to ensure that your repair will not show. For more information, see the *Sunset* book *Wall Coverings.*

### PAINT SELECTION GUIDE

| Surface | Latex flat | Latex semigloss | Oil-base flat | Oil-base semigloss | Oil-base gloss | Wood stain | Polyurethane | Varnish | Shellac |
|---|---|---|---|---|---|---|---|---|---|
| Gypsum board | • | • | • | • | • | | | | |
| Plaster | • | • | • | • | • | | | | |
| Wood paneling | | • | • | • | • | • | • | • | • |
| Bathroom & kitchen walls | | • | | • | • | | | | |
| Wood trim | | • | • | • | • | • | • | • | • |
| Window sills | | • | | | | | • | • | |
| Masonry | • | | | | | | | | |

# Wood Flooring

A good wood floor will last the life of your home and actually improve with age. But even the best wood floors are subject to damage or other problems. The problem may be in the surface flooring or related to defects in the supporting structure. To successfully repair the floor, it's important to know what type of flooring you have and how it's attached to the subfloor, as well as the cause of the damage or problem.

Flooring structure, types of wood flooring, and common problems are described below. On the following pages you'll find directions for repairing surface damage, fixing individual boards, replacing damaged sections of flooring, and silencing squeaky floors both from the surface and from underneath.

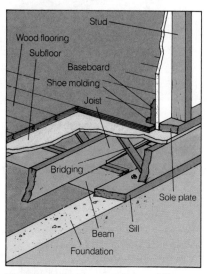

**Wood flooring** is secured to a subfloor usually supported on joists and beams.

**Flooring structure.** A wood floor consists of a finished floor laid over a subfloor supported by joists and beams (see drawing above). Joists may have solid or diagonal bridging between them to provide extra strength. Joists, beams, posts, and, in a two-story house, bearing walls carry the weight of the flooring material and subfloor and transfer it to the foundation.

The finished floor may be hardwood—red or white oak, maple, beech, or birch—or one of the less expensive softwoods, such as hemlock, larch, or elm.

The subfloor may be constructed from 1 by 4, 1 by 6, or 2 by 6 lumber, or plywood panels. In a lumber subfloor, boards are laid diagonally across joists. A plywood subfloor has panels laid in a staggered fashion with the ends of the panels butted together over and nailed to the joists.

If your house is built on a concrete slab, the floor may be laid over wood 2 by 4s (called sleepers) and nailed, or laid on a base of plywood and fastened with nails or adhesive.

**Types of wood floors.** Two common types of wood flooring are strip and plank. Boards for strip flooring come in random lengths and uniform widths. (Common widths are 1½, 2, 2¼, and 3¼ inches.) Plank flooring, a holdover from colonial days, was originally made from maple planks more than a foot wide. Today, it differs little from strip flooring, except that it comes in random widths (usually 3, 5, and 7 inches), as well as random lengths. In both types, board length usually ranges from 2 to 8 feet; most boards are ¾ inch thick.

Both strip and plank boards may be milled with square or tongue-and-groove edges and ends, or with a combination of both. Depending on the milling, strip and plank floorings may be blind nailed, face nailed, or screwed to the subfloor (see drawing below).

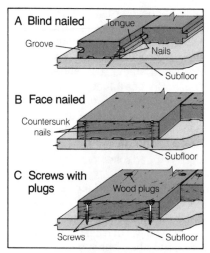

**Wood flooring** may be blind nailed (A), leaving no visible signs of the nails; face nailed with the nails countersunk (B); or attached with screws that are concealed under wood plugs (C).

Tongue-and-groove strip flooring is almost always blind nailed; square-edged strip flooring is usually face nailed. Tongue-and-groove plank flooring may be blind nailed, screwed, or both; square-edged planks may be face nailed, screwed, or both. Plugs usually indicate that flooring is screwed to the subfloor, though plugs are sometimes used just for decoration.

**Common floor problems.** Problems can range from minor surface damage to serious structural defects. Daily wear and tear on a wood floor causes surface scratches and gouges. The natural expansion and contraction of wood occurring with changes in temperature or humidity, as well as alternate drying and wetting due to leaks, can cause nails to pull out of the wood, allowing flooring boards to separate or warp; even the joists and the subfloor can separate. The natural settling of a house can also cause separations between the joists and the subfloor.

If your floor is sagging or uneven, there could be a serious structural problem; consult a professional.

**Repairing the floor.** You can repair most minor surface damage yourself (see facing page). If your floor has separated, split, loose, or warped boards, first determine the cause and correct it, if necessary; then make the repair (see facing page).

If the damage is too extensive for a simple repair, you may need to replace boards or sections of flooring as described on pages 100–101. (Directions for replacing damaged sections depend on how the boards are milled and the way they're secured to the subfloor, so be sure to make these determinations before going ahead.) To eliminate squeaks in floors, you can choose one of several methods, from lubricating the squeak with graphite to installing wood shims (page 102).

Finally, if your floor's overall appearance and condition are suffering, you may want to make repairs and replacements where necessary, then refinish the entire floor. For refinishing techniques, see the *Sunset* book *Do-It-Yourself Flooring*.

# Repairing Wood Floors

Surface damage on wood floors, as well as separated, split, loose, or warped boards, can be successfully repaired. When you're refinishing the repaired area, match its color and protective finish as closely as possible to the surrounding area to effectively hide the repair.

## Repairing surface damage

To preserve the beauty of your wood floors, repair surface damage, such as water or burn marks, scratches, and gouges, immediately after it occurs. In most cases, you'll first have to remove the protective wax or oil finish from the damaged area with a wax stripper. Once you complete the repair, you must rewax or oil the area. When stripping and rewaxing, follow the manufacturer's directions for the product you're using.

**Water marks.** After removing the protective finish, rub the marks with fine-grade steel wool and a little paste wax or a solvent-base liquid floor wax. If the marks don't disappear, wipe the wax with a soft cloth and rub again with fine-grade steel wool and odorless mineral spirits. Wipe clean and finish.

**Burn marks.** For burn marks that just darken the wood's surface, lightly sand; wipe up sanding residue with a damp cloth. When dry, finish as desired.

For deeper burns, carefully scrape out the burned wood with a sharp knife. Apply one or more coats of a commercial scratch hider, putty stick, or stick shellac; then finish.

**Scratches and gouges.** You can conceal a shallow scratch with one or two applications of a commercial scratch hider or crayon. To repair deep scratches and gouges, remove wax or oil from the damaged area. Fill the scratch or gouge with matching wood putty, putty stick, or stick shellac. Let dry; then sand smooth with fine-grade sandpaper and finish.

## Fixing damaged floor boards

It's best to repair separated, split, loose, or warped floor boards as soon as trouble appears.

For long or wide separations between boards, fill the gaps with a wood strip (see below). For the best fit, angle the saw blade to cut a strip that tapers in slightly at the bottom.

Loose, split, or warped boards can be satisfactorily repaired, as shown below. Sand any putty when it's dry with fine-grade steel wool and finish the floor as desired.

---

## SEPARATED BOARDS

**Measure the gap between boards;** transfer the measurements and cut a wood strip from a new board using a table saw with blade guard, omitted here for clarity (A). Glue the strip in the gap; weight it until the glue dries (B).

## SPLIT BOARDS

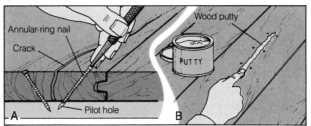

**Drill pilot holes at an angle** every few inches along the length of the crack. Drive and countersink annular-ring nails (A). Fill the nail holes and crack with wood putty (B). Finish to match the rest of the floor.

## LOOSE BOARDS

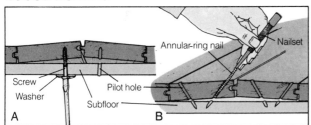

**From below:** Drill pilot holes through the subfloor and just into the boards; insert screws (A). **From above:** Drill pilot holes; drive and countersink nails (B), fill with wood putty, and finish.

## WARPED BOARDS

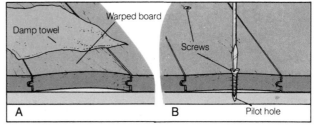

**Cover the warped board** with a damp towel for 48 hours (A). Drill pilot holes every few inches along the board. Insert and tighten screws (B); fill the holes with wood putty and finish.

# ...Wood Flooring

## Replacing Wood Flooring

If your damaged flooring doesn't respond to the remedies on pages 98–99 and 102, you may need to replace some boards. The job doesn't require exceptional skill, but it does take patience and finesse.

Ideally, replacing boards will be one step in an overall floor refinishing project. If not, you'll have to take special care to match and finish the replacement boards. To ensure a good match, take the old boards when you shop for replacements. With plank flooring, make a drawing of the damaged area showing the dimensions of the planks you're removing.

Before replacing flooring, look for evidence of the nailing method. In blind nailing, nails are driven through each board's tongue, and they don't show from the finished surface. Dots of wood putty indicate face nailing. Plugs on

plank flooring often cover screws; if the plugs are just decorative, the flooring is blind nailed (some flooring secured with screws may be blind nailed as well). For any of these, you can use one of two approaches.

One approach, shown below, is to remove the damaged boards in a staggered pattern. This produces a less noticeable repair and is best for an open floor area. The other approach (see facing page), good for areas that will be covered by a rug or furniture, is to cut out a rectangle, remove the damaged boards, and replace them.

Illustrated here are directions for replacing blind-nailed tongue-and-groove boards. You'll follow the same general sequence to replace other types of flooring, but because they're attached differently to the subfloor, note special instructions that follow.

**Face-nailed square-edged boards.** Use a nailset to drive the nails through the boards and into the subfloor. If you're using the rectangular pattern, cut only the ends of the boards. Starting at one end, use a prybar to remove them. With the staggered pattern, follow Steps 1–3 below.

Lay new boards (cut to size) in place; use a hammer and 2 by 4 wood block to tap the last one into place. Face nail boards to the subfloor, matching the nail pattern in the original flooring. Countersink the nail heads with a nailset and hammer; fill the holes with wood putty. After the putty is dry, sand it smooth and finish the area to match the existing flooring.

**Plugged planks.** After marking the area to be cut, use an electric drill to drill out the wood plugs down to the screw

---

### REPLACING TONGUE-AND-GROOVE BOARDS (STAGGERED)

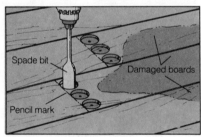

**1)   Mark cutting lines** on the damaged boards. Using an electric drill with a large spade bit, drill a series of holes just inside the lines (be careful not to drill into the subfloor).

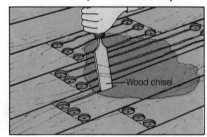

**2)   Split the defective area** of each board, using a large wood chisel and hammer. Tap the chisel lightly to avoid splitting or cracking the surfaces of adjacent boards.

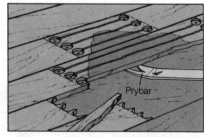

**3)   Pry out split lengths** of boards; use a small wood block for leverage, if needed. Carefully trim the board ends square, using a wide, sharp-bladed wood chisel and a hammer.

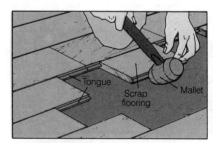

**4)   Measure and cut** the new boards. Slip the first board's groove over an existing one's tongue. Tap in place with a mallet and wood scrap; then blind nail.

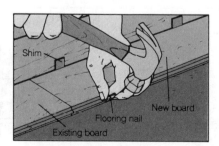

**5)   Continue positioning boards,** removing tongues where necessary. Blind nail in place. Use shims to align the new boards' edges with the existing ones.

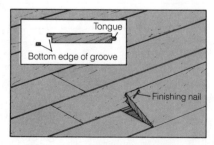

**6)   Remove the bottom edge** of the last board's groove. Insert tongue side first; press in place. Face nail at each end. Countersink nails, fill holes, and finish.

heads; then remove the screws. If your planks are also face nailed (look for dots of wood putty), use a nailset and hammer to drive nails through the planks and into the subfloor.

To cut a rectangular pattern, set the blade of a power circular saw to the thickness of the planks and cut the four sides, using a wood guide strip; carefully remove the planks with a prybar. To remove planks in a staggered pattern, follow Steps 1–3 (facing page).

Mark the replacement planks and cut them to length. Using the plugs in the existing planks as guides for spacing, mark the locations of screw holes on the ends of each replacement plank and on the ends of each existing plank adjacent to the opening. At each location, use an electric drill with combination bit to drill a hole for the plug and a pilot hole for the screw shank (page 15). The diameter and depth of the holes should be the same as those in the existing flooring.

Lay the planks one at a time. Insert and tighten the screws. Daub glue in the plug holes and seat the plugs, removing excess glue. When the glue is dry, sand the plugs flush with the surface and finish the boards to match the existing flooring.

---

**QUICK FIX-UP**
CARING FOR WOOD FLOORS

To clean minor spots and stains from a wood floor, wipe the floor with a barely damp sponge mop. If the stains remain, use a mild cleanser, such as a solution of ammonia or white vinegar, to remove them. Rinse the floor with a clean, damp (not wet) sponge mop to remove any residue.

To restore the floor's luster, buff it lightly; wax, if necessary, and buff again. In general, vacuum or dry-mop flooring about once a week; wax once or twice a year.

---

## REPLACING TONGUE-AND-GROOVE BOARDS (RECTANGULAR)

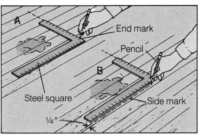

**1)  Mark area** to be cut with a pencil and steel square (A). Make side marks ¼ inch from joints so saw won't hit any nails (B).

**2)  Adjust the blade depth** to the boards' thickness (test with a drill). Start cuts in the center; work toward ends.

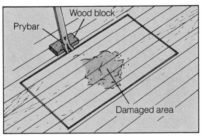

**3)  Lift boards** with a prybar, starting at the midpoint of a side cut. Use a wood block for leverage and to protect the floor.

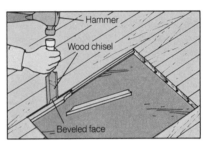

**4)  Cut away the ¼-inch edges** outside the saw cuts, using a hammer and wood chisel. Countersink exposed nail heads.

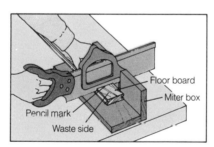

**5)  Cut one end** of each new board at a 90° angle; use a back saw and a miter box to make the cuts.

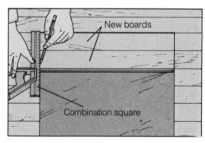

**6)  Lay each board** in place, fitting the cut end tightly. Mark the other end and saw on the waste side.

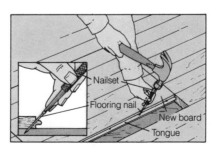

**7)  Slip the new board's groove** over the tongue of the board in place; blind nail. Remove the last board's tongue.

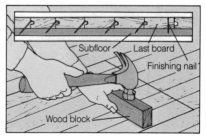

**8)  Tap the last board down** and face nail the ends. Countersink nails, fill holes with wood putty, and finish.

# ...Wood Flooring

## Silencing Squeaky Floors

It's often relatively simple to eliminate floor squeaks once you pinpoint the cause. Knowing why floors squeak and how to determine the cause of the squeaks you hear will help you choose the appropriate repair method illustrated below.

**What causes squeaks.** The squeaks you hear when you walk across a floor occur when pieces of wood rub together. Squeaks in wood floors can originate in the finished floor, subfloor, joists, bridging, or other parts of the supporting structure (page 98). Common causes are separations between the joists and subfloor (due to drying, inadequate nailing, or settling), weak or loose bridging, and ill-fitting or warped floor boards.

**Locating squeaks.** In a house where joists are visible from the basement or crawl space, you'll be able to pinpoint squeaks more easily than in homes where joists aren't exposed or where it's an upper floor that's making the noise.

If joists are exposed, watch from below while another person walks across the floor above; you should be able to detect the probable cause of the squeak. For example, you may spot slight movement between joists and the subfloor, or loose bridging between joists. If the joists are not exposed, you'll have to confine your investigations to the finished flooring.

**Correcting squeaks.** Simple remedies include squirting powdered or liquid graphite between boards or dusting cracks between boards with talcum powder. You can also apply floor oil to the floor or a few drops of mineral oil between boards. (Use mineral oil sparingly; too much can stain the surface of the floor.)

If the squeaks are coming from ill-fitting or warped boards, you can often fix them from above. Work wood putty between boards or try one of the remedies below. Nail through the flooring from above only when you can't work from below; the areas where you nail may be somewhat conspicuous.

In a home where joists are exposed, you can work on the floor from underneath. Toenail loose bridging (page 98); tighten other loose areas as shown below.

## THREE WAYS TO SILENCE SQUEAKS FROM ABOVE

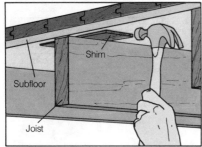

**Place a carpeted 2 by 4** at a right angle to squeaky boards. Move it in a rectangular pattern, tapping it sharply with a hammer to reseat any loose boards.

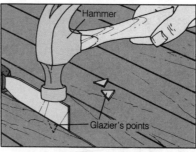

**Coat glazier's points** with graphite, then hammer them between boards. Sink the points well using a hammer and the edge of a putty knife.

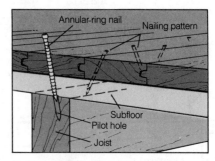

**Drill angled pilot holes** through the board, into the subfloor, and, if possible, into a joist. Drive in nails; countersink and fill.

## THREE WAYS TO SILENCE SQUEAKS FROM BELOW

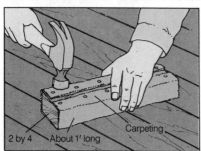

**Tap a shim** into the gap between a joist and the subfloor. Don't force it or you may widen the gap.

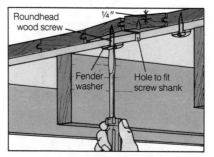

**Drill holes** slightly smaller than screw threads; install washers and wood screws (¼ inch shorter than total floor thickness).

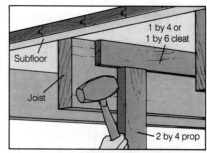

**Mount a cleat** against a joist under loose boards; prop and tap so the cleat is snug against the subfloor. Nail to the joist.

# Resilient Flooring

The family of floor coverings described as resilient flooring includes linoleum, cork, polyurethane, vinyl, vinyl-asbestos, rubber, and asphalt materials. Resilient flooring comes in individual tiles or in sheets up to 12 feet wide. Both types are usually laid in solvent-base adhesive on concrete, plywood, or hardboard; some tiles are self-sticking.

Resilient floors are flexible, resistant to moisture and stains, and easy to maintain. Even so, they can get scratched, stained, or gouged, and they may develop bumps, bubbles, or curled edges. These may be minor surface problems or indications of problems in the subfloor.

Before you try to repair or replace damaged sections of resilient flooring, you'll need to determine the cause of the damage and, if necessary, correct it. Then you can either touch up the surface to conceal the flaws, or patch or replace the damaged area. If you must replace flooring, take care to match materials and adhesives (see at right).

**Evaluating the damage.** The cause of most surface damage, such as stains, scratches, gouges, or holes, is usually readily apparent. But some minor surface damage can often be traced to more serious problems in the subfloor or supporting structure.

A regular pattern of indentations, running for several feet or forming T's, may be caused by separations in the subfloor due to shrinkage of the wood

or settling of the structure. In such a case, you'll have to remove the floor covering and repair the subfloor (consult the *Sunset* book *Do-It-Yourself Flooring*).

Small bumps that appear in the surface of the floor may be caused by nails that have worked loose. Over a period of time, movement in the structure can cause the subfloor to separate from the joists, forcing the nails up into the resilient flooring. Or, if the original tiles or sheet material was installed when there was too much moisture in the subfloor, the nails may have worked loose as the damp wood dried.

You can place a wood block over the bumps and tap it lightly with a hammer to drive the nail heads flush. If this doesn't work, you'll have to remove the floor covering to gain access to the subfloor.

If tiles have curled at the edge or popped loose in one area, you may have a minor plumbing leak. Stop the leak (page 135) before you fix the flooring. Moisture can also cause sheet vinyl to work loose around the perimeter of a room. Moisture in the floors of rooms at or below grade level often results from poor drainage outside (page 50), a problem you'll have to solve before repairing the flooring.

**Repairing or replacing flooring.** You can make most minor surface repairs effectively using the simple tools and techniques shown on page 104. If damage is more extensive, you'll have to re-

move and replace a tile or even patch a section of sheet flooring (pages 104–105).

**Matching replacement materials and adhesives.** If you have material left over from the original installation or if the floor is relatively new and the material is still available, it's likely you'll be able to make a satisfactory match. But a patch on old or worn flooring may be conspicuous. If so, consider using a complementary or even contrasting color or design. If you can't make repairs that are visually acceptable, it may be time to replace the entire floor covering.

When you repair or replace resilient flooring, use the adhesive specified by the flooring manufacturer. If you're sure of the type of flooring you have, a flooring materials supplier can tell you what adhesive is recommended; if you're not sure, take a sample of the flooring with you. Also be prepared to tell the supplier what kind of subfloor you have.

For all repairs discussed on these pages except repairing bubbles, use a solvent-base adhesive (use a water-base one for bubbles). When working with a solvent-base adhesive, check the container to find out what solvent is recommended for cleaning up smudges or removing stubborn adhesive that remains after the damaged flooring has been removed. Have the solvent on hand so you can quickly remove any smudges before they dry.

---

## THREE CAUSES OF SURFACE FLAWS

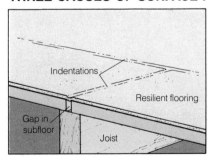

**A regular pattern of indentations,** sometimes in the shape of a T. Cause: Separations in the subfloor due to shrinkage or settling.

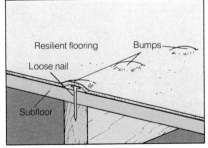

**Small bumps.** Cause: Loose nails due to structural movement, or moisture in the subfloor which pushes nails up as the wood dries.

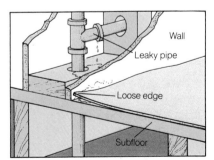

**Loose flooring edges or tiles.** Cause: Moisture due to a plumbing leak or, in rooms at or below grade level, poor outside drainage.

# ...Resilient Flooring

Minor stains or surface damage on resilient tile can be easily corrected, but more serious damage may mean replacing one or more tiles.

To remove surface stains, see the facing page. Directions for refastening curled tiles or repairing bubbles or small holes appear below.

If a tile is badly scratched or gouged, you'll have to take it up and replace it (see at right). If you have an exact match, your repair will be almost invisible, provided the existing tiles aren't discolored.

To remove the damaged tile, you'll need a propane torch with a flame spreader or an iron; use a stiff putty knife to lift up the damaged tile and to remove the adhesive. When you've removed the tile, let the adhesive cool and harden (it will take about an hour) before you scrape it away. Check that the subfloor is smooth and flat. Set the replacement tile in the same type of adhesive used in the original installation or in a solvent-base adhesive.

Be sure the new tile is level with the adjacent ones. If it's too low, lift it up and apply more adhesive. If it's too high, press it down to squeeze out excess adhesive. Use the recommended solvent to remove excess adhesive and let the adhesive dry completely before walking on the floor.

## Repairing Resilient Tile

### REPLACING A DAMAGED TILE

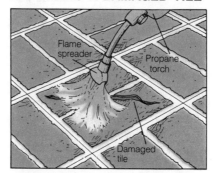

**1)   Use a propane torch** with a flame spreader to soften the adhesive under the damaged tile (tile should be warm but not too hot to touch).

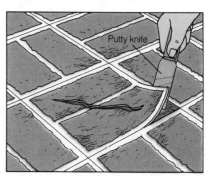

**2)   Pry up** a corner of the tile with a putty knife; free the tile. When the adhesive hardens, scrape it up so the subfloor is smooth and clean.

**3)   Spread a thin, even layer** of adhesive on the subfloor using a notched trowel and following the adhesive manufacturer's directions. Be careful not to get any adhesive on adjacent tiles.

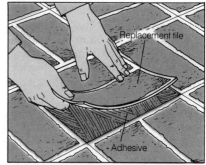

**4)   Butt two adjacent edges** of the new tile against two adjacent tiles, matching the pattern, if any. Press the tile in place, remove any smudges with solvent, and let dry.

## THREE REPAIRS FOR COMMON SURFACE DAMAGE

**Curled tile.** Soften the adhesive with a warm iron; scrape it off the subfloor with a putty knife. Apply solvent-base adhesive to the tile with a notched spreader, press down, and weight overnight.

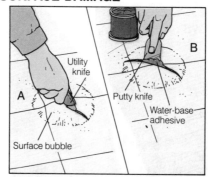

**Bubble.** Soften with a warm iron; slit the bubble edge to edge with a utility knife (A). With a putty knife, force water-base adhesive inside (B). Press flat and weight overnight.

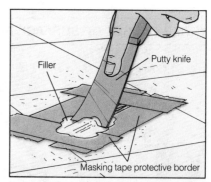

**Small hole or gouge.** Apply a filler made of fine powder scraped from leftover flooring and a few drops of clear nail polish. (Protect the surrounding area with tape.) Buff with fine-grade steel wool when dry.

# Repairing Sheet Flooring

If your sheet flooring is stained or has suffered minor surface damage such as bubbles or small holes, see below and on the facing page for repair instructions. If the damage is more serious, you can patch the area with a new piece of flooring (see at right).

In patching, the trick is to match the patch to the existing floor. If you decide to patch rather than lay all new flooring, you'll need a replacement piece larger than the damaged area.

When you position the patch, be careful to align the pattern on the patch with the pattern on the existing flooring. Use a sharp utility or linoleum knife and a steel straightedge to cut through the flooring; you'll need a putty knife to pry up the damaged area and scrape off the old adhesive on the subfloor. If necessary, apply adhesive solvent to remove the damaged flooring and the old adhesive.

To set the new patch, use solvent-base adhesive or the adhesive used in the original installation. The patch must be level with the existing floor. If the patch is too low, lift it up and apply more adhesive. If it's too high, press it down to squeeze out excess adhesive. Use the recommended solvent to remove excess adhesive. Follow the adhesive manufacturer's directions for drying time.

## PATCHING DAMAGED SHEET FLOORING

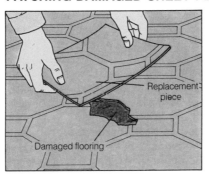

**1)  Cut a piece** from leftover flooring with a sharp utility knife, making sure the piece is large enough to cover the damaged area and matches the floor's pattern.

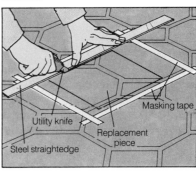

**2)  Tape the piece** to the floor with masking tape, matching the pattern carefully. Use a utility knife and straightedge to cut through the patch and old flooring.

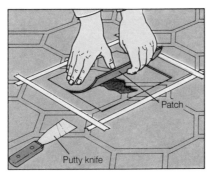

**3)  Set the patch aside.** Use a putty knife or cold chisel to pry up the old flooring and chip out the adhesive, being careful not to mar the existing flooring.

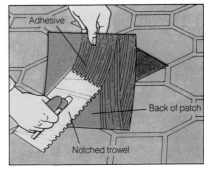

**4)  Spread adhesive** on the patch with a notched trowel; press the patch firmly in place so it's level with the existing flooring. Remove smudges with solvent.

## REMOVING STAINS FROM RESILIENT FLOORING

To prevent stains in resilient tile and sheet flooring, wipe up spills promptly. Stubborn stains or stains that have set require a bit more work, and even some experimentation.

First try to remove the stain by wiping it with a clean white cloth moistened with liquid detergent floor cleaner (use a nylon pad dipped in the detergent for heavy residue).

If detergent doesn't remove the stain, try the following products, one at a time and in order: rubbing alcohol, liquid chlorine bleach, turpentine, nail polish remover, and lighter fluid. CAUTION: Do *not* apply nail polish remover to vinyl and vinyl-asbestos; turpentine, nail polish remover, or lighter fluid to asphalt or rubber tile; or chlorine bleach to natural cork.

Apply each product with a clean white cloth, turning the cloth frequently. Don't walk on the treated area for 30 minutes. When the stain is gone, rinse the area with water and let it dry; reapply floor finish, such as vinyl floor polish or wax, if it's normally used.

Avoid using abrasive scouring powders or pads on resilient flooring, no matter what type you have. Before using any cleaning product, in fact, it's a good idea to test it on an inconspicuous area. If you're in doubt about what cleaning product to use on your floor, consult your flooring dealer.

# Baseboards & Shoe Moldings

Installed where the floor and walls meet, baseboards (also called base molding) and shoe moldings hide uneven floor and wall joints and protect walls from damage caused by foot traffic, furniture, and cleaning tools. Often, they become so dented or marred that they warrant replacement.

Below are directions for replacing lengths of baseboard and shoe molding that have square ends. For lengths that run into corners, you'll have to cut mitered or coped ends (see facing page).

**Buying materials.** When you shop for replacement sections, take a piece of the old ones with you to ensure a good match. Wood baseboards and shoe moldings come in many standard patterns and sizes and several finishes. If yours are old ones, though, you may have to get specially milled replacements.

When ordering, specify thickness first, then width and length (both thickness and width are measured at their widest points). Also buy a supply of finishing nails (size depends on the thickness of the baseboard and molding).

**Replacing baseboards and shoe moldings.** When removing sections of baseboard and shoe molding, be careful not to damage the wall behind them. To protect the wall, use a wood block behind the prybar as you work (see drawings below) and pry only at studs.

Begin by inserting the thin end of a broad-bladed prybar between the baseboard and shoe molding. Pry outward along the molding to loosen it, then pull the molding carefully away from the baseboard.

To remove a length of baseboard, insert the thin end of the prybar between the baseboard and wall. Pry outward to create a gap between the wall and baseboard. As the baseboard comes loose, insert wood wedges in the gap. Continue prying and inserting wedges until the length of baseboard is fairly loose. Then pry with one hand, grab the baseboard with the other, and yank it away from the wall. Remove any nails that remain in the wall, shoe molding, or baseboard.

## REPLACING DAMAGED BASEBOARD & SHOE MOLDING

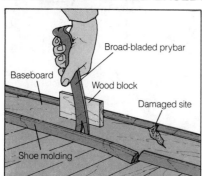

**1)  Insert the thin end** of a prybar between the shoe molding and baseboard; loosen the molding by prying outward. Pull the molding free; remove nails.

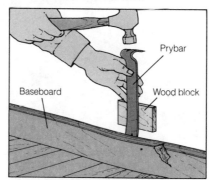

**2)  Place the thin end of the prybar** between the baseboard and wall (use a wood block to protect the wall) and pry outward to make a gap.

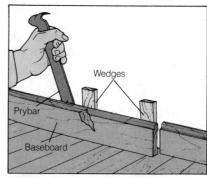

**3)  Insert wood wedges** in the gap as you pry. When the baseboard is loose, pull it free. Remove remaining nails from the baseboard and wall.

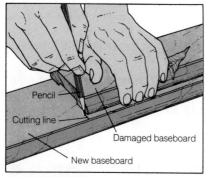

**4)  Measure the replacement baseboard** and shoe molding against the damaged pieces; mark cutting lines with a pencil. For corners, see the facing page.

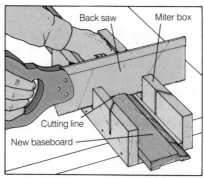

**5)  Use a miter box** and back saw to cut replacement baseboard and shoe molding. Saw the pieces on the waste side of the cutting line.

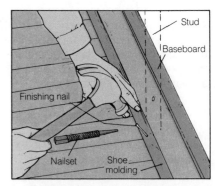

**6)  Position the baseboard;** drive nails at each stud. Position the shoe molding and nail into the sole plate at each stud. Sink nails, fill, and finish.

Measure the lengths of replacement baseboard and shoe molding against the damaged ones for fit. Mark cutting lines with a pencil. To cut replacement pieces, use a miter box and back saw. Holding the wood steady, saw on the waste side of the cutting line.

Place the new baseboard against the wall. Drive finishing nails through the baseboard and into each stud. Then position the shoe molding against the baseboard and drive finishing nails through the molding and into the sole plate at each stud location. Use a hammer and nailset to sink nail heads and fill the holes with wood putty. When it's dry, sand it smooth. Finish the baseboard and shoe molding as desired.

**Cutting and fitting corners.** When you're replacing two lengths of baseboard that meet at an outside corner, you'll have to miter the ends of both pieces and install them as shown above right. If the ends of the baseboards you're replacing meet at an inside corner, cope the end of one replacement to fit over the other (see at right). Cut and fit the ends of both shoe molding pieces in the same way.

## ANATOMY OF A BASEBOARD

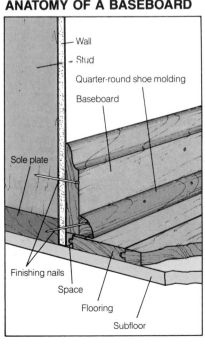

Wall
Stud
Quarter-round shoe molding
Baseboard
Sole plate
Finishing nails
Space
Flooring
Subfloor

## INSTALLING AN OUTSIDE CORNER

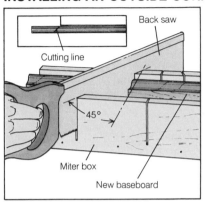

Cutting line
Back saw
45°
Miter box
New baseboard

**1)   Use a miter box and back saw** to cut the replacement baseboard at a 45° angle after measuring the new pieces against the damaged ones and marking the cutting lines on them with a pencil.

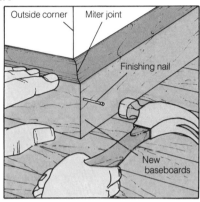

Outside corner
Miter joint
Finishing nail
New baseboards

**2)   After nailing one new piece in place,** butt the end of the second baseboard section against it and drive two nails through the joint. Sink the nails, fill the holes, and finish.

## INSTALLING AN INSIDE CORNER

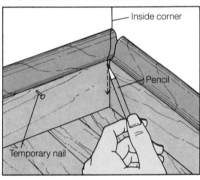

Inside corner
Pencil
Temporary nail

**1)   Temporarily nail the new piece** that you want to cope in the corner. Butt the end of the other new piece against it and trace the outline with a pencil.

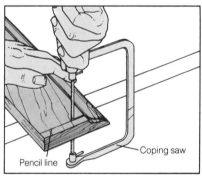

Pencil line
Coping saw

**2)   Remove the marked piece;** holding the piece steady, use a coping saw (page 17) to cut carefully and accurately along the pencil line.

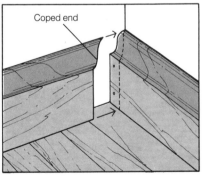

Coped end

**3)   Nail the uncoped piece in place;** then cut the coped piece to length. Butt it against the uncoped piece and nail it in place.

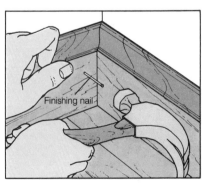

Finishing nail

**4)   Nail the coped piece in place** by driving nails through the baseboard and into the studs and sole plate. Sink the nails, fill the holes, and finish.

# Stairs

Squeaks in stairs are usually caused by a loose tread rubbing against a riser or the stringers when someone steps on the stair. Treads become loose when joints open due to shrinkage or when supporting blocks or nails work loose. Once you pinpoint the location of the noise, you can usually remedy it.

You probably already know which steps are the noisemakers in your staircase. If the noise comes from where you step, concentrate your repair efforts there. If the noise comes from one side when you step in the center, or if it comes from the rear of the tread when you step at the front, first secure the place where you step, then move to the apparent source of the noise.

If the stairs are accessible from underneath, work on them from below so your repairs won't show. You can use wedges, brackets, or wood blocks to secure the treads to the risers (see below at right).

If you don't have access from below, you'll have to work from above. First, try lubricating the stairs with powdered graphite or talcum powder. Forcefully blow the powder into the joints, especially where the backs of the treads meet the risers.

## PARTS OF A STAIRCASE

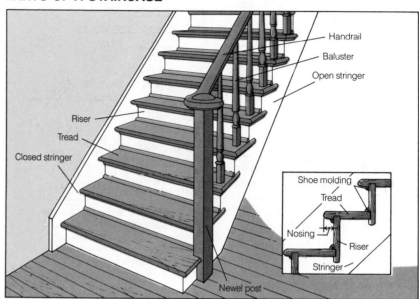

If this doesn't help, try one of the repairs illustrated below at left. To prevent the wood from splitting, drill pilot holes before inserting nails or screws; counterbore the holes (page 15) if you plan to fill them with dowel plugs rather than wood putty.

If you drive in wedges, you'll have to remove any shoe molding first (see inset above). After driving in the wedges with a hammer as shown below left, cut them flush with the riser, using a utility knife, and replace the shoe molding to conceal them.

## SIX WAYS TO FIX SQUEAKY STAIRS

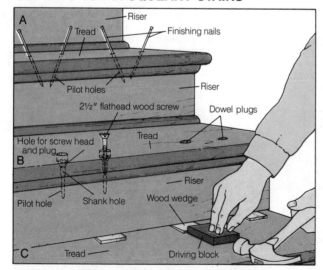

**From above:** Drive and sink nails into angled pilot holes drilled through the tread into the riser; cover with wood putty (A). Insert screws into pilot holes drilled through the tread into the riser; glue in dowel plugs (B). Tap in glue-coated wedges between the tread and riser (C); trim and cover with molding.

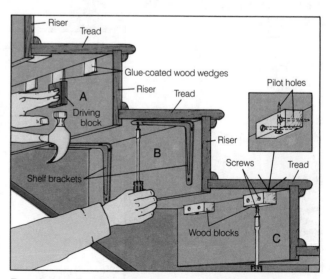

**From below:** Tap glue-coated wedges between the tread and riser, using a hammer and driving block (A). Install brackets under the tread and riser (B). Glue and screw wood blocks under the tread and against the riser, keeping the screw ends at least ¼ inch beneath the surface (C).

# Banisters

Most wood banisters consist of one or two handrails, balusters, and one or more supporting newel posts (see facing page). Repeated use can weaken the banister, resulting in loose handrails, balusters, or posts.

Methods for tightening loose parts involve inserting wedges or securing loose joints with screws. If you're using screws, drill pilot holes for them to prevent the wood from splitting. Use an electric drill with a combination bit (page 16) so you can sink the screw heads. To conceal them, fill the screw holes with wood putty—preferably colored to match the wood—and sand the putty smooth.

## TWO WAYS TO TIGHTEN A LOOSE HANDRAIL

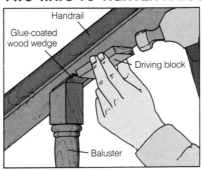

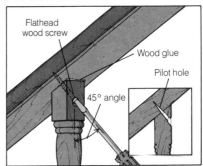

**Tap a glue-coated wedge** between the handrail and baluster (don't pry up the handrail). Using a utility knife, trim the wedge flush with the baluster.

**Drill an angled pilot hole** through the baluster and into the handrail; countersink. Apply wood glue; insert screw and tighten. Fill hole, sand, and finish.

## TWO WAYS TO TIGHTEN A LOOSE BALUSTER

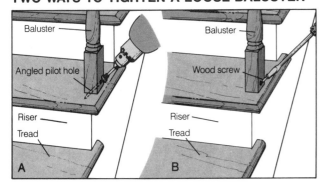

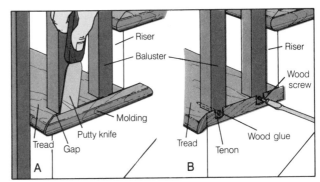

**For balusters nailed to treads,** drill an angled pilot hole through the baluster and into the tread; countersink the hole (A). Insert a wood screw and tighten (B). Fill the hole with wood putty, sand smooth when dry, and finish.

**For notched and tenon balusters,** pry off the molding with a putty knife or chisel (A). Drill a pilot hole through the tenon and into the tread; countersink. Apply wood glue around the notch and tenon. Insert screw and tighten (B). Replace molding.

## TWO WAYS TO TIGHTEN A LOOSE NEWEL POST

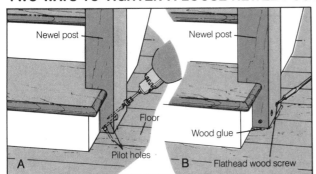

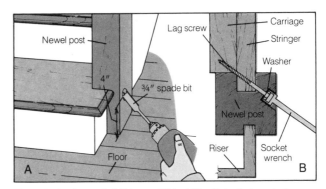

**Drill angled pilot holes** near the base of the newel post through the post and into the floor; countersink the holes (A). Apply wood glue between the post and floor; insert flathead wood screws and tighten (B). Fill the holes with wood putty, sand smooth when dry, and finish.

**Use a ¾-inch spade bit** (page 16) to drill a ¾-inch-deep hole into the newel post (A). With a $7/32$-inch bit, extend the hole into the carriage; then use a $5/16$-inch bit to enlarge it through the newel. Screw in a $5/16$ by 4-inch-long lag screw (B). Glue in a dowel plug, sand, and finish.

# The Plumbing System

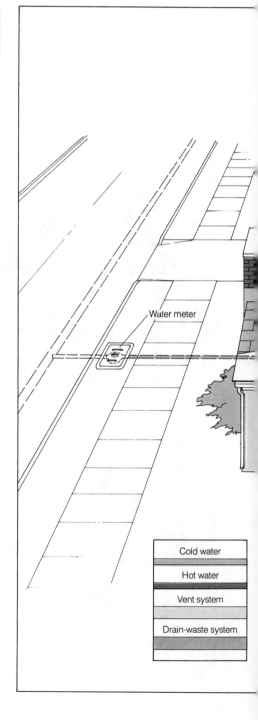

Water meter

| Cold water |
| Hot water |
| Vent system |
| Drain-waste system |

This behind-the-scenes look at a typical home plumbing system shows three separate but interdependent systems: supply, drain-waste, and vent. Hot and cold water flow through the supply pipes; drain-waste pipes carry away used water and waste. The vent system gets rid of sewer gas at each fixture and maintains proper pressure in the drainpipes.

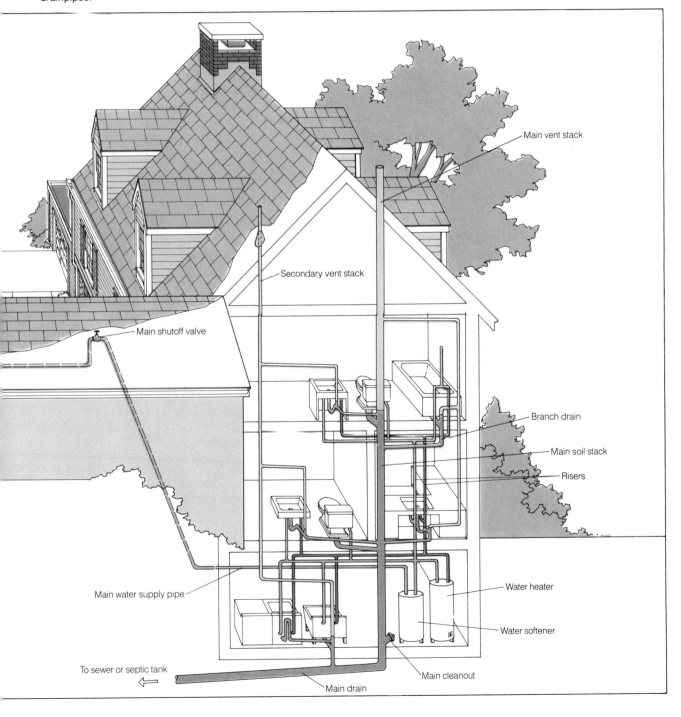

Main vent stack

Secondary vent stack

Main shutoff valve

Branch drain

Main soil stack

Risers

Main water supply pipe

Water heater

Water softener

To sewer or septic tank

Main cleanout

Main drain

# How the System Works

When you're making plumbing repairs, it helps to understand the plumbing system hidden behind your home's walls and under its floors. In a typical plumbing system, three systems are at work: supply, drain-waste, and vent.

- **The supply system** carries water from a water utility or other source into your house and around to all the fixtures (sinks, tubs, toilets) and to such appliances as the dishwasher and washing machine.

- **The drain-waste system** carries used water and waste out of the house into a sewer or septic tank.

- **The vent system** carries away sewer gases and maintains proper pressure inside the drainpipes, preventing toxic gases from entering your home.

## The supply system

Water enters your house through a main supply pipe connected to a water utility main or to a source on your property. In most homes a water meter monitors usage from a water utility; a main shutoff valve (usually located near where the supply pipe enters the house) turns the water for the house on and off (page 111).

Once inside the house, the main supply pipe divides into two branches, one for hot water and one for cold. If the system is equipped with a water softener, it may be either on the main supply line before it divides or on the branch supplying just the water heater.

For most of their distance, hot and cold water pipes run parallel and horizontally until they reach the vicinity of fixtures and water-using appliances. There, vertical branches, called risers, connect the fixture or appliance to the water system. Risers are usually concealed inside walls. Horizontal pipes are fastened to floor joists or buried under a concrete slab.

Supply pipes, installed with a slight pitch in the runs, slope back toward the lowest point so all pipes can be drained through a valve or faucet at that point.

Some fixtures and water-using appliances have their own shutoff valves (shown at right) so you can shut off the water to repair them without cutting off the water supply for the entire house. To be prepared for an emergency, everyone in the household should learn how to turn off the water supply both at the individual fixtures and at the main shutoff valve (page 7).

## The drain-waste system

The drain-waste system takes advantage of gravity to channel waste water and solid wastes to the house sewer line. Drainpipes lead away from all fixtures at a carefully calculated slope. If the slope is too steep, water will run off too fast, leaving particles behind; if it's not steep enough, water and waste will drain too slowly and may back up into the fixtures. The normal pitch is ¼ inch for every horizontal foot of pipe.

The workhorse in the drain-waste system is the soil stack, a vertical section of 3 or 4-inch-diameter pipe that carries waste away from toilets and other fixtures and connects with the main house drain in the basement or crawl space, or under the slab. From here, the wastes flow to a sewer or septic tank.

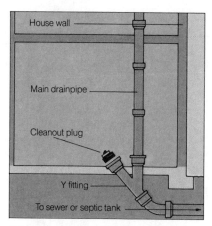

**Y (shown here) or T fitting** provides access to clean out clogs in the drainpipe.

Since any system will clog occasionally, cleanouts are placed in the drainpipes. Ideally, there should be one cleanout in each horizontal section of drainpipe, plus cleanouts in a U-shaped house trap, sometimes located outdoors, to give access to sewer or septic tank connections. A cleanout is usually a 45° Y fitting or 90° T fitting, designed for cleaning with a snake.

## The vent system

To prevent dangerous sewer gases from entering the home, each fixture must have a trap in its drainpipe and must be vented. A trap is a bend of pipe that remains filled with water at all times to keep gases from coming up the drain.

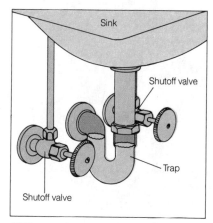

**All fixtures have a trap;** some have one or two valves to shut off the water.

The vents in the drain-waste system are designed to get rid of sewer gas and to prevent pressure buildups in the pipes. The vents come off the drainpipes downstream from the traps and go out through the roof. This maintains atmospheric pressure in the pipes and prevents the siphoning of water from the traps.

Each plumbing fixture in the house must be vented. Usually, a house has a main vent stack (which is the upper part of the main soil stack) with 1½ to 2-inch vent pipes connecting to it. In many homes—especially single-story ones—widely separated fixtures make it impractical to use a single main vent stack. In this situation, each fixture or fixture group has its own waste connection and its own secondary vent stack.

# Sink Faucets

The first step in fixing a leaking or sluggish faucet is identifying which of the two basic types of faucets you're dealing with. One is a long-standing design —usually with two handles and one spout—called a compression faucet (see below). The other is a more recent type called a washerless faucet. It usually has a single lever or knob that controls the flow and mix of hot and cold water by aligning interior openings with the water inlets.

Washerless faucets may be one of several types—disc, valve, ball, or cartridge. An example of each is described on pages 115–118. Because models vary with the manufacturer, it's important to get identical replacement parts.

Directions for disassembling and repairing compression and washerless faucets appear here and on the following pages. When you're taking the faucet apart, douse stubborn connections with penetrating oil before trying to loosen them with a wrench. Tape-wrap the wrench's jaws to prevent marring visible parts of the fixture.

Before starting any faucet repair, plug the sink so small parts can't fall down the drain; then line the sink with a towel to prevent damage from tools or parts accidentally dropped. As you disassemble the faucet, line up the pieces in the order that you remove them so you can put them back together properly.

CAUTION: Before you work on a faucet, turn off the water at the fixture shutoff valves or the main shutoff valve (page 111), and open the faucet to drain the pipes.

## Leaking Compression Faucets

If your faucet has separate hot and cold water handles, it's probably a compression faucet (also called a stem or washer faucet). In this faucet, a rubber seat washer is secured to the stem, which has very coarse threads on the outside. When you turn the handle to shut off the faucet, the stem is screwed down, compressing the washer against the valve seat in the faucet body. The stem is secured by a packing nut, which compresses the packing (twine, a washer, or an O-ring) and prevents water from leaking around the stem.

If water leaks around the handle, tighten the packing nut. If that fails, replace the packing (see next page).

If the faucet leaks from the spout, either a washer is defective or a valve seat is badly corroded. To find out which side needs work, turn off the shutoff valves one at a time; the leak will stop when one or the other is turned off. Then you'll need to take off the handle, remove the stem, and either replace the washer, or replace or recondition the valve seat (see next page).

When you reassemble the faucet, lubricate the stem threads with plumber's grease before installing the stem. If the threads are worn or stripped, consider replacing the stem.

Before doing any work, turn off the water at the fixture shutoff valves or at the main shutoff valve (page 111). Open the faucet to drain the pipes.

### COMPRESSION FAUCET

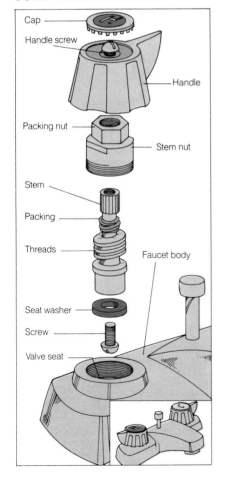

Cap
Handle screw
Handle
Packing nut
Stem nut
Stem
Packing
Threads
Faucet body
Seat washer
Screw
Valve seat

### TAKING THE FAUCET APART

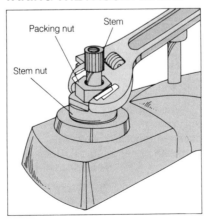

Packing nut
Stem
Stem nut

**1) With the handle removed,** lift off the stem and packing nuts by turning the nuts counterclockwise with an adjustable-end wrench or a pair of rib-joint pliers. (Be careful not to strip the nuts.)

Stem
Packing
Worn threads
Seat washer

**2) Unscrew the stem,** lifting it straight out of the faucet body. Examine the threads. If they're damaged or worn, replace the stem; if not, check the packing for wear (see next page).

# ... Sink Faucets

## REPLACING THE PACKING & WASHER

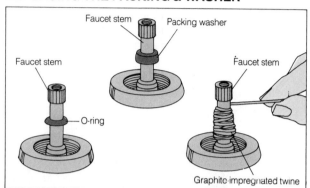

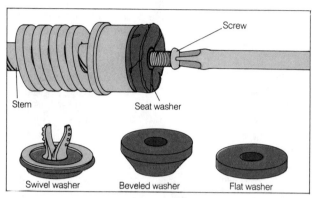

**To replace worn packing,** either remove the O-ring or packing washer and slide on an exact duplicate, or scrape off the twine and wrap new twine clockwise around the stem.

**To replace a cracked or worn seat washer,** remove the screw and washer; install a duplicate washer. If the threads are too worn to hold a screw, snap in a swivel washer.

## WORKING ON THE VALVE SEAT

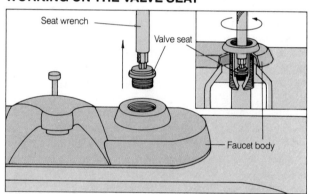

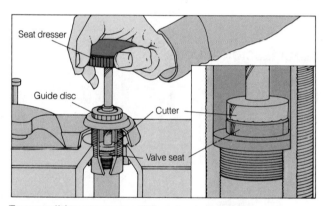

**To replace a removable valve seat** that's pitted or corroded, insert a seat wrench (page 21) into the valve seat and turn it counterclockwise until the seat lifts out. The new valve seat should be an exact duplicate. Coat the threads of the new seat with pipe joint compound before installing it.

**To recondition a nonremovable valve seat,** grind down its burrs with a seat dresser (page 21), an inexpensive tool you can buy from a plumbing supply dealer. Insert and turn it clockwise once or twice until the seat is smooth; remove metal filings with a damp cloth.

## CLEANING YOUR FAUCET AERATOR

If the flow from your faucet is sluggish, the trouble may be in the faucet aerator. This device, at the tip of most faucet spouts, mixes air and water for a smooth flow. But minerals or dirt particles in the water often build up on the screen and disc, blocking the flow.

If mineral deposits are to blame or if aerator parts are damaged, it's best to replace the aerator. But if dirt is the problem, simply unscrew the aerator from the end of the spout (to loosen stubborn connections, douse them with penetrating oil). Disassemble and set the parts aside in order.

Clean the screen and disc with a brush and soapy water; use a pin or toothpick to open any clogged holes in the disc. Flush all parts with water before putting them back together.

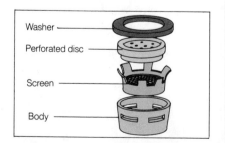

**Aerator comes apart** for easy cleaning.

# Leaking Disc Faucets

In disc faucets, the mix and flow of hot and cold water are controlled by two discs (not shown in drawing) inside the cartridge. Raising the faucet handle lifts the upper disc, controlling the amount of flow; rotating the handle turns the lower disc, controlling the mix. The disc assembly seldom wears out, but if it does, you'll need to replace the entire cartridge. Most often, the rubber inlet and outlet seals in the cartridge are the problem.

If you have a leak at the base of the faucet, a seal may be worn. Take the faucet apart as shown below; you'll find the set of seals under the cartridge. Replace them with exact duplicates.

If the water flow is sluggish, first check the faucet aerator (see facing page). If that's not the problem, the faucet inlet and outlet holes may be obstructed by sediment buildup; if so, scrape away any deposits.

When reassembling a dismantled faucet, be sure to realign the seals on the bottom of the cartridge with the holes in the faucet body.

Before doing any work, turn off the water at the fixture shutoff valves or the main shutoff valve (page 111).

## DISC FAUCET

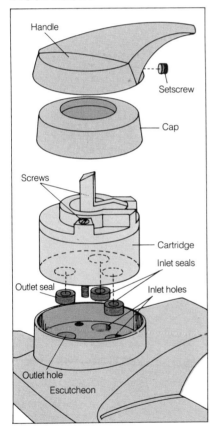

## TAKING THE FAUCET APART

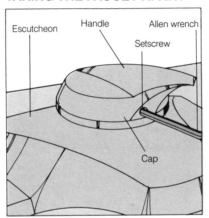

**1)** **To remove the handle,** lift it as high as it can go and loosen—but don't remove—the setscrew with an Allen wrench. Take off the handle and cap.

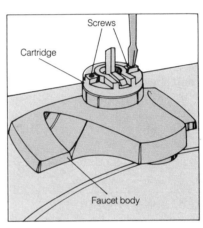

**2)** **To remove the cartridge,** loosen the two screws that fasten it to the faucet body. Then lift the entire cartridge straight off the body.

## WORKING ON THE INLETS & OUTLETS

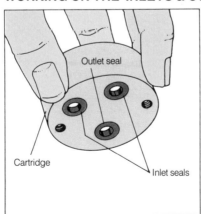

**1)** **Check the rubber inlet and outlet seals** in the bottom of the cartridge for signs of wear. While you have the faucet taken apart, it's best to remove all the seals and replace them with exact duplicates.

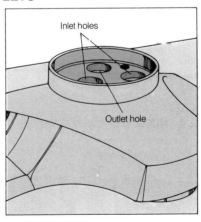

**2)** **Examine the inlet and outlet holes** for sediment buildup. Scrape away any deposits with a blunt knife. Aligning the seals on the cartridge with the holes, replace the cartridge, then the cap and handle.

---

**QUICK FIX-UP**
STOPPING FAUCET LEAKS

When water's leaking from around a faucet handle, wrap a wide rubber band around the trouble spot to keep it under control until you can fix it.

# ... Sink Faucets

## Leaking Valve Faucets

A valve faucet has a valve assembly on each side (one for hot water, one for cold) through which water flows up and out the spout. Moving the handle from side to side controls the mix; moving it forward and backward controls the flow.

The main problems you may encounter with a valve faucet are spout leaks, loose handle assemblies, and sluggish flow. A leak at the base of the spout may be due to a faulty spout O-ring; if the spout drips, you may need to replace one or more of the valve assembly parts. If the handle is loose, a simple adjustment to the handle screw or cam assembly at the back of the faucet can remedy it. Finally, if sluggish flow is the problem, the strainers or aerator (page 114) may be clogged with sediment and need cleaning.

Before doing any work, remember to shut off the water supply to the faucet.

### VALVE FAUCET

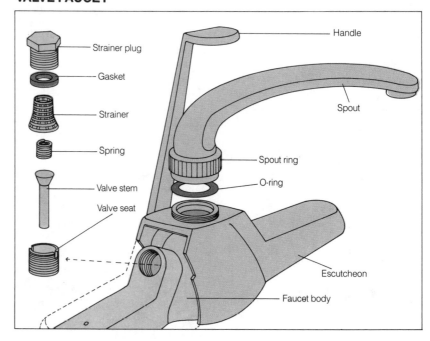

### REPAIRING THE SPOUT

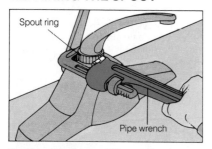

**1)  Remove the spout** by turning the spout ring counterclockwise, using a tape-wrapped pipe wrench.

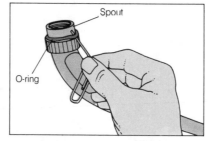

**2)  To remove a worn O-ring,** pry it off with a bent paper clip. Roll on a new one lubricated with plumber's grease.

### ADJUSTING THE HANDLE

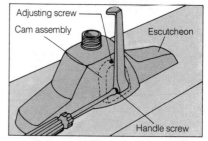

**To tighten a loose handle,** secure the handle screw or remove the escutcheon and turn the adjusting screw on the cam.

### CLEANING THE VALVE ASSEMBLY

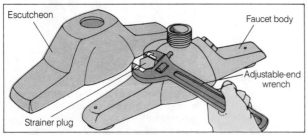

**1)  To remove the valve assembly,** unscrew the strainer plug with an adjustable-end wrench after removing the escutcheon.

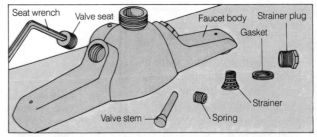

**2)  Remove the valve parts** by hand, the valve seat with a seat wrench. Clean all parts and replace, or install new ones.

# Leaking Ball Faucets

In a ball faucet, water flows when openings in the rotating ball align with hot and cold water inlets in the faucet body.

If water leaks from under the handle, leave the water on and tighten the adjusting ring; if the leak persists, turn off the water and replace the cam. For a dripping spout, replace the inlet seals and springs or the ball.

Cure any leaks around the spout sleeve by replacing the O-rings on the faucet body.

## BALL FAUCET

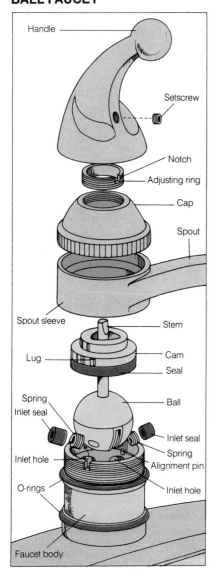

## TIGHTENING THE ADJUSTING RING

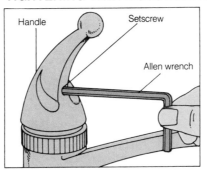

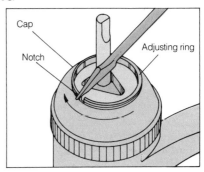

**1)    Loosen the setscrew** under the handle of the faucet with an Allen wrench and lift the handle off.

**2)    Tighten the adjusting ring** in the cap by turning it clockwise with a screwdriver inserted in the notch.

## REPLACING THE FAUCET PARTS

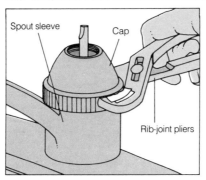

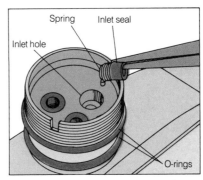

**1)    Unscrew the cap,** using tape-wrapped rib-joint pliers. Lift out the ball and cam; underneath are the inlet seals and springs. Remove the spout sleeve to expose the faucet body.

**2)    Lift out the inlet seals and springs,** using needle-nose pliers. With a penknife, remove any sediment in the holes; replace the inlet seals. Examine the O-rings and replace them if they're worn.

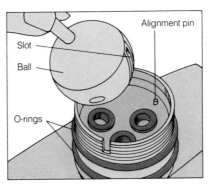

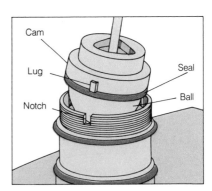

**3)    If the old ball is corroded,** replace it with a duplicate. When you install the new ball, carefully line up the slot in the ball with the alignment pin in the faucet body.

**4)    To replace the cam,** fit the lug on the new cam into the notch on the faucet body. Then replace the spout sleeve and cap, tighten the adjusting ring, and replace the faucet handle.

# ... Sink Faucets

## Leaking Cartridge Faucets

A cartridge faucet has a series of holes in the stem-and-cartridge assembly that align to control the mix and flow of water. Usually, leaks occur because of worn O-rings or a faulty cartridge.

First, look at the O-rings on the faucet body. If they're in good shape, remove the cartridge (look under the spout sleeve or on the outside of the faucet for the retainer clip that holds the cartridge in place). If the cartridge is worn, replace it with a duplicate.

Cartridges vary, so read the manufacturer's instructions before installing a new one. The most common type has a flat side that must face front; otherwise, the hot and cold water supply will be reversed. Be sure to fit the retainer clip snugly into its slot.

Before doing any work, remember to shut off the water supply.

### CARTRIDGE FAUCET

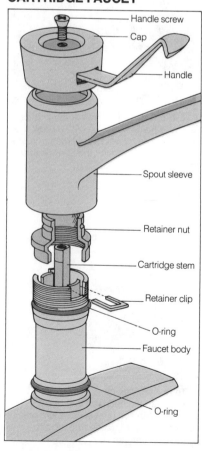

- Handle screw
- Cap
- Handle
- Spout sleeve
- Retainer nut
- Cartridge stem
- Retainer clip
- O-ring
- Faucet body
- O-ring

### TAKING THE FAUCET APART

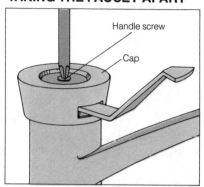

Handle screw
Cap

**1)** **Remove the handle screw** with a screwdriver; lift off the cap and handle. Remove the retainer nut.

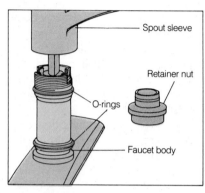

Spout sleeve
Retainer nut
O-rings
Faucet body

**2)** **Move the spout sleeve** back and forth and gently pull it off the faucet body. Replace any worn body O-rings.

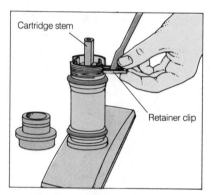

Cartridge stem
Retainer clip

**3)** **Pull the retainer clip** out of its slot in the faucet body using a screwdriver or needle-nose pliers.

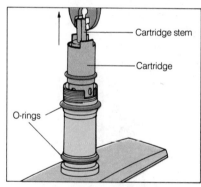

Cartridge stem
Cartridge
O-rings

**4)** **To remove the cartridge,** grip its stem with pliers and lift it straight out of the faucet body.

### REPLACING THE CARTRIDGE

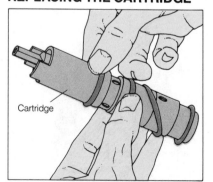

Cartridge

**1)** **A defective cartridge** may or may not show signs of wear; replace it anyway to get the faucet working again. Take the old cartridge along when you shop for a new one to be sure of getting an exact duplicate.

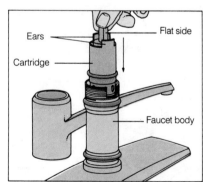

Ears
Cartridge
Flat side
Faucet body

**2)** **Push a new cartridge** down into the faucet body. If there's a flat side, be sure it faces forward. Reassemble the faucet, fitting the retainer clip snugly into its slot in the faucet body.

# Sink Sprays & Diverters

A kitchen sink spray has a spray head attached to a hose, which is connected to a diverter valve in the faucet body. When you squeeze the spray head handle, the diverter valve reroutes water from the faucet to the spray head hose. Illustrated is one of several types of diverter valves.

If the flow is sluggish, make sure the hose isn't kinked; then clean the aerator in the spray nozzle. Continued sluggishness may indicate diverter valve problems. You'll have to clean the valve or replace it.

If the spray head leaks, remove it from the hose and replace the washer. For a leak at the faucet end of the hose, tighten the hose coupling. If the hose itself leaks, it's probably cracked; you'll need to replace it.

## SINK SPRAY ASSEMBLY

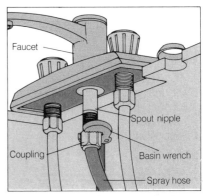

## CORRECTING THREE SINK SPRAY PROBLEMS

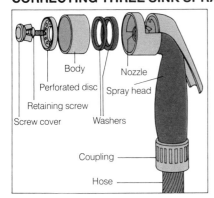

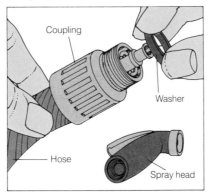

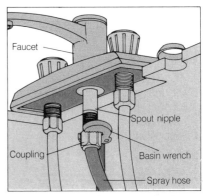

**To unclog a spray nozzle,** remove the retaining screw and clean the perforated disc with a brush and soapy water; open clogged holes with a pin.

**To correct a leaking spray head,** turn off the water; unscrew the spray head and replace the hose washer if worn. Also try tightening the coupling.

**To replace a spray hose,** use a basin wrench to unfasten the coupling under the sink; also unfasten the spray head coupling. Replace the hose with a duplicate.

## CLEANING A DIVERTER VALVE

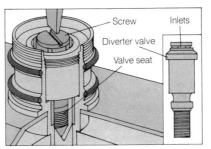

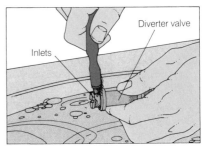

**1)   Unscrew the spout nut** to reach the diverter valve in a compression faucet (diverters vary in washerless faucets).

**2)   Loosen the screw** on the diverter valve just enough to lift the valve out of the faucet body.

**3)   Take the valve apart;** clean inlets and surfaces with a brush and soapy water. Reassemble, or replace if defective.

# Tub Faucets & Shower Heads

## Leaking Tub Faucets

Like sink faucets, tub faucets can be compression style or washerless. If you need to repair a leaking tub faucet, refer to the directions for sink faucets on pages 113–118.

To take apart any style tub faucet, pry off the cap, unscrew the handle, and remove the escutcheon. In a compression faucet, you'll see the stem and packing nut. You may need to use a deep-socket wrench (page 21) to grip and loosen a recessed packing nut.

The washerless tub faucet shown here is repaired in almost the same way as a cartridge-type sink faucet (page 118). You remove the stop tube and draw out the retainer clip to get at the cartridge. The other kind of washerless tub faucet (not shown here) is repaired like a ball-type sink faucet (page 117).

---

**PROFESSIONAL TIP**
LOOSENING FROZEN CONNECTIONS

Instead of using a wrench to force nuts and couplings frozen in place, douse the connection with penetrating oil. Wait half an hour; then loosen with a wrench.

---

**TWO TYPES OF TUB FAUCETS**

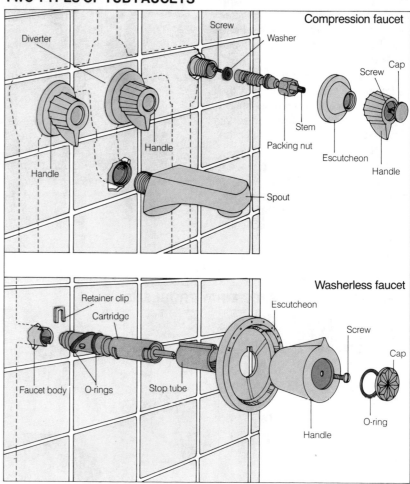

## Faulty Shower Heads

If your shower head leaks where it meets the arm, you probably need to replace the washer. To reach it, loosen the collar, using tape-wrapped rib-joint pliers; then unscrew the head from the adjusting ring.

Erratic or weak pressure usually indicates mineral buildup. To restore proper flow, clean outlet holes with a pin or unscrew a perforated face plate and soak it overnight in vinegar; then scrub it clean.

If the shower head pivots stiffly, check the washer for wear and coat the swivel ball with petroleum jelly before reassembling.

**TWO TYPES OF SHOWER HEADS**

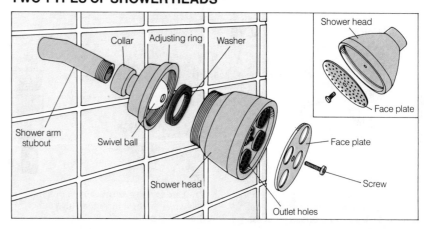

# Pop-up Stoppers

As its name implies, a pop-up stopper moves up or down to open or close the drain. The primary stopper problem is a bad fit between the stopper and the sink or tub.

When a stopper doesn't seat properly, you need to remove and inspect it. Some sink stoppers sit atop the pivot rod and simply lift out; others require a slight twist to free them because a slot on the body hooks them to the rod. Still others are attached to the pivot rod.

To remove a tub stopper, pull it out along with the rocker arm. (They should come out readily, since the striker spring rests unattached on the rocker arm.)

Clean the stopper of hair and debris. If there's a rubber seal, pry it off and check for damage. Slip on a new one if needed. Also make sure the flange is tightly seated and in good shape.

If a sink stopper still doesn't seat properly, adjust the clevis screw, pivot rod, or retaining nut (see below). If a tub stopper doesn't fit after cleaning, remove the overflow plate and pull the entire lever assembly out through the overflow. Loosen the adjusting nuts; slide the middle link up the striker rod. Lower the link for a sluggish drain.

## SINK POP-UP ASSEMBLY

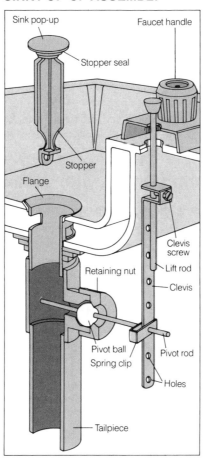

## TUB POP-UP ASSEMBLY

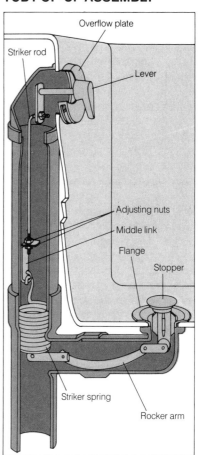

## ADJUSTING A SINK POP-UP

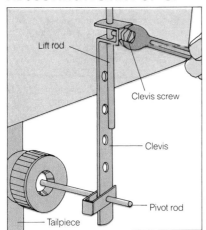

**If a sink pop-up doesn't seat tightly,** loosen the clevis screw with a wrench, push the stopper down, and retighten the clevis screw. When the drain is closed, the pivot rod should slope slightly uphill from the clevis to the tailpiece.

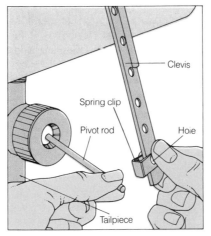

**If the sink stopper is so tight** that it impedes drainage and adjusting the clevis screw doesn't help, reset the pivot rod. Squeeze the spring clip and free the pivot rod. Move the clip up to the next clevis hole; insert the rod.

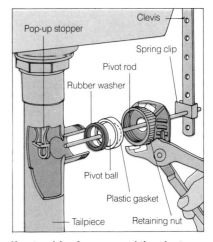

**If water drips from around the pivot ball,** use tape-wrapped rib-joint pliers to tighten the retaining nut that holds the ball in place. Still leaking? Replace the gasket or washer (or both) inside the pivot ball-and-rod assembly.

# Sink Drains

A stopped sink drain isn't just an inconvenience; it can sometimes be an emergency.

It's always best to prevent clogs before they happen (for hints, see page 127). Be alert to the warning sign of a sluggish drain—it's easier to open a drain that's slowing down than one that's stopped completely.

When it's too late for preventive medicine, a dose of scalding water— especially effective against grease buildups—may be treatment enough. If not, it could be that something foreign—a button, coin, or small utensil—has slipped down the drain. To check, remove and thoroughly clean the sink pop-up stopper (page 121) or strainer.

Often, a clog will be close to the sink. You can determine this by checking the other drains in your home. If more than one won't clear, something is stuck in the main drain (pages 126–127). Otherwise, you're probably dealing with a clog in the sink trap or drainpipe. The most effective way to clear a clog is with a snake (see facing page). You can try using a plunger or a chemical drain cleaner first; in any case, pay special attention to the cautions on these pages before you begin work.

## Clearing Drains with a Plunger

What's the first reaction to a clog? Reach for the plumber's helper—the plunger. The plunger is a good drain-clearing tool, but it often fails to work because it's incorrectly used. Don't make the typical mistake of pumping up and down two or three times, expecting the water to whoosh down the drain.

Though no great expertise is needed to use this simple tool, here are a few tips to guide you:

■ **Choose a plunger** with a suction cup large enough to cover the drain opening completely, as shown in the drawing at right.

■ **Fill the clogged fixture** with enough water to cover the plunger cup.

■ **Coat the rim** of the plunger cup with petroleum jelly to ensure a tight seal.

■ **Block off all other outlets** (the overflow, second drain in a double sink, adjacent fixtures) with wet rags.

■ **Insert the plunger** into the water at an angle so no air remains trapped under it.

■ **Use 15 to 20 forceful strokes,** holding the plunger upright and pumping vigorously.

■ **Repeat the plunging** two or three times before giving up.

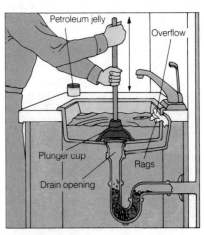

**To unclog a sink,** pump the plunger vigorously up and down.

## Using Chemical Drain Cleaners

Though routine use of chemical drain cleaners to *prevent* clogs may eventually damage your pipes (see "Preventing Drain Clogs," page 127), these cleaners can be helpful in opening clogged drains. If water is draining somewhat but plunging has failed to open the drain completely, you may want to try using a drain cleaner.

Whenever you use chemicals, do so with caution and in a well-ventilated room. Be sure to take these precautions:

■ **Never use a plunger** if a chemical cleaner is present in the drain; you risk splashing caustic water on yourself.

■ **Wear rubber gloves** to prevent the chemical from burning your skin. Avoid splashing the cleaner.

■ **Don't use a chemical cleaner** if the blockage is total, especially if the fixture is filled with water. It won't clear the blockage, and you'll face another problem—how to get rid of the caustic water.

■ **Never use** a chemical cleaner in a garbage disposer.

■ **Read labels** and match cleaners with clogs. Alkalis cut grease; acids dissolve soap and hair.

■ **Don't mix chemicals.** Mixing an acid and an alkali cleaner can cause an explosion.

■ **Don't look down the drain** after pouring in a chemical. The solution often boils up and gives off toxic fumes.

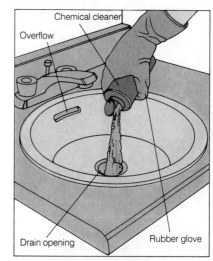

**Pour in chemical drain cleaner,** protecting your hands with rubber gloves. Avoid splashing or breathing the fumes.

# Clearing Drains with a Plumber's Snake

Should the plunger and chemical treatment fail, try the snake (also called a drain-and-trap auger). This tool is a very flexible metal coil that you feed through the pipes to reach the clog.

The most effective way to snake out a clog is to remove the trap and snake directly through the drainpipe. If you don't want to remove the trap, you can try snaking through the sink drain opening or the trap cleanout, if any. But be forewarned that if a metal trap is thin or badly corroded, you may punch through it with the snake.

To use the snake, feed it into the drain, trap, or pipe until it stops. If the snake has a movable handle, position it about 6 inches above the opening and tighten the thumbscrew; rotate the handle to break the blockage. If there's no handle, maneuver the cable by simultaneously pushing and twisting until it hits the clog.

The first time the snake stops, it probably has hit a turn in the piping rather than the clog. Guiding the snake past a sharp turn takes patience and effort. Keep pushing it forward, turning it as you do. Once the head of the snake hooks some of the blockage, pull the snake back a short distance to free some material from the clog; then push the rest on through.

If snaking doesn't succeed, the clog is probably too deep in the pipes to reach through the drainpipe. This means you're dealing with a main drain clog that needs to be attacked through the soil stack, main cleanout, or house trap (pages 126–127).

## PLUMBER'S SNAKE

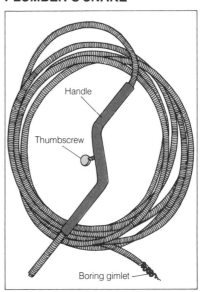

Handle

Thumbscrew

Boring gimlet

## THREE WAYS TO USE A SNAKE

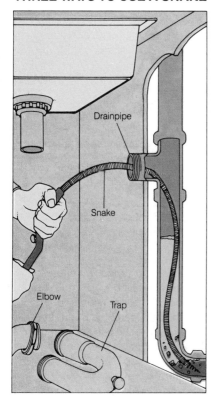

Drainpipe

Snake

Elbow

Trap

**To snake through the drainpipe,** remove the trap (page 124), spilling the contents into a pail. Feed the snake as far as possible behind the wall until it hits the clog.

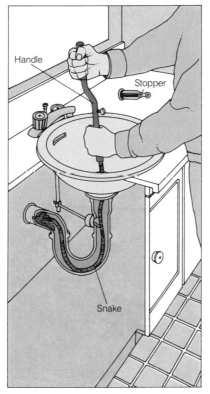

Handle

Stopper

Snake

**To snake through the drain,** remove the stopper (page 121) or strainer and insert the snake; twist it down through the trap until you reach the clog.

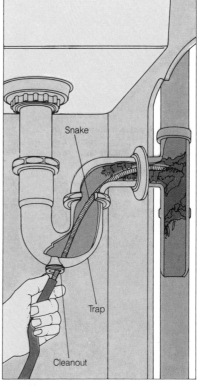

Snake

Trap

Cleanout

**To snake through a trap cleanout,** set up a pail, then remove the plug. Direct the snake up toward the drain or toward the wall (as shown) to reach a deeper blockage.

# Sink Traps

Sink traps often develop leaks or clogs. Corrosion or a loose or stripped coupling can produce leaks. If the drain is clogged and resists all attempts to unclog it (pages 122–123), suspect a mineral buildup inside the trap.

To resolve these problems, you'll need to install a new trap and possibly a new tailpiece. Determine what type of trap you have—swivel or fixed P—and replace it with an exact duplicate. The new unit comes complete with washers and threaded couplings. Tailpieces are sold separately.

To remove the tailpiece only, see below. Don't force a stubborn unit; remove the trap instead.

## TYPES OF TRAPS

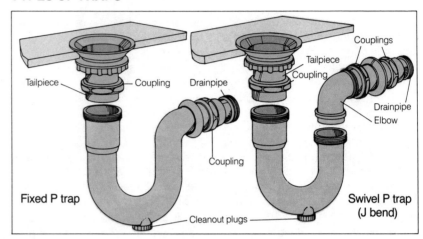

## REPLACING A TRAP

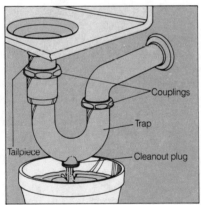

**1)  Remove the cleanout plug,** if any, to drain water into a pail under the trap. Use penetrating oil to loosen the connections.

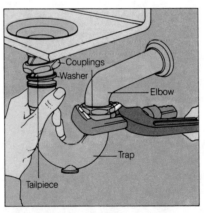

**2)  Loosen the couplings** at the tailpiece and elbow with a tape-wrapped pipe wrench; pull out the old trap.

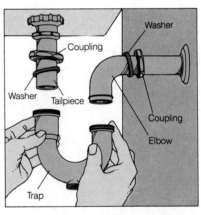

**3)  Slide new couplings and washers** onto the tailpiece and elbow. Attach the trap and tighten the couplings.

## REPLACING A TAILPIECE

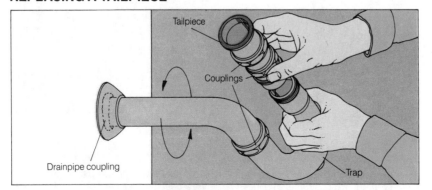

**Unscrew sink drain and trap couplings;** push the tailpiece into the trap. Loosen the drainpipe coupling; swivel the unit and remove the tailpiece. Attach a new one.

---

**QUICK FIX-UP**
TAPING A LEAKY TRAP

Here's a stopgap measure to fix a leaking trap until you can get a replacement. Dry the outside of the trap. Then wrap plastic electrical tape several times around the area that's leaking. Though the fix may last longer than you expect, it's best to install a new trap as quickly as possible.

# Tub & Shower Drains

Before trying any drain-clearing methods on a plugged tub, check that the tub's pop-up stopper is opening fully (page 121) and is free of hair and debris.

If the stopper isn't the problem, then the drainpipe is probably clogged. First try a plunger or chemical drain cleaner (page 122). If these fail to do the job, you'll have to clear the trap with a snake.

Most tubs have a P trap in the drain. In some homes, the tub may have a drum trap in the floor near the tub instead (it will have a removable metal cover and a rubber gasket).

Using a snake in a tub P trap is much like snaking a sink trap (page 123). If you have a drum trap, first try snaking it clear through the tub overflow. If that doesn't work, bail out all the standing water from the tub. Then, using an adjustable-end wrench, unscrew the trap cover slowly. Have rags ready for any water that wells up. Remove the cover; bail out and clean the trap. If, after this, water does not well up, snake toward the tub; if water does well up, snake toward the main drain.

If you can't reach the clog from the trap, it's probably deeper in the main drain (pages 126–127).

### UNCLOGGING TWO TYPES OF TUB DRAINS

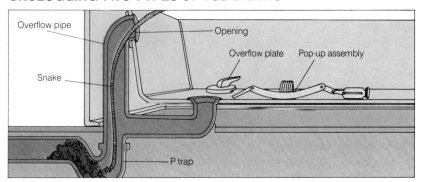

**To unclog a tub P trap,** remove the overflow plate and pull out the pop-up assembly, including the rocker arm and spring. Feed the snake down the overflow pipe and maneuver it toward the clog.

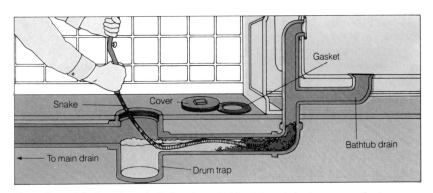

**To unclog a tub drum trap,** bail all water out of the tub and slowly unscrew the trap cover to control any water that wells up. Clean out the trap. If it's still clogged, snake toward the tub, as shown, or toward the main drain.

Though it may be difficult to unclog a shower drain with a plunger, it's worth a try. If that doesn't work, maneuver a snake down the drain opening into the trap.

As a last resort, you can use a garden hose. Attach the hose to an outdoor faucet or to an indoor faucet with a threaded adapter. Push the hose deep into the drain and pack rags into the opening. Turning the water on in short, hard bursts should open the drain.

CAUTION: Never leave a hose in any drain; a sudden drop in water pressure could siphon sewage back into the fresh water supply.

### TWO WAYS TO UNCLOG A SHOWER DRAIN

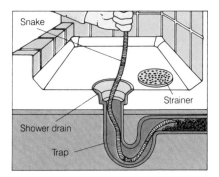

**Unscrew the strainer** from the shower drain. Direct the snake down into the trap, maneuvering it to the clog.

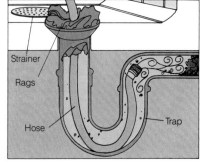

**Feed a hose** deep into the trap; pack rags in the opening. Turn the water alternately on full force and abruptly off.

# Main Drain & Soil Stack

If a clog is too deep in the pipes to get at from a fixture (pages 122–123 and 125), the trouble lies somewhere in the main drain or soil stack. A blockage in either one can stop up all the fixtures above the clog.

To troubleshoot a clog, trace the pipes from the plugged fixtures to the main soil stack. You can clear the soil stack from above, through the vent. The main drain is cleared through the main cleanout, vent, or house trap.

**Drain-clearing tools.** You'll need a special 50 to 75-foot-long snake—hand-operated or powered—to work on a vent stack. You can rent either tool; if you choose a power snake, use caution and work with a partner—this tool can be dangerous.

Instead of using a snake on a main cleanout or house trap, you can use a garden hose with rags stuffed around it or a balloon bag attached to a hose nozzle.

CAUTION: Exercise extreme care when using a hose; you're dealing with raw sewage. Never leave a hose in any drain; a sudden drop in water pressure could siphon sewage back into the fresh water supply.

**Clearing the soil stack and main drain.** First try clearing the stack by feeding a snake in through the roof vent. (Be especially careful on a steep or slippery roof.) If the clog's not in the stack, attack the clog from the main cleanout or house trap.

The main cleanout, usually a Y or T-shaped fitting, is near the bottom of the soil stack where it meets the main drain. Look for it in the basement or crawl space, or on an outside wall. Use a pipe wrench to remove the cleanout plug. Have pails, mops, and rags handy; open the plug slowly to control the flow of waste and not release a flood.

If a snake, hose, or balloon bag doesn't break up the clog, move downstream to the house trap.

The house trap has two adjacent cleanout plugs near where the main drain leaves the house. With a pipe wrench, slowly loosen the plug nearest the outside sewer line. Probe with a snake, but be ready to withdraw it and

## THE DRAIN-WASTE SYSTEM

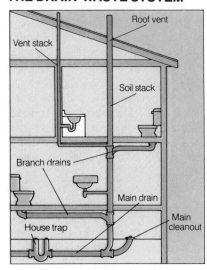

cap the trap quickly when water flows. When it subsides, reopen the trap and clean it out from both ends with a wire brush.

After clearing any clog, always flush the pipes thoroughly from upstream in the system, using plenty of clean water.

## DRAIN-CLEARING TOOLS

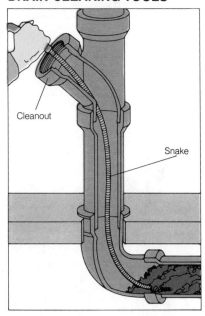

**A snake can probe** and maneuver around pipe bends to break up a stubborn clog deep in the pipes.

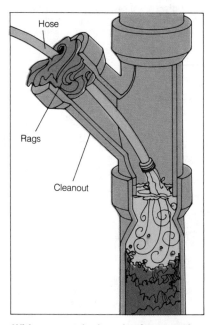

**With a rag-packed garden hose,** apply abrupt water pressure to force out a deep clog. Use this technique with caution.

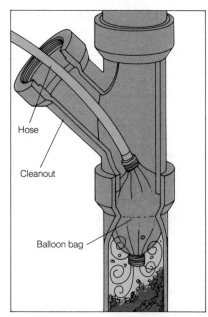

**Use a balloon bag** to deliver a powerful surge of pressure to break up a clog. Exercise caution when using this technique.

## THREE WAYS TO CLEAR CLOGS

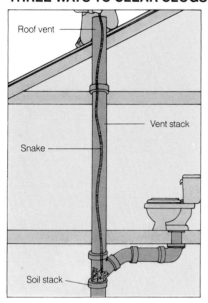

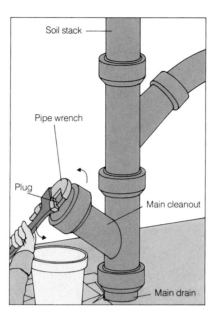

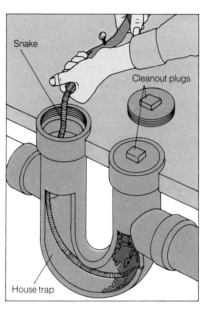

**Thread the snake through the vent stack** to the soil stack, working it from side to side. Exercise caution on the roof.

**Remove the main cleanout plug slowly;** snake the clog free. Flush, apply pipe joint compound to the plug, and recap.

**Slowly loosen the plug** at the house trap and probe with a snake; cap when water flows. Open both plugs and clean out.

## PREVENTING DRAIN CLOGS

No plumbing problem is more common or more frustrating than a clogged drain. Kitchen sink drains clog most often because of a buildup of grease that traps food particles. Hair and soap are often at fault in bathroom drains. Drains can usually be cleared easily and inexpensively, but taking some simple precautions will help you avoid stop-ups.

**Proper disposal of kitchen waste** will keep sink drain clogs to a minimum. Be especially careful not to pour grease down the kitchen sink. Another villain is coffee grounds—throw them out, don't wash them down.

**Be sparing with chemical cleaners,** particularly if you have brass, steel, or cast-iron traps and drainpipes; some caustic chemicals can corrode metal pipes. (Plastic drainpipes are more resistant to damage from caustic chemicals.) If used no more than once every few months, cleaners containing sodium hydroxide or sodium nitrate can be safe and effective.

Safety precautions for using drain cleaners are on page 122. Be sure to follow these, as well as the instructions on the package. You'll need to let the cleaner sit in the bend of the trap for awhile for it to be effective. Be careful not to splash the cleaner around or get any on your skin. Rinse the area thoroughly with clean water when you're finished.

**Clean floor drain strainers.** Some tubs, showers, and basement floor drains have strainers that are screwed into the drain opening. You can easily remove these strainers and reach down into the drain with a bent wire to clear out accumulated debris. And be sure to scrub the strainer.

**Clean pop-up stoppers** (page 121) in the bathroom sink and tub regularly. Lift out sink pop-ups once a week and rinse them off.

Every few months, remove the overflow plate on a tub and pull up the pop-up assembly to reach the spring or rocker arm. Remove accumulated hair and rinse thoroughly.

**Keep the sewer pipes** from the house free of tree roots that may invade them. If roots are a particular problem in your yard, you may need to call in professionals once a year or so to clear the pipes. They'll use an electric auger to cut out the roots.

**Finally, flush the drain-waste and vent systems** whenever you go up onto your house roof to clean out downspouts or gutters. Run water from a garden hose into all vents, giving them a minute or two of full flow.

# Toilets

Two assemblies are concealed under the lid of a toilet tank: a ball cock assembly, which regulates the filling of the tank, and a flush valve assembly, which controls the flow of water from the tank to the bowl.

Here's what happens when someone presses the flush handle. The trip lever raises the lift wires (or chain) connected to the tank stopper. As the stopper goes up, water rushes through the valve seat into the bowl via the flush passages. The water in the bowl yields to gravity and is siphoned out the trap.

Once the tank empties, the stopper drops into the flush valve seat. The float ball trips the ball cock assembly to let a new supply of water into the tank through the tank-fill tube. As the tank water level rises, the float ball rises until it gets high enough to shut off the flow of water. If the water fails to shut off, the overflow tube carries water down into the bowl to prevent an overflow.

On the next five pages are instructions for making toilet repairs. For quick reference, see the chart below.

## THE PARTS OF A TOILET

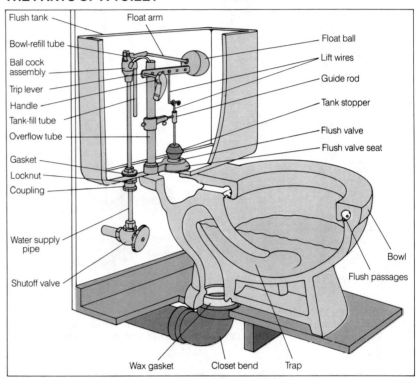

## TROUBLESHOOTING A TOILET

| Problem | Possible Causes | Remedies | Pages |
|---|---|---|---|
| **Noisy tank fill** | Defective ball cock | Oil trip lever, replace faulty washers, or install new ball cock assembly | 129 |
| | Restricted water supply | Adjust shutoff valve | 129 |
| **Running toilet** | Float arm not rising high enough | Bend float arm down or away from tank wall | 130 |
| | Water-filled float ball | Replace ball | 130 |
| | Tank stopper not seating properly | Adjust stopper guide rod and lift wires or chain; replace defective stopper | 130 |
| | Corroded flush valve seat | Scour valve seat or replace | 130, 131 |
| | Cracked overflow tube | Replace tube or install new flush valve assembly | 131 |
| | Ball cock valve doesn't shut off | Oil trip lever, replace faulty washers, or install new ball cock assembly | 129 |
| **Clogged toilet** | Blockage in drain | Remove blockage with plunger or closet auger | 132 |
| **Inadequate flush** | Faulty linkage between handle and trip lever | Tighten setscrew on handle linkage or replace handle | 133 |
| | Tank stopper closes before tank empties | Adjust stopper guide rod and lift wires or chain | 130 |
| | Leak between tank and bowl | Tighten tank bolts or couplings, or replace gasket | 133 |
| | Clogged flush passages | Clear obstructions from passages with wire | 133 |
| **Sweating tank** | Condensation | Install tank insulation or a tempering valve | 133 |

# Noisy Toilets

If you hear a high whine or whistle as the toilet tank fills after a flush, the problem may be simply restricted water flow or, more importantly, a defective ball cock assembly.

The ball cock in your toilet tank may be one of several types (see at right). The conventional diaphragm-type ball cock is shown in the repair sequences in this section. Two newer types—the float-cup ball cock and the adjustable-fill valve—eliminate the need for a float arm and ball.

To correct a noisy toilet, try adjusting the shutoff valve first; the problem may be restricted water flow. Still noisy? Oil the trip lever or replace the ball cock washers. If that doesn't work, replace the entire ball cock assembly.

CAUTION: First turn off the water at the fixture shutoff valve; then flush the toilet to empty the tank and sponge out any remaining water.

---

**PROFESSIONAL TIP**
LOOSENING
CONNECTIONS

To avoid slipping with a wrench and cracking the fixture, douse stubborn connections with penetrating oil.

---

## TYPES OF BALL COCK ASSEMBLIES

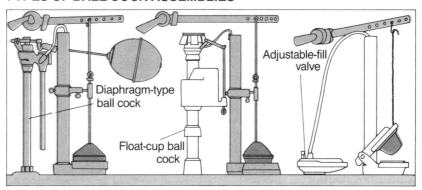

## REPLACING BALL COCK WASHERS

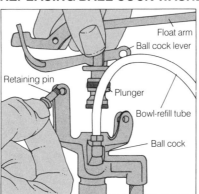

**1)**   **Remove the retaining pins** in the ball cock lever (they may be threaded) and lift out the float arm. Pull the plunger up and out of the ball cock.

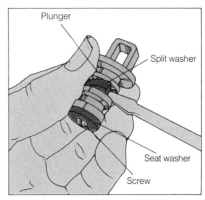

**2)**   **Pry the split washer** from its groove with a screwdriver and unscrew the seat washer from the plunger's base. Replace the washers.

---

## REPLACING THE BALL COCK ASSEMBLY

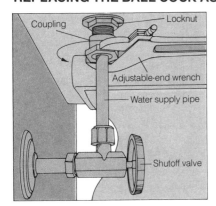

**1)**   **Disconnect the coupling** joining the water supply pipe under the tank to the ball cock. Remove the float arm.

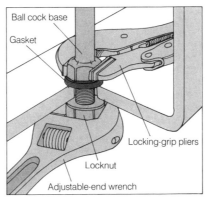

**2)**   **Using pliers and a wrench, loosen the locknut** holding the ball cock. Unclip the refill tube; remove the ball cock.

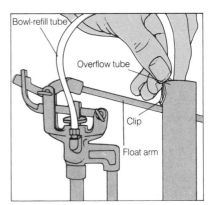

**3)**   **To install the new assembly,** reverse the removal procedure; reconnect the float arm and reattach the refill tube.

# ... Toilets

## Running Toilets

If water in your toilet tank trickles incessantly, refer to the chart on page 128 for help in diagnosing the cause. If the problem isn't in the ball cock assembly (page 129), you may need to adjust or replace the float mechanism or one or more parts of the flush valve assembly—the overflow tube, valve seat, tank stopper, guide rod, or lift wires. Or you may need to replace the entire assembly.

**Float mechanism.** Bending the float arm downward or away from the back of the tank may stop the water from running. Replace a water-filled float ball.

**Flush valve assembly.** A defective or badly fitting valve seat or stopper may cause a running toilet. If the valve seat is rough and pitted, scour it smooth.

If the tank stopper isn't seating properly, try adjusting the guide rod and lift wires or chain. Or replace the stopper with a duplicate or a flapper.

If a metal overflow tube is cracked, replace it. If the toilet is still running, replace the entire flush valve assembly (you'll have to disconnect the tank from the bowl to get at the valve seat).

CAUTION: First turn off the water at the fixture shutoff valve; then flush the toilet to empty the tank and sponge out any remaining water.

### WORKING ON THE STOPPER & VALVE SEAT

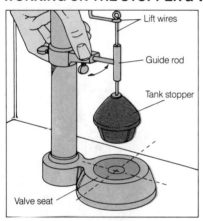

**1)** **Loosen the thumbscrews** and re-align the guide rod or bend the lift wires if the stopper doesn't seat properly.

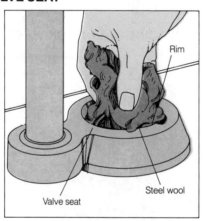

**2)** **Gently scour** a rough and pitted valve seat and rim with fine steel wool to smooth the surfaces.

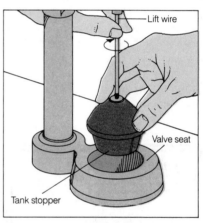

**3)** **To replace a worn-out tank stopper** with a duplicate, unscrew it from the lift wire and screw on a new one.

### INSTALLING A FLAPPER STOPPER

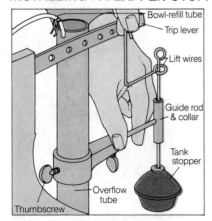

**1)** **To remove the old stopper,** unhook the lift wires and loosen the thumbscrew. Lift off the guide rod and stopper.

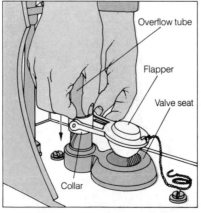

**2)** **To install the flapper,** slide its collar to the base of the overflow tube. Position the flapper over the valve seat.

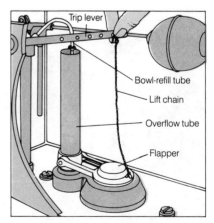

**3)** **Adjust the length of the lift chain** and fasten it to the trip lever, leaving about ½-inch slack.

## REPLACING THE FLUSH VALVE ASSEMBLY

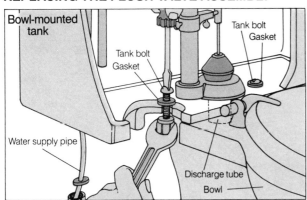

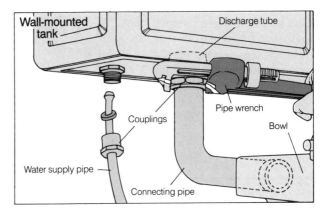

**1) Disconnect the tank.** First disconnect the water supply pipe. Then, for a bowl-mounted tank (left), remove the tank bolts and gaskets; lift off the tank. For a wall-mounted tank (right), loosen the pipe couplings and remove the connecting pipe.

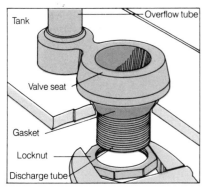

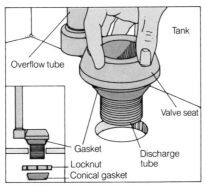

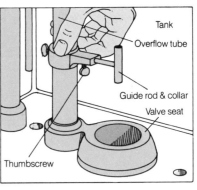

**2) Unscrew the locknut** on the discharge tube under the tank after removing the conical gasket. Remove the lift wires, guide rod, and stopper; lift out the valve seat and overflow tube.

**3) Assemble the gasket** on the new flush valve; insert the assembly through the tank bottom. Position the overflow tube; assemble and tighten the conical gasket and locknut under the tank.

**4) To install a stopper with lift wires,** slide the guide rod and collar down the overflow tube. Center the guide rod over the valve seat and tighten the thumbscrew to hold it in place.

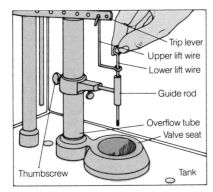

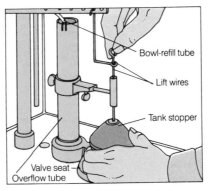

**5) Hook the upper lift wire** into the trip lever. Slide the lower lift wire down through the upper wire and the guide rod. Adjust the guide rod's height with the thumbscrew on the collar.

**6) Screw the tank stopper** onto the lower lift wire so the stopper will drop straight down. Reposition the bowl-refill tube and reconnect the tank, reversing the removal procedure.

**PROFESSIONAL TIP**
DETECTING A TANK LEAK

If you can't tell whether your toilet is leaking around the tank bolts or just sweating, add food coloring to the tank water. Wait an hour; then touch the bolt tips and nuts under the tank with white tissue. If the tissue shows coloring, you have a leak; otherwise, it's condensation. For remedies to either problem, see page 133.

# ... Toilets

## Clogged Toilets

If you suspect a toilet is clogged, don't flush or it may overflow.

To unclog the toilet, first bail out or add water so the bowl is half-full. Then use a funnel-cup plunger, specially designed to fit the bowl's trap. If the plunger doesn't clear the clog, use a closet auger (page 21). Its curved tip reaches deep-set clogs and its protective housing won't scratch the bowl.

---

**QUICK FIX-UP**
PREVENTING AN
OVERFLOW

If a toilet is about to overflow, quickly reach into the tank; push the tank stopper down into the valve seat and hold it while you turn off the water.

---

### TWO WAYS TO UNCLOG A TOILET TRAP

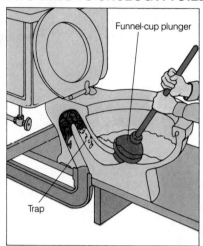

**Use a funnel-cup plunger** to dislodge a clog in the toilet trap. Rapidly pump the plunger a dozen times or more to push the obstruction through the trap.

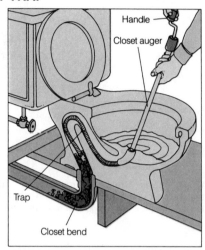

**Use a closet auger** to break up a deep-set clog in the toilet trap or closet bend. To maneuver the auger, simultaneously push it and turn the handle.

---

## MAINTAINING YOUR SEPTIC TANK

A good septic tank system doesn't require a great deal of maintenance or call for many special precautions. But the maintenance it does require is crucial, since failure of the system can constitute a serious health hazard. You should have a diagram of your septic tank's layout, showing the location of the tank, pipes, manholes, and disposal field. If you don't, the information may be on a lot plan filed with the county or city clerk.

**Chemicals, drain cleaners with lye, and thick paper products** should never be disposed of through the system. Some chemicals destroy the bacteria necessary to attack and disintegrate solid wastes in the septic tank. Paper products can clog the main drain to the tank and smaller pipes to the disposal field, making the entire system useless. Also, don't let

cooking grease enter the system; it will coat the surface of the earth in the disposal field and prevent absorption.

**Have your septic tank checked** by a professional about once a year. To function properly, the tank must maintain a balance of sludge (solids remaining on the bottom), scum (gas containing small solid particles), and liquid, as shown on the drawing at right. The proportion of the sludge and scum layers to the liquid layer determines whether pumping is needed.

**Have your septic tank pumped** by a professional whenever necessary to remove sludge and some of the scum. The best time to do the work is in the spring, since during the winter the bacterial action is slowed down and the tank will have become loaded with solid waste.

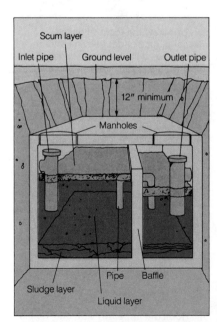

**This schematic drawing** shows sludge, liquid, and scum layers in a concrete tank.

# Leaks, Tank Sweating & Flush Problems

Other toilet problems you may need to repair include leaks, tank sweating, and flush problems.

CAUTION: Some repairs require an empty tank. Turn off the water at the fixture shutoff valve; flush the toilet and sponge the tank dry.

**Leaks.** Toilet leaks, a common problem, may be confused with toilet sweating. For a tip on how to detect leaks, see page 131.

To stop a leak between the tank and bowl of a bowl-mounted toilet tank, tighten the bolts in the tank, or remove them and replace their gaskets. To seal the connections on a wall-mounted tank, tighten the couplings on the pipe connecting the tank and bowl, or unscrew the couplings, remove the pipe, and replace the washers.

If the base of the bowl leaks, the bowl will have to be lifted up and resealed. For this job, call a plumber or see the *Sunset* book *Basic Plumbing Illustrated*.

**Tank sweating.** This problem occurs most often in the summer when cold water in the tank cools the porcelain, and warm, moist air condenses on the outside. Tank sweating encourages mildew, loosens floor tiles, and rots subflooring.

An easy solution is to insulate the inside of the tank by draining it; and then gluing a liner made of foam rubber pads to the inside walls. A more costly remedy, and one that's usually a job for a professional, is to install a tempering valve that mixes hot water with the cold water entering the tank.

**Flush problems.** A loose handle or trip lever can cause an inadequate or erratic flush cycle. Adjusting the setscrew on the handle or lever or replacing the handle can often solve the problem. Clogged flush passages under the bowl's rim may also be restricting the flow of water during a flush. Clean obstructed passages with a piece of wire.

## FIXING A LEAKY TANK

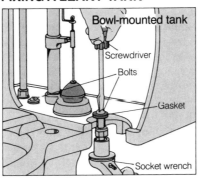

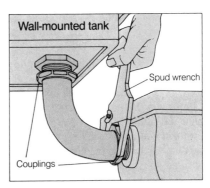

**Tighten the bolts** between the tank and bowl of a bowl-mounted tank or replace their gaskets.

**Tighten the couplings** on the connecting pipe of a wall-mounted tank or remove the pipe and replace the washers (not shown).

## PREVENTING TANK SWEATING

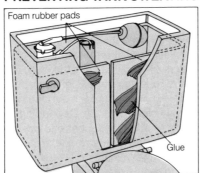

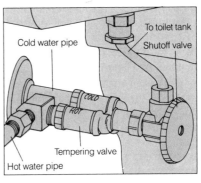

**Glue pieces of ½-inch-thick foam** to the inside of the tank. Be sure the foam doesn't touch moving parts.

**Install a tempering valve** at the shutoff valve to mix hot water with cold (have a professional run in a hot water pipe).

## SOLVING FLUSH PROBLEMS

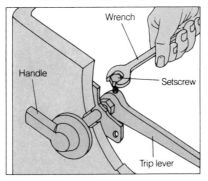

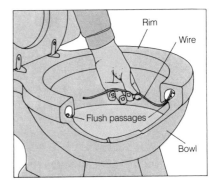

**Tighten the setscrew** on a loose handle or trip lever.

**Use a thin piece of wire** to clean out a blockage in the bowl's flush passages.

# FACE-LIFTS FOR FIXTURES

As time goes by, moisture and daily use take their toll on plumbing fixtures. Once-gleaming porcelain and fiberglass surfaces can dull, discolor, or become damaged. Separations can appear where the bathtub joins the wall.

Before you put a stained, chipped, or cracked fixture out to pasture, consider giving it a face-lift with some bleach, touch-up paint, glue, or caulk. You can even have it professionally recoated. Often, such repairs can extend the life of an aging fixture, postponing an expensive replacement.

**Stains and mineral deposits.** You can renew a fixture by removing discolorations, rust stains, and mineral deposits. An effective treatment for discolorations and rust stains is a liquid chlorine bleach solution. Commercial products are available to remove mineral deposits. Polish with a mixture of cream of tartar and peroxide to improve the appearance of an enameled fixture.

To remove rust stains from porcelain or fiberglass, try rubbing the stain with a cut lemon, or try applying lemon juice. If the fixture is badly stained, use a 5 percent solution of oxalic acid or a 10 percent solution of hydrochloric acid. Apply the acid solution with a cloth and leave it on only a

second or two; then rinse it off thoroughly. Be sure to protect your skin and eyes by wearing rubber or plastic gloves and protective goggles.

**Small scratches and chips.** You can cover a small scratched or chipped area of porcelain or fiberglass by building up thin coats of enamel paint or epoxy paint, available in touch-up kits in many colors to match the color of your fixture.

Before applying the paint, clean the surface of the damaged area with alcohol. Then check that the area is clean, dry, and dustfree. Using a small brush, apply several coats of touch-up paint, blending it toward the edges of the scratch or chip. Allow the paint to dry for an hour between coats; keep the touched-up area dry for 24 hours. Don't expect perfection—you may be able to see where the touch-up was done once the paint dries.

**Large chips.** If the corner or edge of a porcelain or fiberglass fixture has broken off and you have the chip, you can glue it back in place with epoxy resin. Again, be sure the surfaces are entirely clean and dry. Depending on the label directions, coat one or both surfaces with adhesive and press the pieces together firmly. Use masking tape to secure the repair for at least an hour. Keep the area dry overnight.

**Separated bathtub-wall joint.** One of the most common bathroom repairs is sealing cracks in the joint between the bathtub and the wall. It's a chore you'll have to repeat every year or so because the weight of the tub changes as it's filled and emptied again and again.

The simplest way to seal the troublesome joint is with flexible waterproof caulking compound, sometimes called plastic tub-and-tile sealer. The sealer comes in a tube. (For information about the most common types of caulking compounds for home use, see page 25.)

Before applying the sealer, scrape away the old caulking. Clean and dry the area thoroughly to ensure a good seal. Holding the tube at a 45° angle, slowly squeeze the sealer into the joint, using a steady, continuous motion. If you can do each side of the tub without stopping, the line of caulking will be smoother and neater. Wait at least 24 hours before using the bathtub.

If you find that caulking won't last in the bathtub-wall joint, you can apply quarter-round ceramic edging tiles. Available in kits, the tiles are installed around the rim of the tub, using the caulking compound just described as an adhesive. Be sure to scrape away old caulking and clean and dry the area before you begin.

## MENDING CHIPPED FIXTURES

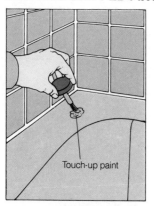 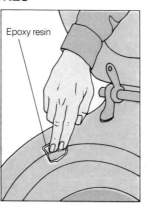

Touch-up paint

Epoxy resin

**Apply enamel or epoxy touchup paint** over a small scratch or chip. If possible, glue the chip back on with epoxy resin.

## SEALING A TUB-WALL JOINT

 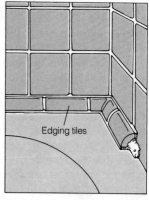

Caulking compound

Edging tiles

**Seal a tub-wall separation with a continuous bead of caulking** or install quarter-round ceramic edging tiles.

# Water Pipes

## Leaking Pipes

A higher than normal water bill might be your first indication of a leaking pipe. Or you might hear the sound of running water even when all your fixtures are turned off.

When you suspect a leak, check the fixtures first to make sure all the faucets are tightly closed. Then go to the water meter, if you have one. If the dial is moving, you're losing water somewhere in the system.

**Locating the leak.** Finding the leak isn't always easy. The sound of running water helps; if you hear it, follow it to its source. You can buy a listening device that amplifies sounds when it's held up to a pipe.

If water is staining the ceiling or dripping down, the leak is probably directly above. Occasionally, though, water may travel along a joist and then stain or drip at a point some distance from the leak. If water stains a wall, it means there's a leak in a section of pipe. Any wall stain is likely to be below the actual location of the leak, and you'll probably need to remove part of the wall to find it.

Without the sound of running water and without drips or stains as evidence, leaks are more difficult to find. Using a flashlight, check all the pipes in the basement or in the crawl space.

**Fixing the leak.** If the leak is major, turn off the water immediately, either at the fixture shutoff valve or the main shutoff valve. You'll probably have to replace the leaky section of pipe. You may want to call in a plumber. Or, to fix it yourself, see the *Sunset* book *Basic Plumbing Illustrated*.

If the leak is small, the ultimate solution is to replace the pipe; but there are temporary solutions until you have time for the replacement job. These methods work for small leaks only.

Clamps should stop most leaks for several months if they're used with a solid rubber blanket. It's a good idea to buy a sheet of rubber, as well as some clamps sized to fit your pipes, at a hardware store and keep them on hand just for this purpose.

A sleeve clamp that exactly fits the pipe diameter works best. Wrap a rubber blanket over the leak, then screw the clamp down over the blanket. An adjustable hose clamp used with a rubber blanket stops a pinhole leak. If nothing else is at hand, use a C-clamp, a small block of wood, and a rubber blanket.

In a pinch, try applying epoxy putty around a joint where a clamp won't work. The pipe must be dry for the putty to adhere. Turn off the water supply to the leak and leave the water off until the putty hardens completely on the pipe.

If you don't have a clamp or putty, you can still stop a small leak temporarily by plugging it with a pencil point (see the Quick Fix-up below).

### QUICK FIX-UP
STOPPING A SMALL LEAK

You can temporarily plug a small pipe leak by breaking off a pencil point in the hole. Then wrap the pipe with three layers of plastic electrical tape, extending the tape 3 inches on either side of the leak.

## FOUR WAYS TO STOP A SMALL LEAK

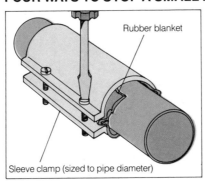

**Place a sleeve clamp** over a rubber blanket at the place where the pipe leaks. Screw the clamp down tightly.

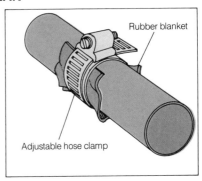

**Position an adjustable hose clamp** around a rubber blanket over a small pipe leak and tighten the clamp.

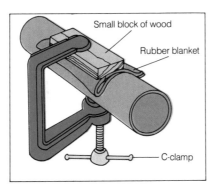

**Secure a C-clamp** and a small block of wood over a rubber blanket to stop a small leak.

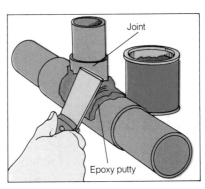

**Apply epoxy putty** to a leaking pipe joint, using a putty knife or your fingers. Dry the joint and turn off the water before applying.

# ... Water Pipes

## Noisy Pipes

Pipe noises range from loud hammering sounds to high-pitched squeaks. The causes may be loose pipes, waterlogged air chambers, or water pressure that's too high. Anchoring exposed pipes is a simple solution; other remedies, such as anchoring pipes concealed inside walls, floors, or ceilings, may call for a professional.

**Banging.** Pipes are usually anchored with metal pipe straps every 6 to 8 feet for horizontal runs, 8 to 10 feet for vertical runs. If your pipes bang when you turn on the water, you may need to add straps, cushion the pipes with a rubber blanket, or both. When you anchor a pipe—especially a plastic one—leave room for expansion. Also, don't use galvanized straps on copper pipes.

**Squeaking.** Only hot water pipes squeak. As the pipe expands, it moves in its strap, and friction causes the squeak. Solution: Cushion it as you would a banging pipe.

**Water hammer.** This noise occurs when you turn off the water at a faucet or an appliance quickly. The water flowing through the pipes slams to a stop, causing a hammering noise. The cause could be loose pipes; anchor them as shown below.

In some homes, the problem may be faulty air chambers (see below).

These lengths of pipe, installed behind fixtures and appliances, hold air that cushions the shock when flowing water is shut off. They can get filled with water and lose their effectiveness.

To restore air to the chambers, turn off the water at the main shutoff valve (page 111) and open all the faucets to drain the system. Close the faucets and turn the water on again. The air chambers should fill with air.

Another cause of water hammer is water pressure that's above 80 psi (pounds of pressure per square inch). To lower the pressure, install a pressure-reducing valve (you can call a plumber or see the *Sunset* book *Basic Plumbing Illustrated*).

### THREE WAYS TO STOP BANGING PIPES

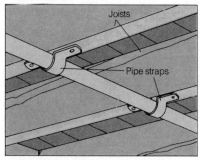

Nail additional pipe straps to joists to stop horizontal pipes from vibrating.

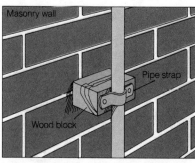

Nail a wood block to a masonry wall with masonry nails; strap the vertical pipe to it.

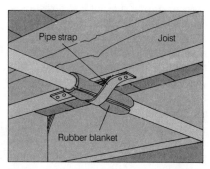

Wrap a rubber blanket or piece of hose around a noisy pipe to cushion it in its strap.

### HOW AN AIR CHAMBER WORKS

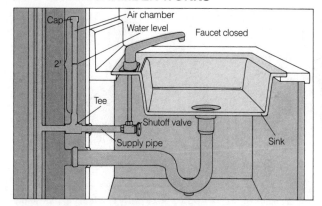

When the faucet is closed, the moving water stops at the faucet and rises up into the air chamber.

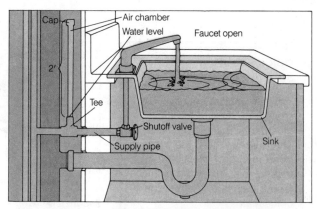

When the faucet is open, the water flows up the supply pipe and out the faucet, without moving up into the air chamber.

# Frozen Pipes

A faucet that won't yield water is the first sign of frozen pipes. If a severe cold snap hits, prevent freezing and subsequent bursting of pipes by following the suggestions below. Even if the pipes do freeze, you can thaw them before they burst if you act quickly.

**Preventing frozen pipes.** When temperatures fall very low, here's how to keep your pipes from freezing:

- **Keep a trickle of water** running from the faucets.

- **Beam a heat lamp or small heater** at exposed pipes.

- **Wrap uninsulated pipes** with newspapers, heating wires, foam, or self-adhesive insulating tape.

- **Keep doors ajar** between heated and unheated rooms.

**Thawing frozen pipes.** If a pipe freezes, first shut off the water at the main shutoff valve (page 111) and open the faucet nearest the frozen pipe so it can drain as it thaws. Waterproof the area with containers and plastic dropcloths in case leaks occur; then use one of the following methods to gradually warm the frozen pipe. Be sure to work from the faucet toward the iced-up area.

## A VARIETY OF PIPE-THAWING TECHNIQUES

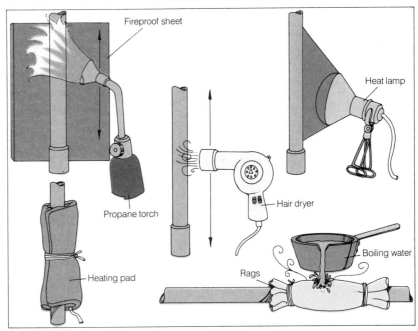

- **Propane torch.** With a flame-spreading nozzle, the torch will quickly thaw a frozen pipe.

  CAUTION: Shield flammable areas with a fireproof sheet; don't let the pipe get too hot to touch.

- **Hair dryer.** Used like the torch, a dryer will gently defrost the pipe.

- **Heating pad.** Wrap a length of pipe with a heating pad.

- **Heat lamp.** For pipes behind walls, floors, or ceilings, beam a heat lamp 8 or more inches from the surface.

- **Hot water.** If no other method is available, wrap the pipe (except plastic) in rags and pour boiling water on it.

## WINTERIZING YOUR PLUMBING SYSTEM

Homeowners who used to simply turn down the thermostat in a vacated house for the winter are now closing down the plumbing system because of prohibitively high energy costs. Winterizing your plumbing is a virtually cost-free alternative to frozen pipes.

First, turn off the main shutoff valve (page 111) or have the water company turn off service to the house. Starting at the top floor, open all faucets, both indoors and outside.

When the last of the water has dripped from the taps, open the plug at the main shutoff valve, if possible (you may have to contact the water company), and let it drain.

Turn off the power or gas to the water heater and open its drain valve.

To freezeproof the system, empty toilet bowls and tanks. Remove the cleanout plugs on all sink traps or remove the traps, if necessary (page 124). Once emptied, replace them and fill with automotive antifreeze mixed with water in the proportions specified for cars in your climate.

You won't be able to drain tub and shower traps. Instead, add at least a quart of full-strength antifreeze. Don't put antifreeze into a dishwasher or clothes washer.

Finally, if your home has a basement floor drain or a main house trap, fill each with full-strength antifreeze.

# Major Appliances

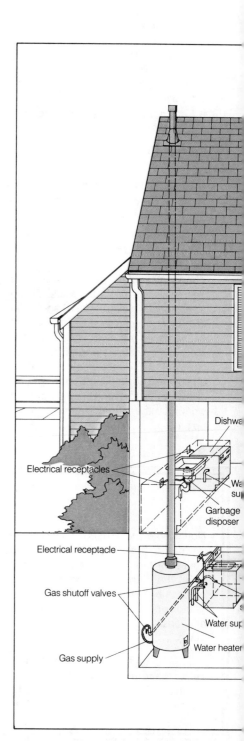

Electrical receptacles

Dishwa...

Wa...
su...

Garbage
disposer

Electrical receptacle

Gas shutoff valves

Water sup...

Gas supply

Water heater

Once called ''modern conveniences,'' the appliances shown below—refrigerator, range, dishwasher, garbage disposer, washer, dryer, and water heater—have today become standard equipment in most homes. Should you experience problems with any of these appliances, turn to the appropriate diagnostic and repair guide in this chapter.

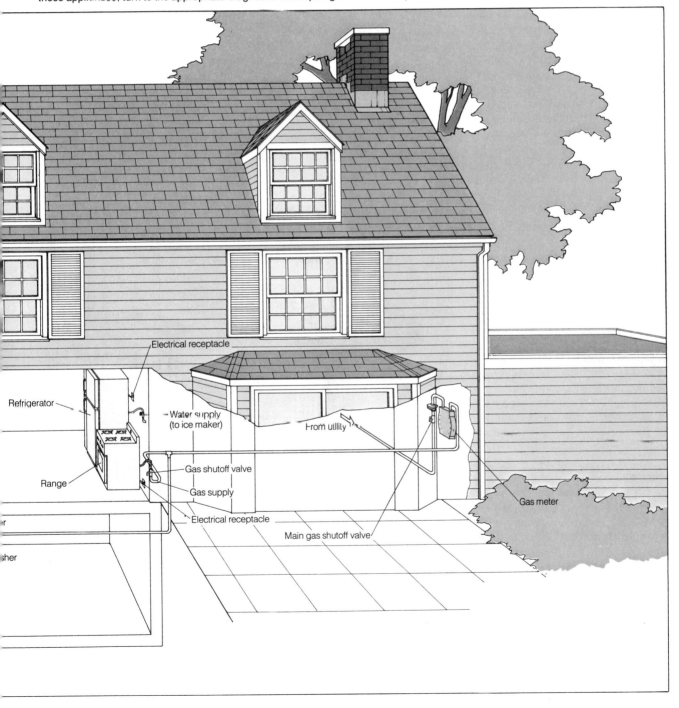

Electrical receptacle

Refrigerator

Water supply (to ice maker)

From utility

Range

Gas shutoff valve

Gas supply

Electrical receptacle

Main gas shutoff valve

Gas meter

# Water Heaters

Most problems with water heaters are announced by noises or by water that's either too hot or not hot enough. Often you can correct the problem yourself. A possible exception is a water leak, which may require professional service or tank replacement. Gas leaks call for immediate help from the utility company.

**How a water heater works.** Whenever someone turns on a hot water faucet, heated water is drawn from the top of the tank and is replaced by cold water that is carried to the bottom through the dip tube. When the water temperature drops, a thermostat activates the heat source—a burner in a gas model, two heating elements in an electric.

A gas heater has a flue running up the center and out the top to vent deadly gases. An electric heater needs no venting. In both, an anticorrosion anode attracts corrosion that would otherwise attack the tank's walls.

**Maintenance for good, safe service.** Open the drain valve at the bottom about every 6 months—letting the water run into a bucket until it looks clear (usually about 5 gallons) will prevent sediment accumulation. Annually test the temperature-pressure relief valve, which guards against hazardous pressure buildup: lift or depress its handle, and water should drain from the overflow pipe; if it doesn't, shut off water to the heater, open a hot water faucet somewhere in the house, and replace the valve.

CAUTION: If steam or boiling water ever comes out of the valve or the hot water faucets, shut the heater off at once. And if you ever hear a rumbling sound, assume the heater is overheating and turn it off.

**Water temperature.** If temperature is a problem, consult the chart; also consider the following possibilities.

If yours is a gas heater, check that the temperature control is on and is set correctly (normally 160°F; lower if there's no dishwasher). Should you suspect a faulty control, test it by opening a hot water faucet for 3 minutes. If the heater doesn't turn on, reset the control to a lower temperature and test again. If it still fails, have it replaced.

Long pipe runs let water cool en route to the faucet. You can insulate the pipes, move the heater, or install a second heater. Leaking hot water faucets should be repaired (pages 113–118).

To save energy, consider an insulating foam or fiberglass heater jacket; buy a kit, or buy materials and make one from scratch.

**Draining and flushing a tank.** Turn off the gas or electricity, close the cold water valve, and attach a hose to the drain valve to route water into a floor drain or outdoors. Open the drain valve and open one hot water faucet somewhere in the house to let in air. When all water has drained, turn the cold water valve on and off until the water from the drain looks clear. Then close the drain valve and the hot water faucet, open the cold water valve, and restore power.

## Gas heaters

Knowing how to light the pilot is one key to living with a gas water heater; see the instructions on the tank. For safety, a gas heater has a thermocouple, a thermoelectric device that impinges on the pilot flame and shuts off the gas if the pilot light goes out.

CAUTION: If you ever smell gas, get out of the house immediately and call the gas company.

The gas flame should be blue. If it's orange, adjust the shutter; if it's still orange, call for service.

## TWO TYPES OF WATER HEATERS

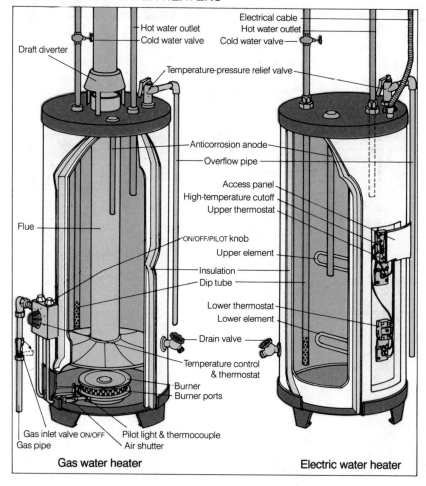

Draft diverter
Hot water outlet
Cold water valve
Electrical cable
Hot water outlet
Cold water valve
Temperature-pressure relief valve
Anticorrosion anode
Overflow pipe
Access panel
High-temperature cutoff
Upper thermostat
Flue
ON/OFF/PILOT knob
Upper element
Insulation
Dip tube
Lower thermostat
Lower element
Drain valve
Temperature control & thermostat
Burner
Burner ports
Gas inlet valve ON/OFF
Gas pipe
Pilot light & thermocouple
Air shutter

**Gas water heater**          **Electric water heater**

Twice a year, inspect the flue assembly to be sure it's properly aligned and all its joints are sealed. Then check the flue by placing your hand near the draft diverter (with the burner on); air flowing out indicates an obstruction that should be removed. Every year or two, shut off the gas, remove the access panel, and clean the burner ports, using stiff wire or a needle.

### Electric heaters

When an electric heater has problems, suspect the heating elements, their thermostats, and the high-temperature cutoff. The two heating elements (upper and lower), immersed in water, are controlled by thermostats which, along with the high-temperature cutoff, are concealed behind a panel on the side (insulation must be cut away for access after removing the panel). If the high-temperature cutoff has tripped due to water that's too hot, the solution may be as easy as pushing the reset button. High voltage and inaccessibility warrant a service call to adjust the thermostats, reset the high-temperature cutoff, or to replace any of these components or the heating elements themselves.

## TROUBLESHOOTING A WATER HEATER

| Problem | Possible Causes | Remedies |
|---|---|---|
| **No hot water** | Ⓔ Ⓖ Temperature control or thermostat off, or defective | Ⓖ Turn temperature control up, or test (see text); **if defective, replace** * |
| | | Ⓔ **Replace defective thermostat** * |
| | Ⓖ Pilot light out | Relight (see instructions on tank) |
| | Ⓖ Closed gas inlet valve | Turn handle parallel to gas line; relight pilot |
| | Ⓖ Pilot won't light | Clean orifice; **if defective, replace thermocouple** * |
| | Ⓖ Burner won't light (pilot on) | Turn temperature control to ON; adjust pilot (page 176) |
| | Ⓔ Power off at heater | Check heater master switch and circuit breaker or fuse (pages 152–153) |
| | Ⓔ Defective heating element | **Replace element (preferably both elements)** * |
| | Ⓔ Tripped high-temperature cutoff | **Remove panel and push reset button** * |
| **Too little hot water, or water not hot enough** | Ⓔ Ⓖ Temperature control or thermostat too low, or defective | Ⓖ Turn temperature control up, or test (see text); **if defective, replace** * |
| | | Ⓔ **Turn thermostat up, or replace** * |
| | Ⓖ Partly closed gas inlet valve | Open valve fully (handle parallel to gas line) |
| | Ⓖ Burner flame not blue | Adjust shutter on burner (page 176) |
| | Ⓖ Clogged burner ports | Clean burner ports with stiff wire |
| | Ⓖ Slow heater recovery | Clean burner ports with stiff wire |
| | Ⓔ Defective heating element | **Replace element (preferably both elements)** * |
| | Ⓔ Low voltage | Call utility company |
| **Water excessively hot** | Ⓔ Ⓖ Temperature control or thermostat too high, or defective | Ⓖ Turn temperature control down; **if defective, replace** * |
| | | Ⓔ Turn thermostat down, **or replace** * (see also "Noises") |
| | Ⓖ Blocked flue | Disassemble flue and clear obstruction |
| | Ⓔ Defective heating element or high-temperature cutoff | **Replace defective part** * |
| **Noises** | | |
| Rumbling | Ⓔ Ⓖ Overheating | Open temperature-pressure relief valve; if steam or boiling water escapes, shut heater off immediately |
| Whistling and sizzling | Ⓔ Sediment buildup in tank | Drain and flush tank (see text) |
| | Ⓔ Encrusted heating elements | **Replace elements** * |
| Whistling and popping | Ⓖ Misadjusted burner | Adjust burner (page 177) |
| Rumbling and cracking | Ⓖ Sediment buildup in tank | Drain and flush tank (see text) |
| **Water leaking from heater** | Ⓔ Ⓖ Leaking drain valve | Tighten valve; if defective, replace valve washer |
| | Ⓔ Ⓖ Temperature-pressure relief valve open | Close valve; **if defective, replace** * |
| | Ⓔ Ⓖ Corroded tank | **Replace heater** * |
| | Ⓔ Leaking heating elements | **Tighten mounting bolts and replace gaskets** * |

Ⓔ Electric heater only    Ⓖ Gas heater only    Appliance models vary; see your owner's manual for information specific to your water heater
*This repair is best left to a professional

# Garbage Disposers

The two types of garbage disposers are batch feed (activated by turning a stopper) and continuous feed (activated by a wall switch). Problems usually involve jams or clogs, or occasionally leaks.

CAUTION: If dismantling the disposer or working on electrical connections, shut off power at the main disconnect (page 153). **Never** put your hand in the disposer—use pliers or tongs to remove an object. And never pour a chemical drain cleaner into a disposer.

If your disposer makes a loud whirring noise or stops, it has jammed. Turn it off and wait 5 minutes; then firmly press the reset button on the bottom of the motor housing. (Machines without buttons reset automatically.)

If the disposer still doesn't work, see if it's designed to be unjammed from below—it may have a small crank (or a socket for an Allen wrench) to turn the flywheel. Or it may have a reversing switch. Lacking these, angle a broom handle against an impeller blade and work the blade back and forth until the jam dislodges. Then press the reset button.

To cure a clog, disassemble the trap and use a snake (page 123).

Water dripping from the disposer usually indicates one or more seals are worn and need to be replaced.

When professional help is required, take the disposer to the repair service to avoid paying for a service call. To remove it, separate it from the drain elbow and loosen the mounting screws to release it from the support flange.

For best service from your disposer, run cold water during disposal and for a minute after. And be careful about what you put in it—never glass, metal, or rubber. Disposers vary, so consult your owner's manual.

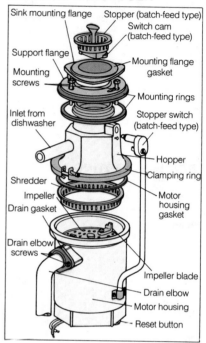

### PARTS OF A DISPOSER

## TROUBLESHOOTING A GARBAGE DISPOSER

| Problem | Possible Causes | Remedies |
|---|---|---|
| **Disposer doesn't run; no sound** | Power off at disposer | Check fuse or circuit breaker (pages 152–153) |
| | Defective motor | **Repair or replace motor\*** |
| | Tripped overload switch | Push reset button firmly (if no button, wait for switch to reset automatically) |
| | Faulty switch | Replace wall switch (page 158); **or replace stopper switch\*** |
| **Disposer doesn't run; motor hums** | Jammed impeller | Clear jam (see text); push reset button firmly |
| | Defective motor | **Repair or replace motor\*** |
| **BATCH-FEED disposer stops when you let go of stopper** | Worn switch cam on stopper | Replace stopper |
| **Disposer grinds or drains slowly** | Insufficient water flow | Open cold water faucet fully |
| | Unsuitable waste in disposer | Remove waste; see owner's manual for guidelines |
| | Broken impeller blade or dull shredder | **Replace blade or shredder\*** |
| **Water leaks from disposer** | Loose drain elbow | Tighten drain elbow screws or replace drain gasket |
| | Badly sealed motor housing and hopper | Replace motor housing gasket |
| | Sink mounting flange not sealed | Tighten mounting screws or replace gasket |
| **Unusual disposer noises** | Foreign object in disposer | Remove object with pliers or tongs |
| | Loose mounting screws | Tighten mounting screws |
| | Broken impeller blade | **Replace blade or impeller\*** |
| | Defective motor | **Repair or replace motor\*** |

\*This repair is best left to a professional
Appliance models vary; see your owner's manual for information specific to your disposer

# Automatic Dishwashers

A dishwasher has its full share of parts that can become blocked, jammed, or clogged. Let the drawing and the chart guide you through the various problems and their remedies.

Very hot water—140 to 160°F—is basic to good service from a dishwasher.

Some dishwashers are equipped with an air gap (see inset) to prevent waste water from backing up into the washer. Because it collects bits of waste, the air gap must be cleaned regularly (remove the cap and cover and use a wire). A dishwasher without an air gap has a high loop in the drain hose; be sure it's not kinked, and clear any obstructions from it with a length of wire when necessary.

CAUTION: Before making repairs, pull the plug from the receptacle. Turn off the hot water valve under the sink before working on the water inlet valve or disconnecting the hot water hose.

## PARTS OF A DISHWASHER

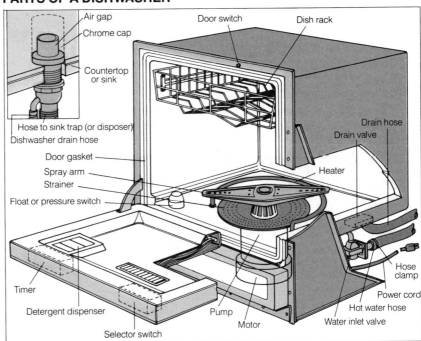

## TROUBLESHOOTING A DISHWASHER

| Problem | Possible Causes | Remedies |
|---|---|---|
| **Dishwasher leaks** | Faulty hose connection | Tighten hose clamps or replace hose |
| | Door gasket not sealing | Replace door gasket |
| | Dishes deflecting water | Reposition dishes |
| **Dishwasher runs noisily** | Low water level | Clean or replace screen on water inlet valve |
| | Defective water inlet valve | **Replace water inlet valve** * |
| **Dishwasher doesn't run** | Door not fully closed | Close door tightly |
| | Defective door switch | **Replace switch** * |
| | Defective timer or selector switch | **Replace timer or selector switch** * |
| **Dishwasher won't fill** | Blocked water inlet valve screen | Remove buildup from screen; **or replace water inlet valve** * |
| | Faulty water inlet valve | **Repair or replace water inlet valve** * |
| | Jammed float switch or defective pressure switch | Remove obstruction from beneath float; **replace pressure switch if defective** * |
| | Defective timer or selector switch | **Replace timer or selector switch** * |
| **Dishwasher continues to fill** | Defective water inlet valve | **Repair or replace water inlet valve** * |
| | Blocked fill spout in water inlet valve | **Disassemble valve and clean fill spout** * |
| | Defective timer or selector switch | **Replace timer or selector switch** * |
| | Jammed float switch or defective pressure switch | Remove obstruction from float; **replace pressure switch if defective** * |
| **Dishwasher won't drain** | Dirty air gap | Clean air gap with wire |
| | Plugged strainer | Remove strainer and clean with a brush |
| | Defective drain valve | **Repair or replace drain valve** * |

*This repair is best left to a professional
Appliance models vary; see your owner's manual for information specific to your dishwasher

# Clothes Washers

When your washer doesn't work, think first of the power supply. Be sure the cord is plugged in and isn't defective (pages 156–157); then check the fuse or circuit breaker (pages 152–153).

A kinked water supply or drain hose can be the culprit. Straighten the kink; if you can't, replace the hose.

Oversudsing causes leaks and blocks drains. To reduce the suds, pour ½ cup white vinegar mixed with some cold water into the washer. Next time, use less detergent (try a low-suds type).

Water temperature not right? Be sure the faucets are fully open, screens in the water inlet valve or hoses aren't clogged, and there's lots of hot water.

If the washer won't spin or begins to vibrate, the wash load may be too large or out of balance. Try removing some items or redistribute the load.

For causes and remedies of these and other problems, see the chart.

CAUTION: Before making repairs, pull the plug and turn off the faucets.

## PARTS OF A CLOTHES WASHER

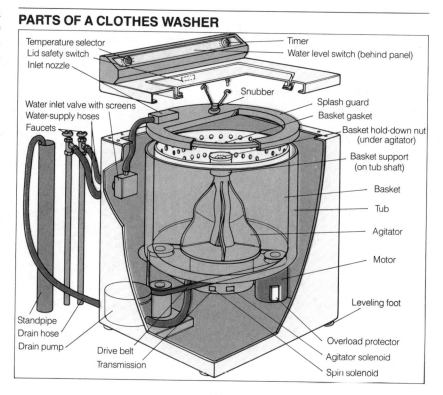

Temperature selector
Lid safety switch
Inlet nozzle
Water inlet valve with screens
Water-supply hoses
Faucets
Standpipe
Drain hose
Drain pump
Drive belt
Transmission
Timer
Water level switch (behind panel)
Snubber
Splash guard
Basket gasket
Basket hold-down nut (under agitator)
Basket support (on tub shaft)
Basket
Tub
Agitator
Motor
Leveling foot
Overload protector
Agitator solenoid
Spin solenoid

## TROUBLESHOOTING A CLOTHES WASHER

| Problem | Possible Causes | Remedies |
|---|---|---|
| **Washer doesn't fill** | Blocked water inlet screens | Clean or replace water inlet screens |
| | Defective timer or temperature selector | **Replace timer or temperature selector\*** |
| **Washer doesn't agitate** | Loose or broken drive belt | Tighten or replace belt |
| | Defective agitator solenoid | **Replace agitator solenoid\*** |
| **Washer doesn't spin** | Loose or broken drive belt | Tighten or replace belt |
| | Defective lid safety switch, timer, or spin solenoid | **Replace switch, timer, or spin solenoid\*** |
| **Washer doesn't drain** | Jammed or defective drain pump | Clear jam; **or replace pump\*** |
| **Washer leaks** | Loose or broken hoses | Tighten clamps and couplings, or replace hoses |
| | Defective basket gasket | **Replace gasket\*** |
| **Washer vibrates excessively** | Machine isn't level | Adjust leveling feet |
| | Defective snubber | **Repair or replace snubber\*** |
| | Loose basket or worn basket support | Tighten basket hold-down nut; **replace support\*** |
| **Water doesn't shut off** | Disconnected air hose | Reconnect hose (not shown) to water level switch |
| | Defective water inlet valve | **Replace water inlet valve\*** |
| **Washer fills but motor doesn't start** | If motor hums: jammed drain pump or defective motor | Unjam pump; **replace motor if defective\*** |
| | Tripped or defective overload protector | Reduce wash load, let protector reset; **replace if defective\*** |

\*This repair is best left to a professional
Appliance models vary; see your owner's manual for information specific to your washer

# Clothes Dryers

Dryers are classified according to the kind of power that provides their heat—either electricity or gas. But even a gas dryer uses electricity for all its non-heating actions. The parts of a dryer are shown at right; the inset illustrates the gas heater that heats a gas dryer.

When your dryer doesn't do its job, look first to the basics. Is it plugged in? Is the cord defective (pages 156–157)? Has the dryer's fuse blown or circuit breaker tripped (pages 152–153)?

Clean the lint trap and use a vacuum or a piece of wire to remove any lint from the exhaust duct. If the load seems too wet to dry efficiently, put it through the washer's spin cycle again.

For other problems and remedies, see the chart below.

CAUTION: Before doing any work on your dryer, pull the plug. Turn off the gas supply to a gas dryer, at either the appliance shutoff or the main shutoff valve (page 9). Should you smell gas, get out ouf the house immediately.

## PARTS OF A CLOTHES DRYER

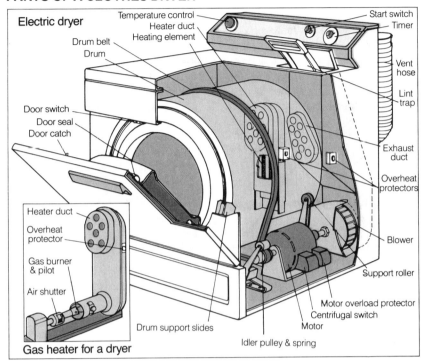

Gas heater for a dryer

## TROUBLESHOOTING A CLOTHES DRYER

| Problem | Possible Causes | Remedies |
|---|---|---|
| **Drum doesn't rotate, though dryer turns on** | Defective start switch, door switch, or timer | Replace start switch, door switch, or timer* |
| | Loose or broken drum belt | Tighten loose belt; **replace broken belt*** |
| | Loose or broken idler pulley or spring | **Replace idler pulley or spring*** |
| | Defective support roller, centrifugal switch, or motor | **Replace support roller, centrifugal switch, or motor*** |
| **Dryer doesn't heat, though drum rotates** | Defective temperature control or timer | **Replace temperature control or timer*** |
| | Defective overheat protector | **Replace overheat protector*** |
| ⒠ | Power off | Check fuse or circuit breaker (pages 152–153) |
| ⒠ | Defective heating element | **Replace heating element*** |
| ⒢ | Pilot light out | Relight; or replace flame switch (not shown)* |
| ⒢ | Defective electric pilot | **Replace pilot*** |
| ⒢ | Incorrect air-gas ratio | Adjust shutter on burner (page 176) |
| **Clothes don't dry** | Clogged lint trap or exhaust duct | Clean lint trap or exhaust duct (see text) |
| | Worn door seal | Replace door seal |
| ⒢ | Incorrect air-gas ratio | Adjust shutter on burner (page 176) |
| **Dryer runs noisily** | Worn drum belt | **Replace drum belt*** |
| | Defective idler pulley or support roller | **Replace idler pulley or support roller*** |
| | Loose blower | Tighten setscrew holding blower to shaft |
| | Worn motor bearings | **Replace bearings or motor*** |

⒠ Electric heater only   ⒢ Gas heater only   *This repair is best left to a professional
Appliance models vary; see your owner's manual for information specific to your dryer

# Kitchen Ranges

A kitchen range has electric elements or gas burners that provide heat to the cooktop and oven. Most gas ranges also have some electric features, such as a clock and lights, and sometimes an electric pilot.

If your electric range or the electrical parts of your gas range don't work, first check the fuse or circuit breaker (pages 152–153). Also, be sure the power cord and terminal block on a freestanding range aren't defective. Replace them if necessary.

With an electric or a gas range, a common complaint is unreliable oven temperature. The thermostat that maintains oven temperature is part of the oven control. If the thermostat fails, have the entire control replaced. But if it's only out of calibration, you may be able to adjust it.

To gauge the problem, place an accurate oven thermometer in the center of a 350° oven. After 20 minutes, check the reading. If it's more than 100° too high or too low, replace the control. If the difference is less than 100°, pull the oven control knob off and locate the calibration screw—either inside the hollow control shaft or on a movable disc on the back of the knob. Tighten or loosen the screw; keep testing until the temperature is correct.

## Electric ranges

The cooktop heating elements of most modern electric ranges simply plug

## TROUBLESHOOTING A RANGE

| Problem | Possible Causes | Remedies |
|---|---|---|
| **Oven doesn't hold set temperature** | Oven control out of adjustment or defective | Recalibrate oven control (see text); **if defective, replace\*** |
| **Oven sweats** | Oven not preheated | Preheat with door ajar |
| | Blocked oven exhaust vent | Remove obstruction from vent |
| | Worn or cracked door gasket | Replace door gasket |
| | Oven temperature too high | Reset oven control or recalibrate (see text) |
| **Uneven baking** | Worn or cracked door gasket | Replace door gasket |
| | Range not level | Adjust leveling feet |
| **Baked food is burned** | Oven temperature too high | Reset oven control or recalibrate (see text) |
| | Blocked oven exhaust vent | Remove obstruction from vent |
| | Pan too dark | Use bright pans |
| | Pans too near oven bottom | Reposition oven racks |
| **Baked food is soggy** | Oven temperature too low | Reset oven control or recalibrate (see text) |
| Ⓖ **Surface burner doesn't light, or burns improperly** | Gas supply shut off | Turn on gas supply |
| | Gas pilot light out | Relight pilot (see owner's manual) |
| | Defective electric pilot | **After verifying that power is on, replace pilot\*** |
| | Clogged surface burner ports | Clean burner ports with stiff wire |
| | Incorrect air-gas ratio | Adjust shutter to get steady blue flame (see text) |
| Ⓖ **Oven doesn't light, or burns improperly** | Gas supply shut off | Turn on gas supply |
| | Gas pilot light out | Relight pilot (see owner's manual) |
| | Defective electric pilot | **After verifying that power is on, replace pilot\*** |
| | Pilot flame too low | Turn pilot adjusting screw to raise pilot flame (page 176) |
| | Defective flame switch | **Replace flame switch\*** |
| | Clogged oven burner ports | Clean burner ports with stiff wire |
| Ⓔ **Surface element doesn't work** | Defective element or element control | Replace element or element control |
| | Defective range wiring | **Replace range wiring\*** |
| Ⓔ **Bake or broil element doesn't work, or works improperly** | Defective element | Replace element |
| | Defective oven control | Replace oven control |

Ⓔ Electric range only    Ⓖ Gas range only
**\*This repair is best left to a professional**
Appliance models vary; see your owner's manual for information specific to your range

into a receptacle, allowing for easy cleaning or replacement. The same is true of the baking and broiling elements. In some ovens, though, you'll need to unscrew the brackets from the oven wall and then unplug the element; or pull it gently forward and then remove the wires from the terminals. Finally, lift out the element.

If an element isn't working, check for breaks or bubbles on the smooth surface of the element. Check, too, for corrosion on the terminals, as well as for broken connections and scorched wires or insulation near the element receptacle.

CAUTION: Turn off power to the range or, if necessary, to the entire circuit before making any electrical checks or repairs.

## Gas ranges

Whether on the cooktop or in the oven, a gas burner that doesn't work may lead you to a pilot that has gone out. Pilots may be gas or electric (in the latter, a spark ignites the gas). Both types are easily relighted (see your owner's manual). A gas pilot that continually goes out calls for cleaning and adjusting, and perhaps gas company help.

The flame of a cooktop or oven burner should be a bright, steady blue. If it's not, you'll need to change the air-gas ratio by adjusting the burner's air shutter. To reach the shutter for a cooktop burner, lift off the cooktop. You can adjust an oven burner's shutter from the compartment under the oven.

If the flame is jumpy, loosen the screw securing the shutter and gradually close it until the flame burns properly. If the flame is a mixture of blue, yellow, and white, increase the air supply by gradually opening the shutter. When the flame is properly adjusted, tighten the screw.

CAUTION: If you smell gas and the pilots are lighted, get out of the house immediately and call the gas company from a neighbor's house.

Be sure to turn off the power to a gas range if you'll be working on its electrical parts.

## PARTS OF AN ELECTRIC RANGE

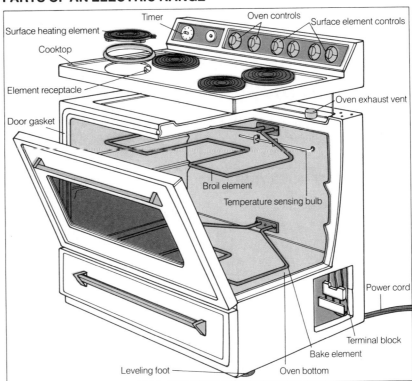

## PARTS OF A GAS RANGE

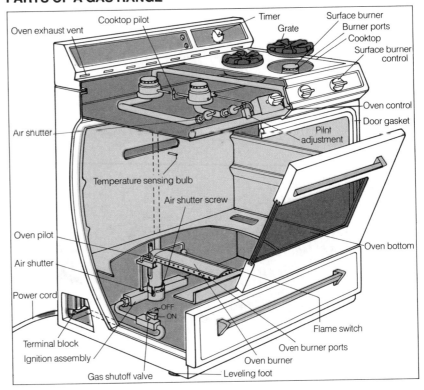

# Refrigerators

Given conscientious routine care, a refrigerator will usually perform its task for years, with a minimum of problems.

Refrigerators are categorized according to the way frost is removed from them.

A *standard* refrigerator defrosts when the power is turned off and the frost is permitted to melt slowly away on its own—or with the aid of pans of hot water placed in the freezer.

In a *cycle-defrost* model, a heater, turned on when the temperature on the evaporator reaches a preset point, keeps the refrigerator compartment free of frost, but the freezer requires manual defrosting every few months.

In a *frost-free* refrigerator, frost from both compartments is continually melted away by a heater that turns on for 20 to 30 minutes, two or three times a day. Clearly, this type of refrigerator

offers the ultimate in convenience, though it's somewhat more prone to problems and is considered less energy-efficient.

In both of the automatically defrosted models, water from the melting frost flows out a drain in the floor of the refrigerator and into a pan, where it evaporates. It's not uncommon for food particles to be carried along, clogging the drain and causing odors. Clean the

## PARTS OF A REFRIGERATOR

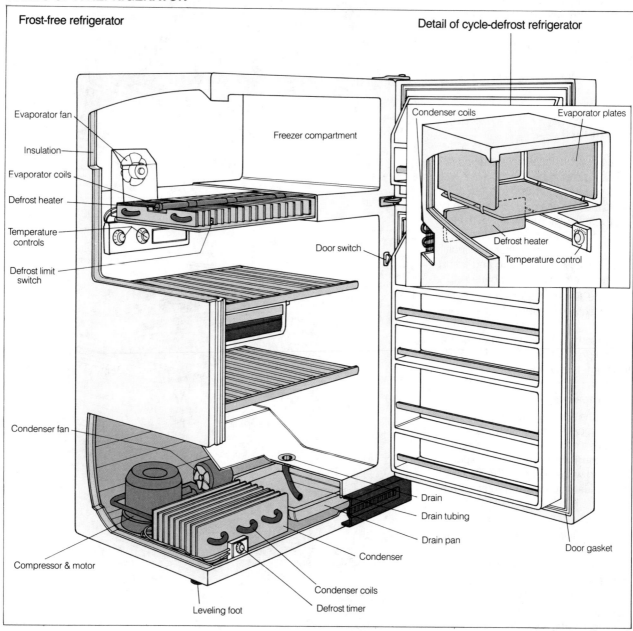

Frost-free refrigerator

Detail of cycle-defrost refrigerator

Evaporator fan
Insulation
Evaporator coils
Defrost heater
Temperature controls
Defrost limit switch
Condenser fan
Compressor & motor
Leveling foot
Defrost timer
Condenser coils
Condenser
Drain pan
Drain tubing
Drain
Door switch
Freezer compartment
Condenser coils
Evaporator plates
Defrost heater
Temperature control
Door gasket

drain regularly—remove the stopper, use a pipe cleaner or similar device to push any accumulations through to the drain pan below, and force a solution made from soap, ammonia, and water through the drain. Finally, empty the pan and wash it.

The door gasket, if washed often with soapy water, will usually last as long as the refrigerator. If you suspect it's no longer sealing well, test it by holding a dollar bill so it's caught in the closed door; you should feel resistance when you pull it out. Repeat the test in several places. A gasket that doesn't pass the test, or one that is obviously cracked or torn, should be replaced. Replacing it is no small task—you'll need patience. Follow the manufacturer's directions.

Temperature settings for refrigerator and freezer compartments are given arbitrary numbers (for example, 1 through 9, warmest to coldest) by manufacturers, but generally 37°F is ideal for the refrigerator compartment and 0°F for the freezer. If you suspect a problem, test the temperatures with a refrigerator or outdoor thermometer.

CAUTION: If you're making an electrical repair, such as replacing a door switch, be sure to turn off the power to the refrigerator.

## TROUBLESHOOTING A REFRIGERATOR

| Problem | Possible Causes | Remedies |
|---|---|---|
| **Refrigerator doesn't run** | Power off at refrigerator | Check that refrigerator is plugged in; check fuse or circuit breaker (pages 152–153) |
| | Defective power cord | Replace cord |
| | Defective temperature control | **Replace temperature control\*** |
| | Defective compressor motor relay | **Replace relay (on back of compressor)\*** |
| | Defective compressor motor | **Repair or replace motor\*** |
| | Obstructed or defective condenser fan | Remove obstruction; **if defective, replace condenser fan\*** |
| **Refrigerator doesn't cool properly** | Defective temperature control | **Replace temperature control\*** |
| | Door doesn't seal tightly | Clean or replace door gasket; adjust door hinges to correct sagging or warped door |
| | Defrost heater stays on constantly | **Replace defrost heater timer\*** |
| | Light stays on when door is closed | Test by depressing door switch manually; replace switch if defective |
| | Obstructed or defective evaporator fan | Remove obstruction; **if defective, replace evaporator fan\*** |
| | Obstructed or defective condenser fan | Remove obstruction; **if defective, replace condenser fan\*** |
| | Refrigerant lost | **Replace refrigerant\*** |
| **Refrigerator runs noisily** | Refrigerator not level | Adjust leveling feet |
| | Loose compressor or hardened rubber compressor mounts | Tighten compressor mounts; **if defective, replace compressor mounts\*** |
| | Evaporator or condenser fan blades striking obstruction | Remove obstruction |
| | Drain tubing vibrating against cabinet | Reposition tubing |
| | Drain pan vibrating | Reposition drain pan |
| **Water leaks onto floor** | Clogged drain | Clean drain (see text) |
| | Cracked drain tubing or pan | Replace drain tubing or pan |
| **STANDARD REFRIGERATOR frosts too quickly** | Door sags or doesn't close properly | Adjust door hinges to correct sagging; adjust leveling feet so door swings shut when half-open |
| | Defective door gasket | Replace door gasket |
| **FROST-FREE OR CYCLE-DEFROST REFRIGERATOR doesn't defrost properly** | Clogged drain | Clean drain (see text) |
| | Defective defrost heater, defrost timer, or defrost limit switch | **Replace defrost heater, defrost timer, or defrost limit switch\*** |

*This repair is best left to a professional
Appliance models vary; see your owner's manual for information specific to your refrigerator

# The Electrical System

Utility company wires

Sub

240-volt circuit

Though we depend on it daily, few of us understand electricity and the circuitry of a typical home's electrical system. But it needn't be a mystery; as the drawing below shows, circuitry is not as baffling as you may think. Though major electrical work is most safely left to experienced hands, even a beginner can repair or replace such common devices as switches, receptacles, and light fixtures. The instructions you'll find in this chapter—and a little know-how—are all it takes.

Switch

Receptacles

120-volt branch circuits

Doorbell

Doorbell transformer

Distribution center

Switch

120-volt, 20 amp circuit to kitchen appliances

240-volt circuit to dryer in basement

120-volt, 20 amp circuit to washer in basement

# How the System Works

Electrical systems seem mysterious and complex because they're mostly hidden within walls. But repairing a visible part of the electrical system in your home isn't necessarily complicated. Even inexperienced do-it-yourselfers can replace plugs, cords, switches, and receptacles, repair light fixtures and lamps, and diagnose circuit problems when these devices won't work.

Understanding the electrical system in your home will help you solve many of the problems you may encounter. So before you turn to the repair instructions on the following pages, read the information below and refer to the drawing of the electrical system on page 151.

The word "circuit" refers to the course electric current travels, from the point where power enters your house (the service entrance panel or a subpanel wired to it) through wires to a device using electricity (such as a light fixture) and back to its starting point.

### How your home is wired

Today, most homes have what's called "three-wire service." The utility company connects three wires—two "hot," one neutral—through a meter to your service entrance panel. These wires provide both 120-volt and 240-volt capabilities. One hot wire and the neutral wire combine to supply 120 volts, the amount used for most household applications, such as lights and small appliances. Both hot wires and the neutral wire can form a 120/240–volt circuit for such needs as a range and dryer.

### Service entrance panel and distribution center.

The wires from the meter connect to the service entrance panel, the control center for your electrical service. Housed in a cabinet or box, the panel is often located outside your home, below the electric meter. Or it can be on an inside wall, directly behind the meter. In this panel you'll usually find the main disconnect—the main fuses or main circuit breakers (see drawings on facing page)—to which the wires connect.

After passing through the main disconnect, the wires enter a distribution center, housed in the service entrance panel or in a separate subpanel. Here the current is divided into branch circuits, each protected by a fuse or circuit breaker. The branch circuits run to lights, switches, receptacles, and permanently wired appliances.

## Understanding Circuitry

**Grounding to prevent shock.** The National Electrical Code requires that every circuit have a grounding system. Grounding ensures that, in the event of a short circuit (pages 154–155), all metal parts of the wiring system or of lamps or appliances connected to it will be maintained at zero volts.

The grounding wire for each circuit is connected to the distribution center and then is run with the hot and neutral wires in the branch circuits.

**Wire connections.** Connections between wires are made inside plastic or metal boxes mounted in the walls or ceiling. Switches, receptacles, and wall or ceiling-mounted light fixtures all have their own boxes.

Individual wires are wrapped in color-coded insulation for easy identification. Though hot wires are usually black or red, they may be any color other than white, gray, or green. Neutral wires are white or gray. Grounding wires are bare or green.

Occasionally, a white wire will be used as a hot wire; for easy identification, it should be taped or painted black where it's close to terminals and splices.

### Safeguards in the system

The service entrance panel and distribution center in your home are equipped with either fuses or circuit breakers. These are the weak point of each circuit—the safety devices that keep the branch circuits and anything connected to them from overheating and catching fire. If there's an overload or a short circuit (pages 154–155), a fuse will blow or a circuit breaker will trip, shutting off the flow of current.

**Fuses.** Fuses have a thin metal strip through which current passes into a circuit. If too much current starts to flow, the metal melts and cuts off the current.

Fuses may be one of several types (see below). Plug and Type S fuses have a metal strip (visible through a window) that melts when there's an overload. Time-delay fuses have a spring-loaded strip that allows temporary overloads. Cartridge fuses show no sign of overload; they must be tested to reveal whether they've blown.

When a fuse blows, always replace it with one of the same type and amperage rating; never replace it with one rated higher.

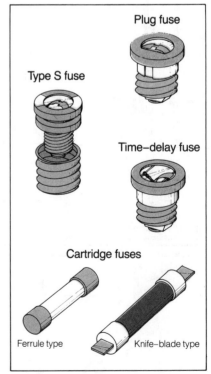

**Fuses in your service panel** and distribution center may be any of these types. Replace a blown fuse with an exact duplicate.

CAUTION: When you need to change a blown fuse, shut off all power (see below) before touching the fuse and be sure you're standing on dry ground.

**Circuit breakers.** Circuit breakers (see drawings below) are heavy-duty switches that serve the same purpose as fuses. When a circuit is carrying more current than is safe, the breaker switches to RESET. On most breakers, the switch has to be pushed to OFF and then to ON after the circuit trips.

A special kind of circuit breaker — the ground fault circuit interrupter (GFCI)—is installed in bathroom, outdoor, and garage locations. If there's a current leakage, or "ground fault," the GFCI opens the circuit instantly, cutting off the electricity.

When a GFCI has tripped, reset it as you would a regular circuit breaker. For a receptacle GFCI, push the RESET button.

### Safety precautions

Working with electricity can be dangerous unless you adhere strictly to certain rules. Above all, NEVER WORK ON ANY LIVE CIRCUIT, FIXTURE, RECEPTACLE, OR SWITCH. Your life may depend on it.

Here are the safety rules you should follow whenever you're working with electricity:

■ **Always shut off power at the main disconnect** before changing a fuse.

■ **Always shut off power to the circuit** before repairing or replacing a switch, receptacle, or fixture.

■ **Always tape over the main switch, empty fuse socket, or circuit breaker** when you're working; leave a note there so no one will accidentally turn on the electricity. Keep any fuses you've removed in your pocket.

■ **Always check that the circuit is actually dead** before you begin working on it. Use a circuit tester or volt-ohm meter (page 22).

■ **Always unplug any appliance or lamp** before repairing it.

---

## SHUTTING OFF THE POWER

A main disconnect allows you to disconnect your entire electrical system instantly whenever you need to change a fuse or make repairs, or in case of an emergency. The disconnect will be one of the following types:

■ **Lever disconnect.** Pull lever to the OFF position to shut off power.

■ **Pull-out fuse block.** Pull firmly on the handgrip to remove the block(s) and shut off power.

■ **Single main circuit breaker.** Push the main breaker handle to the OFF position to shut off power.

■ **Multiple circuit breakers** (up to six). Turn *all* circuit breakers to the OFF position to shut off power.

When you're working on a switch, receptacle, or fixture, you'll need to shut off power to a branch circuit. Flip the circuit breaker for that circuit to OFF. For a circuit with a fuse, first turn off the main power supply, then remove the fuse that controls the circuit you're working on. You can then turn the main power supply on again.

### FOUR TYPES OF DISCONNECTS

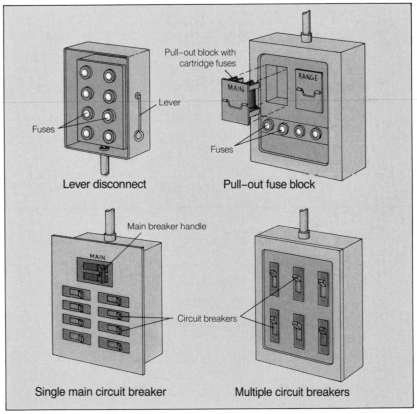

Lever disconnect

Pull-out block with cartridge fuses

Pull-out fuse block

Single main circuit breaker

Multiple circuit breakers

# ...How the System Works

## Diagnosing Electrical Problems

Typically, you discover you have an electrical problem when you turn on a lamp or appliance and it won't work. When that happens, the source of the problem may be the device itself, faulty wiring connections, or an overloaded or a short circuit.

To determine the cause and remedy of your problem, consult the chart below.

Distinguishing between an overloaded or a short circuit can be more difficult. A circuit becomes overloaded when there are more lamps and appliances on it than it can safely handle. When all the lamps and appliances are turned on, the wiring overheats and the fuse blows or the circuit breaker trips.

A short circuit occurs when a bare hot wire touches a bare neutral wire or a bare grounded wire (or some other ground). The flow of extra current blows a fuse or trips a circuit breaker.

Take the steps on the facing page to determine whether you have an overloaded or a short circuit.

NOTE: Plug fuses (page 152) provide a clue to what made them blow: an overload melts the bridge; a short circuit blackens the glass.

## TROUBLESHOOTING ELECTRICAL PROBLEMS

| Problem | Possible Causes | Remedies | Pages |
|---|---|---|---|
| **Light fixture won't work** (check first for burned-out bulb or fluorescent tube) | Defective fluorescent starter | Replace fluorescent starter | 166–167 |
| | Faulty switch | Replace switch | 158–159 |
| | Loose wiring | Tighten connections at switch or fixture | 158–159, 164–165 |
| | Faulty socket | Replace socket | 164–165 |
| **Appliance or lamp won't work** (check first for burned-out bulb or fluorescent tube) | Overloaded circuit | Test for overload; shift appliance or lamp to another circuit* | 155 |
| | Damaged plug | Replace plug | 156–157 |
| | Damaged cord | Replace cord | 156–157 |
| | Loose wiring | Tighten connections at switch or receptacle | 158–161 |
| | Defect in appliance or lamp | Test in another circuit; repair if faulty | |
| **Appliance or lamp won't work in one circuit, but works in others** | Overloaded circuit | Test for overload; shift appliance or lamp to another circuit* | 155 |
| | Loose connection at receptacle | Tighten connections at receptacle | 160–161 |
| | Short circuit | Test for short circuit; make necessary repair* | 155 |
| **Appliance or lamp won't work in one receptacle of circuit** | Loose wiring | Tighten connections at receptacle | 160–161 |
| | Faulty receptacle | Replace receptacle | 160–161 |
| | Short circuit | Test for short circuit; make necessary repair* | 155 |
| **Appliance or lamp won't work in switch-controlled receptacle** | Loose wiring | Tighten connections at switch or receptacle | 158–161 |
| | Faulty switch | Replace switch | 158–159 |
| | Faulty receptacle | Replace receptacle | 160–161 |
| **Some lights on circuit won't work** | Loose wiring | Tighten connections at switch or fixture | 158–159, 164–165 |
| | Faulty switch | Replace switch | 158–159 |
| **All lights on circuit won't work** | Overloaded circuit | Test for overload; make necessary adjustment* | 155 |
| | Short circuit | Test for short circuit; make necessary repair* | 155 |
| | Loose wiring | Tighten connections at switch | 158–159 |
| | Faulty switch | Replace switch | 158–159 |

*After making necessary adjustment or repair, replace fuse or reset circuit breaker (pages 152–153)

# Tracing a Short Circuit or Overload

A blown fuse or tripped circuit breaker is a signal that you may have either a short circuit or an overload in the electrical system as described on the facing page.

Often, when a fuse blows or a circuit breaker trips, the cause is easy to spot. Look for black smudge marks on switch or receptacle cover plates, or for frayed or damaged cords or damaged plugs on lamps and appliances connected to the dead circuit. Replace a damaged cord or plug (pages 156-157); then replace the fuse or reset the breaker.

If the circuit goes dead after an appliance has been in use for a short time, you probably have an overloaded circuit. Move some of the lamps and appliances to another circuit and replace the fuse or reset the circuit breaker for the first circuit.

If you find none of these apparent signs of trouble, you'll have to trace your way through the circuit following the steps below. If following these steps doesn't solve the problem, and your fuse or circuit breaker still blows or trips, your wiring is faulty. Call an electrician to correct the problem.

Turn off all wall switches and unplug every lamp and appliance on the dead circuit. Then install a new fuse or reset the tripped breaker.

If the fuse blows or the breaker trips right away, the problem may be a short circuit in a switch or receptacle. With the circuit dead, remove each cover plate and inspect the device and its wiring. Look for charred wire insulation, wire shorted against the metal box, or a device that's defective. Replace a defective device (pages 158-161); call in an electrician to replace faulty wiring.

If the new fuse doesn't blow or the breaker doesn't trip right away, turn on each wall switch, one by one, checking each time to see if the fuse has blown or the circuit breaker has tripped.

If turning on a wall switch causes a fuse to blow or the breaker to trip, there's a short circuit in a light fixture or receptacle controlled by that switch, or there's a short circuit in the switch wiring. With the circuit dead, inspect the fixture, receptacle, and switch for charred wire insulation or faulty connections. Replace a faulty switch or fixture (pages 158-159 and 164-165); call in an electrician to replace wiring.

If turning on a wall switch doesn't blow a fuse or trip the breaker, the trouble is in the lamps or appliances. Test them by plugging them in one by one. If the circuit doesn't go dead, the circuit was overloaded. Move some of the lamps or appliances to another circuit. If the circuit does go dead just after you've plugged in a lamp or appliance, then you've found the offender.

If the circuit went dead as soon as you plugged in the lamp or appliance, the plug or cord is probably at fault and should be replaced (pages 156-157).

If the circuit went dead as soon as you turned on the lamp or appliance, the appliance or lamp or its switch is probably defective and should be replaced or repaired.

# Cords & Plugs

## Replacing Cords

Cords on appliances and lamps are often subject to pulling and twisting that can sever the wires inside and break down the insulation, resulting in a short circuit. Replace—don't repair—any electrical cord with broken wires or brittle, worn insulation.

Replacing a lamp cord (page 163) or a detachable female appliance cord (see facing page) is easy. Appliance cords that are not detachable are another matter. Unless you're familiar with the construction of the appliance, have a professional replace a faulty cord if the terminals to which it attaches are not easily accessible.

When you're buying a new cord, choose one that has the same size wires and type of insulation as the original.

### TYPES OF CORDS

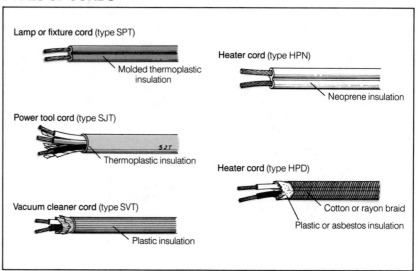

Lamp or fixture cord (type SPT) — Molded thermoplastic insulation

Power tool cord (type SJT) — Thermoplastic insulation

Vacuum cleaner cord (type SVT) — Plastic insulation

Heater cord (type HPN) — Neoprene insulation

Heater cord (type HPD) — Cotton or rayon braid, Plastic or asbestos insulation

## Replacing Plugs

Any plug with a cracked shell or loose, damaged, or badly bent contacts should be replaced. Also replace plugs that transmit power erratically or get warm when used. If a plug arcs when it's pushed into or pulled out of a receptacle, examine the wires; if they're not firmly attached to the terminal screws, tighten any loose connections.

The two kinds of plugs are terminal screw and self-connecting. In plugs with terminal screws, the wires are attached to screws inside the plug body. Self-connecting plugs clamp onto wires, making an automatic connection. These plugs, as well as two-prong plugs with terminal screws, are commonly used for lamps and small appliances. Three-prong grounding plugs are used for large appliances and power tools. Detachable cords for small appliances have female plugs with terminal screws.

NOTE: Many old-style plugs with terminal screws have a removable insulating disc covering the terminals and wires. The National Electrical Code now requires "dead-front" plugs; such plugs have a rigid insulating barrier.

### TYPES OF PLUGS

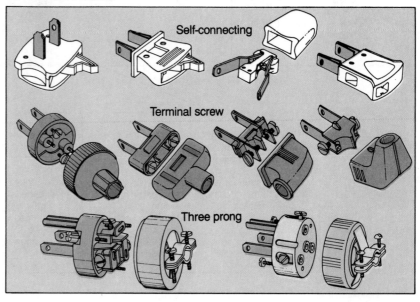

Self-connecting

Terminal screw

Three prong

To replace a plug (see facing page), cut off the old one plus at least an inch of cord. For plugs with terminal screws, split the cord insulation to separate the wires; then strip the insulation from the ends (page 159).

If you're replacing a three-prong grounding plug, attach the wires to the terminal screws as follows: white neutral wire to silver screw, black hot wire to brass screw, and green grounding wire to green terminal screw.

## REPLACING A PLUG WITH TERMINAL SCREWS

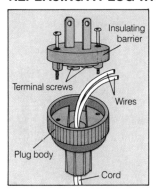

**1) Unscrew and remove** the new plug's insulating barrier. Using a utility knife, split the end of the cord to separate the wires; push the cord through the plug body.

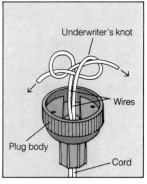

**2) Make 2 loops with the wires,** pass the loose ends of the wires through the loops, and pull tightly to form an Underwriter's knot (this prevents strain on the terminal screws).

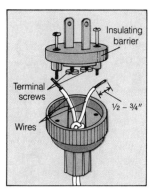

**3) Strip ½ to ¾″ of insulation** off the wire ends, being careful not to nick the wires (page 159). Unscrew the terminal screws on the barrier to allow space for the wires.

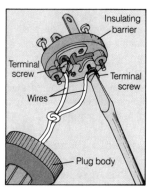

**4) Form loops** on each wire; wrap the wires clockwise ¾ way around the screws. Tighten the screws, trim excess wire, and reattach the barrier.

## REPLACING THREE SPECIAL TYPES OF PLUGS

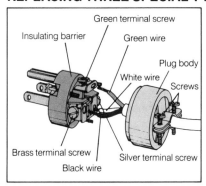

**Three-prong grounded plug.** Unscrew the insulating barrier; push stripped wires through the plug body into the correct terminal slots. Tighten the terminal screws and reassemble the plug.

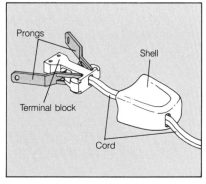

**Self-connecting plug.** Push the cord (don't strip it) through the shell and into the terminal block; squeeze the prongs together to grip the cord and slide into the shell.

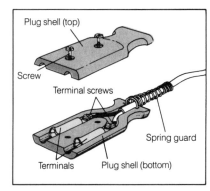

**Female appliance plug.** Unscrew the plug shell; feed the cord through the spring guard. Strip the wire ends (page 159), wrap them clockwise around the terminal screws and tighten; reassemble the plug.

## Replacing 240-Volt Appliance Cords

Replacing cords and plugs on 240-volt appliances is simple if the terminals are easily accessible; use a new pigtail cord with a plug molded to it.

To replace the old cord and plug, unplug the damaged cord and unscrew the other end from the terminal screws on the appliance. Be sure you get an exact replacement for the damaged cord and plug.

Connect the new pigtail cord to the terminal screws on the appliance. If the wires in the cord and the screws on the appliance are color coded, attach the wires to the terminal screws of the same color (black to black, white to white, red to red).

If either the pigtail cord or the appliance terminal screws are not color coded, first attach the center wire of the pigtail to the center terminal screw on the appliance. Then connect the remaining wires to the remaining terminal screws. Plug in the new cord.

### PIGTAIL CORD

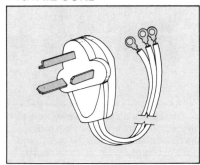

# Wall Switches

When a switch fails, it's usually because the contact points are worn or have oxidized. When this happens, the switch must be replaced. You can replace it with an exact duplicate or with a dimmer or silent switch. Directions below and on the facing page tell how to replace most types of switches and dimmers. Silent switches are simply quiet versions of these types.

**Types of switches.** Most switches in a home are single-pole or three-way. Single-pole switches control a light or receptacle from one location only and have two screws of the same color. Three-way switches operate in pairs to control a light or receptacle from two locations. They have two screws of the same color, either brass or silver, and one—called the common terminal screw—of another color, either copper or black. (The brass or silver screws of a pair of switches connect the switches to each other.) Both types of switches are wired into hot wires only.

Both types may also have a set of backwired terminals (shown at right) as well as terminal screws. Attaching a switch with backwired terminals is easy; simply strip the wires (the wire-stripping gauge on the back shows you how much to strip) and push the ends into the holes (see facing page).

Dimmer switches let you adjust the brightness of a light. Wired like single-pole switches, they have either terminal screws or lead wires (see facing page).

## TYPES OF SWITCHES

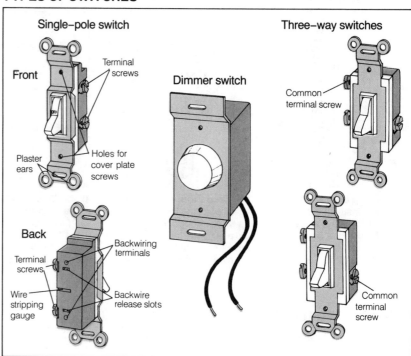

**Replacing a switch.** When you're buying a replacement, carefully read the information stamped on the back of the new switch; the new one should have the same amp and voltage ratings as the old.

If your home's wiring is aluminum, use only replacement switches marked CO/ALR. Replace unmarked switches and switches marked CU/AL with switches marked CO/ALR. Don't backwire switches to aluminum wiring; attach aluminum wires to terminal screws only.

CAUTION: Always shut off the power to the circuit (pages 152–153) before you begin work. Use a circuit tester (page 22) to make sure the circuit you're working on is dead before you touch any wires.

## REPLACING A SINGLE-POLE SWITCH

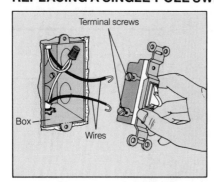

**1) To replace a single-pole switch,** turn off the power to the circuit, then remove the cover plate. Unscrew the switch and pull it out carefully. Unfasten the wires.

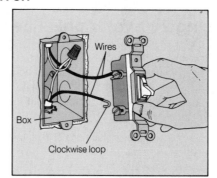

**2) To attach the new switch,** loop the stripped wire ends clockwise around the terminal screws on the switch. Tighten the terminal screws with a screwdriver.

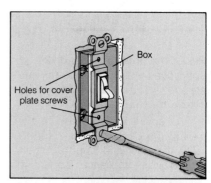

**3) Push the switch carefully** into the switch box to avoid crimping the wires. Screw the switch to the box and reattach the cover plate.

## REPLACING A BACKWIRED SINGLE-POLE SWITCH

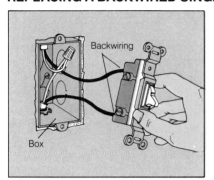

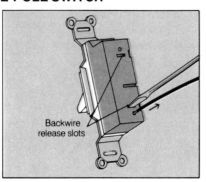

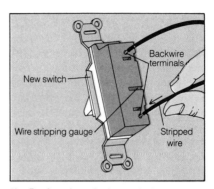

**1)    To replace a backwired switch,** shut off the power. Unscrew the cover plate and set it aside; unscrew and remove the switch from the box.

**2)    Push a small-bladed screwdriver** into the backwire release slots on the back of the switch next to each wire; then pull the wires out.

**3)    Push stripped wire ends** (measure using the wire-stripping gauge) into the terminal on the new switch. Attach the switch to the box; replace the cover plate.

## REPLACING A THREE-WAY SWITCH

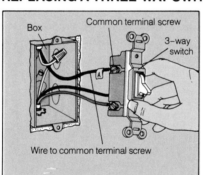

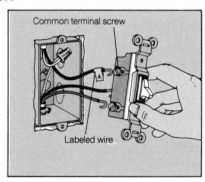

**1)    To replace a 3-way switch,** shut off the power. Remove the cover plate; unscrew and pull out the switch. Label the wire to the common terminal screw with tape.

**2)    Install the new switch,** attaching the labeled wire to the common terminal screw (black or copper). Connect each remaining wire to either of the remaining screws. Insert in the box and fasten.

## INSTALLING TWO TYPES OF DIMMERS

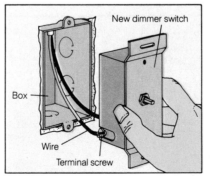

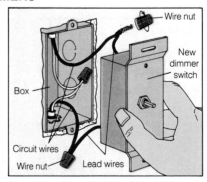

**Dimmer with terminal screws.** Shut off the power; remove the old switch. Loop the circuit wires clockwise around the terminal screws on the dimmer; insert in the box.

**Dimmer with lead wires.** Shut off the power; remove the old switch. Connect the circuit wires to the dimmer's lead wires, twisting them together. Screw on wire nuts and insert the dimmer in the box.

# Receptacles

If appliances or lamps that work properly elsewhere won't work when plugged into a particular receptacle, and you've determined there's no loose wiring or short circuit (page 155), then the receptacle needs to be replaced. Below and on the facing page are instructions for replacing receptacles.

**How receptacles are wired.** Most receptacles in a house have two outlets (known as a duplex receptacle) and are rated at 15 or 20 amps, 120 volts. One or both outlets may be electrically live at all times, or one or both may be controlled by a wall switch. The receptacle may be installed in the middle or at the end of a circuit. The wiring arrangement is different in each case.

Receptacles have three different-colored terminal screws. Brass screws are hot, white or silver screws are neutral, and green ones are for grounding. A receptacle may also be backwired. A backwired receptacle, like a backwired switch (pages 158–159), is easy to install; you simply insert stripped wire ends into the terminal holes.

Receptacles may be grounding or nongrounding types. Always replace a receptacle with a grounding type unless there's no grounding wire in the box or the box isn't grounded; then you can use a nongrounding receptacle. To install a grounding receptacle in an un-

## TYPES OF RECEPTACLES

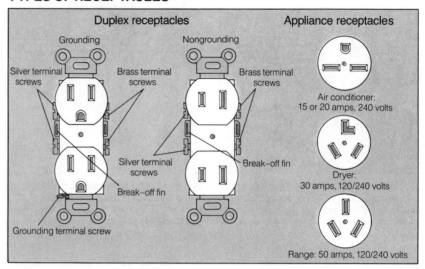

Duplex receptacles

Grounding
Silver terminal screws
Brass terminal screws
Break-off fin
Grounding terminal screw

Nongrounding
Brass terminal screws
Silver terminal screws
Break-off fin

Appliance receptacles
Air conditioner: 15 or 20 amps, 240 volts
Dryer: 30 amps, 120/240 volts
Range: 50 amps, 120/240 volts

grounded box, see the *Sunset* book *Basic Home Wiring Illustrated* or consult an electrician.

Because receptacles are rated for a specific amperage and voltage, be sure to replace an old one with an exact duplicate. If possible, take the old receptacle with you when you buy a new one.

If your wiring is aluminum, your receptacle must be designed to be used with aluminum wire (look for the letters CO-ALR). Use the terminal screws only; backwiring is not suitable for aluminum wires.

**Replacing appliance receptacles.** These receptacles, rated from 15 to 50 amps, 240 volts and from 20 to 50 amps, 120/240 volts, each require a special plug that will fit only that receptacle. Take care when replacing appliance receptacles; these have *two* hot wires—usually red and black—going to them. They may or may not have a separate grounding wire.

CAUTION: Before beginning any work, turn off the power to the circuit (pages 152–153). For a 240-volt circuit, you may have to remove two fuses or trip a two-handled circuit breaker.

## REPLACING A GROUNDED RECEPTACLE (MIDDLE OF CIRCUIT)

Cover plate

**1) To remove a faulty receptacle,** first shut off power to the circuit. Then unscrew the cover plate, and remove and set it aside.

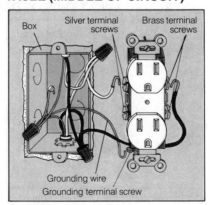

Box
Silver terminal screws
Brass terminal screws
Grounding wire
Grounding terminal screw

**2) Unscrew the receptacle** from its box and carefully pull it out. Note which wire is connected to which terminal screw; then disconnect the wires from the screws.

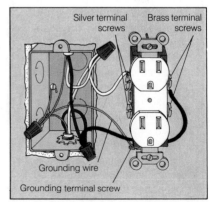

Silver terminal screws
Brass terminal screws
Grounding wire
Grounding terminal screw

**3) To install the new receptacle,** wrap the wires clockwise around the screws (use old receptacle as a guide). Screw the receptacle to the box. Replace the cover plate.

## REPLACING THREE SPECIALLY WIRED RECEPTACLES

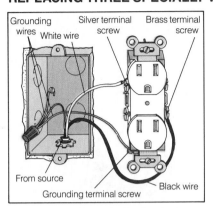

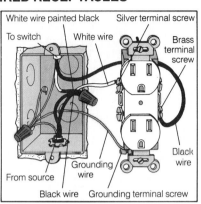

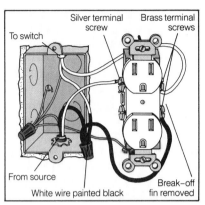

**Receptacle at the end of a circuit.** Attach three wires as shown: black (hot), white (neutral), bare or green (grounding).

**Switch-controlled receptacle.** Attach as shown; note the white wire (painted black) sometimes connected to the black wire.

**Half of the receptacle is switch-controlled** (other half is always live). Label wires and screws carefully; rewire.

## REPLACING A BACKWIRED RECEPTACLE

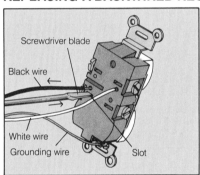

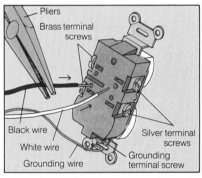

**1) To remove the receptacle,** shut off the power. Push a small-bladed screwdriver into the slots next to the wires; pull them out.

**2) To install the new receptacle,** push the black wire's stripped end into the hole by the brass screws, white wire by the silver ones.

## REPLACING A 120/240-VOLT RECEPTACLE

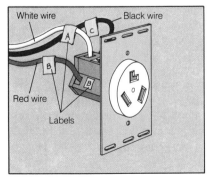

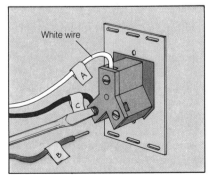

**1) To remove a 125/250-volt receptacle,** shut off the power. Remove the receptacle from its box and label the wires and screws; detach the wires.

**2) Reconnect the wires** to their proper screws on the new receptacle. Reattach the receptacle to the box; replace the cover plate.

---

**PROFESSIONAL HINT**
USING WIRE NUTS

For most simple repairs, you won't need to splice wires. But you may have to splice two or more copper wires to replace a damaged wall or ceiling light fixture, or to make a connection in a receptacle, switch, or junction box.

To splice wires, strip 1 inch of insulation off the wire ends, twist the wires together clockwise, and snip off ⅜ to ½ inch of the ends. Cap the twisted wires with a wire nut, turning it clockwise to secure the connection. Make sure the wire nut is the proper size for the wires.

CAUTION: Don't use wire nuts to splice together a damaged extension cord. For safety, building codes allow you to splice house wires only within junction, receptacle, fixture, or switch boxes. Also, be sure to turn off the power to the circuit (pages 152–153) before you make any splice.

# Doorbells

The parts of a typical doorbell system are the push button, the door bell (or chimes or buzzer), and the transformer. The transformer allows the doorbell to operate on low voltage (6 to 24 volts). Wired into the doorbell circuit at a junction box, it steps down the voltage from the regular 120-volt circuit.

The drawing at right shows how a one-button doorbell system is wired. When your doorbell doesn't ring, or worse, rings constantly, the problem may lie in one of the parts or in the wires that connect them.

NOTE: To diagnose most doorbell problems, you'll need to have the power source connected. But if you're going to work on the transformer or the wires in the junction box, be sure to shut off the power to the circuit. (Remember that the input side of the transformer is high voltage—120 volts.)

## A TYPICAL DOORBELL SYSTEM

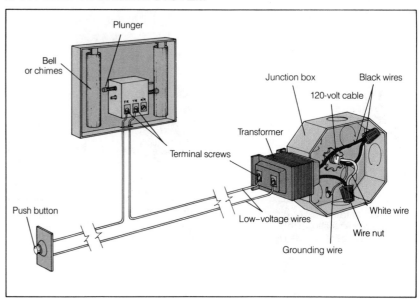

Plunger

Bell or chimes

Terminal screws

Push button

Junction box

Black wires

120-volt cable

Transformer

Low–voltage wires

White wire

Wire nut

Grounding wire

## A silent doorbell

One of a variety of problems—a faulty transformer, push button, or bell, dirt in the mechanism, or poor wiring—can cause your doorbell not to sound. The first place to look is at the source of power. Make sure a fuse or circuit breaker hasn't blown or tripped (pages 152–153). Once you're certain that the 120-volt side of the transformer is getting power, shut off the power and tighten all wire connections. Then turn the power back on and check the low-voltage side, following the steps below to find the source of the trouble.

**Testing the transformer.** The best and safest way to test whether the transformer is functioning properly is to use a volt-ohm meter (page 22). If the transformer is working correctly, the meter reading should match the secondary voltage (6 to 24 volts) marked on the transformer or bell.

Set the voltage range on the meter to 120 volts AC and measure the voltage between the two low-voltage terminals on the transformer. If the meter reads significantly higher than the correct secondary voltage, the transformer is defective and should be

replaced. If the reading is close to the correct secondary voltage, test again by setting the voltage range on the meter to a lower value. If the new reading doesn't agree with the voltage marked on the transformer or bell, replace the transformer.

**Testing the push button.** To check the button, disconnect the two wires connected to it and short them by touching their bare ends together. If this makes the bell ring, the push button is defective and should be replaced. If the bell doesn't ring, the problem is either in the bell or chime mechanism itself or in the wiring.

**Testing the bell or chime mechanism.** Have a helper push the doorbell button while you listen to the bell (or chime). If it makes a buzzing or humming noise, it may be gummed up with dirt. (For example, the striker shaft on a chime mechanism can get stuck because of corrosion, dirt, or excessive grease.) Check the mechanism and clean it as necessary. Use fine-grade sandpaper to remove corrosion from any contacts.

If the bell (or chime) still hums or buzzes after cleaning, replace it. If it

didn't make any noise at all when the button was pushed, disconnect the bell (or chime) and, using new wire, hook it up directly to the transformer. If it works, inspect the old wiring. If it doesn't sound, replace it.

**Repairing the wiring.** Examine the wiring for breaks or frayed insulation that may be causing the wires to short out. Repair any breaks and wrap the repairs with electrician's tape.

## A constantly ringing doorbell

If a doorbell rings constantly, either the button is stuck or the wires going to the button are shorted together.

To test the button, first turn off the power to the transformer. Remove the button from the door frame and disconnect one of the two wires connected to it. Turn the power back on. If the bell doesn't ring, the button should be replaced. If the bell rings, then the problem is a short between the two wires.

With the power turned off, examine the wires for frayed insulation or bare wires rubbing together; use electrician's tape to wrap them where necessary. If you can't find the short, replace the wires.

# Lamps

Most plug-in incandescent lamps have a socket, switch, cord, and plug. (In a simple lamp like the one shown at right, the switch is built into the socket.) Any one of these parts may wear out and need to be replaced.

To check a lamp that doesn't work, first test the light bulb. Next, plug the lamp into another receptacle to be sure the receptacle isn't at fault. Check the plug and cord for wear. To replace the plug, see pages 156–157; to inspect and replace the cord, see at right. If the bulb, cord, and plug are in good shape, use a continuity tester (page 22) to test the socket. To replace the socket and built-in switch, see at right. (If the lamp's switch is attached to the cord, check it and replace if faulty.)

A lamp assembled with rivets instead of nuts and bolts can't be taken apart for repair, so you'll have to replace it.

CAUTION: Before working on any lamp, make sure it's unplugged.

## PARTS OF A LAMP

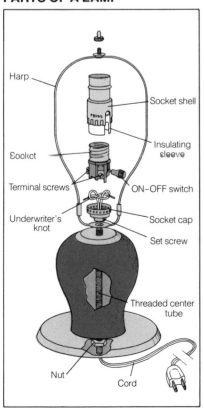

## REPLACING A LAMP SOCKET & CORD

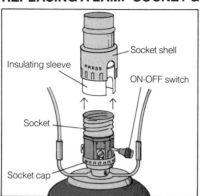

**1)    To remove the socket,** first loosen the socket shell by pushing in where the word "PRESS" is embossed. Lift off the shell and insulating sleeve.

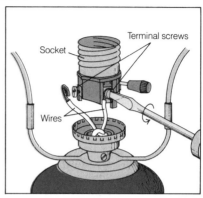

**2)    Unfasten the wires** from the socket terminal screws; inspect the cord insulation. If it's okay, test the socket and replace if necessary; if it's faulty, go to Step 3.

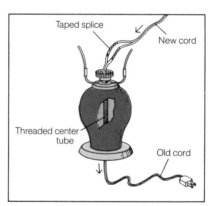

**3)    To replace a faulty cord,** untie the knot. Splice the new cord to the old by twisting the wires' bare ends together and taping them. Pull both cords through; detach the old cord.

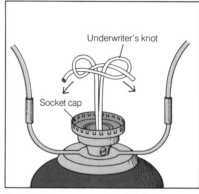

**4)    Split the new cord** to 2½ inches from the end. Tie an Underwriter's knot by making two loops and passing the loose wire ends through the loops. Pull the knot snug.

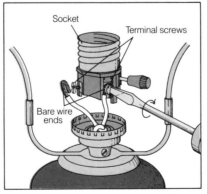

**5)    Strip ½ to ¾ inch** of insulation from the ends of the wires (page 159). Wrap one wire clockwise around each socket terminal screw and tighten the screws.

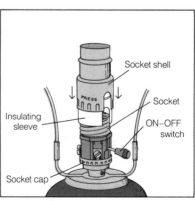

**6)    To reattach the socket,** push the insulating sleeve over the socket; then push in the shell until you hear it click into place. Attach a plug to the cord.

# Incandescent Light Fixtures

Incandescent fixtures include many styles of wall and ceiling-mounted lights—from single-bulb globes to chandeliers. They're connected directly to your home's wiring through a recessed ceiling box hidden by the fixture or by a decorative canopy. Though instructions here are for repairing and replacing ceiling-mounted fixtures, you'll use the same procedures for wall-mounted styles.

When a fixture doesn't work, first check the light bulb. Then check the circuit and light switch (pages 154–155). If the fixture is the problem, the cause may be in the wiring or the socket. Detach the fixture from the ceiling box and check for a loose connection. Tighten it if necessary. If the fixture still doesn't work, you'll have to either replace or repair it as described here and on the facing page.

CAUTION: Before you work on any fixture, shut off the power to the *entire circuit.*

**Replacing a fixture.** The replacement procedure is basically the same for all types of fixtures. You simply detach the old fixture and undo the wiring connections, then make new ones and attach the new fixture, as shown at right. Wiring connections may be made with wire nuts; if there are more than just two black and two white wires, label all wires and make a sketch before undoing them.

NOTE: If the fixture is heavy, have a helper hold it; or hang it from the box with a hook made from a wire coat hanger.

You may have to buy new mounting hardware to hang the new fixture. If the ceiling box has a metallic stud, the fixture may be attached to it with a nipple and hickey, a reducing nut, or a strap (see below). If there's no stud, the strap may be attached to the ceiling box ears. Fixtures heavier than 10 pounds must be hung from a box with a stud and nailed to the ceiling joists.

**Repairing a fixture.** Repair involves removing and replacing the socket(s) and/or wiring. Sockets in all types of fixtures may have terminal screws like a lamp socket (page 163), or they may have permanently attached wires as shown in the center of the facing page. Use a continuity tester (page 22) to determine whether a socket is faulty. When you replace a socket, be sure to connect wires of the same color together.

On a chandelier, the sockets and socket wires in the arms are connected to a main cord running up the center. Usually, the connections are hidden inside the fixture body; you may have to remove a cap or nut on the bottom to reach them. Replace the main cord as you would a lamp cord (page 163); to replace the socket wires and sockets, see the facing page. If you're replacing only sockets or socket wires and not the main cord, you can work with the chandelier in place.

## TYPES OF CEILING FIXTURES

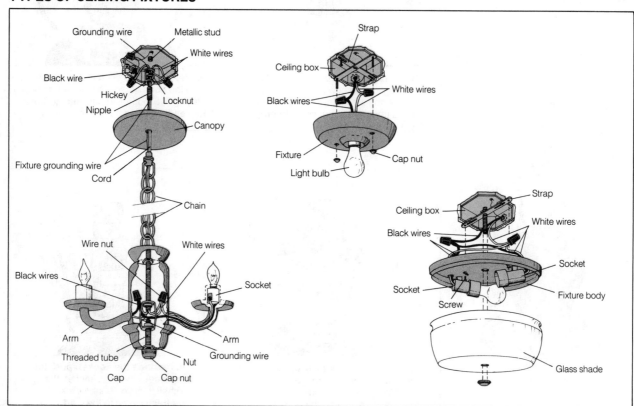

## REPLACING A FIXTURE

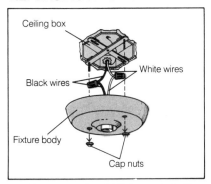

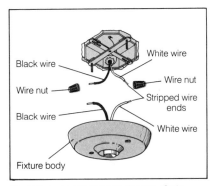

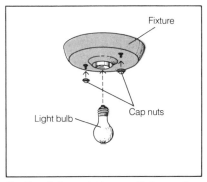

**1)    To remove the old fixture,** shut off power to the circuit. Remove the bulb and unscrew the cap nuts to free the fixture from the screws on the ceiling box.

**2)    Disconnect the old fixture.** Strip ½ inch off the new wires. Wrap the bare ends around circuit wires and bend over; install wire nuts.

**3)    Carefully push the new fixture** onto the screws that hold it to the ceiling box. Screw on the cap nuts to secure the fixture, and replace the bulb.

## REPLACING A PREWIRED SOCKET

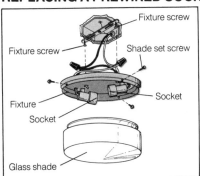

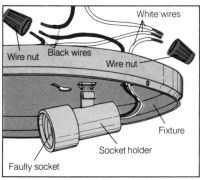

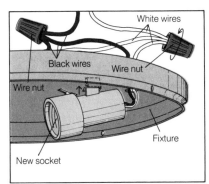

**1)    To replace a prewired socket,** turn off power to the circuit. Remove the glass shade; unscrew the fixture screws to free the fixture.

**2)    Unscrew the wire nuts** to disconnect the socket wires from the circuit wires. Unclip and remove the faulty socket from the fixture.

**3)    Attach the new socket.** Push the wires through and splice them to the circuit wires with wire nuts. Reattach the fixture and replace the cover.

## REWIRING A CHANDELIER ARM

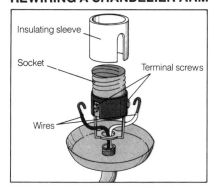

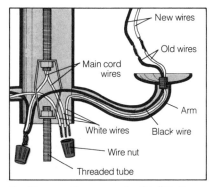

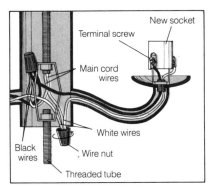

**1)    To replace a socket and its wires,** shut off power to the circuit. Remove the sleeve, detach the wires from the socket terminal screws, and unscrew the socket.

**2)    Remove the cap** under the fixture. Temporarily tape the new socket wires to the old. Detach the old wires from the main cord wires and pull the new wires through.

**3)    Screw on the new socket;** connect the new wires. Remove the old socket wires and attach the new ones to the main cord wires; reassemble the fixture.

# Fluorescent Light Fixtures

Unlike incandescent lights, which use house current directly, fluorescent fixtures require a high-voltage current to produce light. The working parts of a fluorescent light fixture consist of fluorescent tubes, a ballast (transformer) that converts house voltage to a much higher voltage, a tubeholder (socket), and, on some fixtures, a starter that assists the ballast in the initial starting process (see illustration on facing page).

The three types of fixtures are preheat, rapid start, and instant start. On a preheat fixture, an older style, the starter is visible; it looks like a miniature aluminum can. On a rapid-start fixture, the starter is built into the ballast. An instant-start fixture has no starter and is distinguished by a tube with a single pin on each end.

You can easily make most repairs on a faulty fluorescent light fixture. Use the chart below to help pinpoint the cause of the problem. Tubes, ballasts, tubeholders, and starters are the components involved in most repairs; usually you need only replace them. But you must match replacement parts to your fixture—parts are not interchangeable among the three different types. Take the old parts with you when you shop for new ones.

**Replacing a fluorescent tube.** Before you remove a fluorescent tube, be sure to shut off the wall switch to the fixture.

To remove a double-pin tube, rotate it a quarter-turn in either direction and gently pull it out. Install the new tube by pushing it into the tubeholders and then giving it a quarter-turn to lock it into place.

Remove a single-pin tube from the fixture by pushing the tube against the spring-loaded tubeholder until the other end can be removed. To install the new tube, put the tube pin in the spring-loaded tubeholder and push until the other end can be inserted.

CAUTION: Should you accidentally break a tube, handle the broken pieces carefully; the coating on the inside is poisonous.

**Replacing a starter.** Before you replace a starter, be sure to shut off the wall switch to the fixture.

To replace a starter on a preheat fixture, first remove the fluorescent tube. Rotate the starter a quarter-turn counterclockwise and pull it out of its

## TROUBLESHOOTING A FLUORESCENT FIXTURE

| Problem | Possible Causes | Remedies |
|---|---|---|
| **Lamp won't light** | Tube burned out (ends blackened) | Replace tube |
| | Fuse blown or circuit breaker tripped | Replace fuse or reset circuit breaker* |
| | Improper tube installation | Take out and install again |
| | Dirty tube (rapid start only) | Remove tube; wash, dry, and install |
| | Fixture too cold | Raise room temperature to at least 50°F |
| | Oxide film buildup on tube pins | Rotate tube in tubeholders once or twice |
| | Starter burned out | Replace starter on preheat type, ballast on rapid start |
| | Tubeholder broken | Replace tubeholder |
| **Lamp flickers** (new tubes may flicker for a short time after installation) | Improper tube installation | Take out and install again |
| | Tube nearly worn out (ends blackened) | Replace tube |
| | Oxide film buildup on tube pins | Rotate tube in tubeholders once or twice |
| | Fixture too cold | Raise room temperature to at least 50°F |
| | Poor contact with tubeholders | Realign tubeholders; straighten and sand, if necessary |
| **Ends of tubes are discolored** (dark bands about 2 inches from ends are normal) | Tube nearly worn out | Replace tube |
|    **Preheat type with new tubes** | Defective starter | Replace starter on preheat type, ballast on rapid start |
|    **Discolored on one end only** | Temperamental tube | Remove tube; turn end for end |
| **Ends of tube glow, but center doesn't** | Defective starter | Replace starter |
| | Defective ballast | Replace ballast |
| **Lamp fixture hums** | Ballast incorrectly installed | Check wiring diagram printed on ballast and correct |
| | Wrong type of ballast | Check wattage and type; replace ballast |
| | Defective ballast | Replace ballast |

*If fuse blows or circuit breaker trips again, you have a short circuit (page 155)
Check wiring or call an electrician

socket. Place the new starter in the socket and rotate it a quarter-turn in the clockwise direction.

**Replacing a tubeholder or ballast.** Before you replace a tubeholder or ballast, shut off power to that circuit. Then follow the steps illustrated below. To connect the wires, you'll have to strip about ½ inch of insulation from the end of each wire and use wire nuts to connect the ballast or tubeholder wires to the fixture wires. If your new tubeholder has push-in connections or terminal screws instead of permanently connected wires, connect the fixture wires to these, rather than using wire nuts as shown below. A new ballast will have permanently connected wires.

## PARTS OF A FLUORESCENT FIXTURE

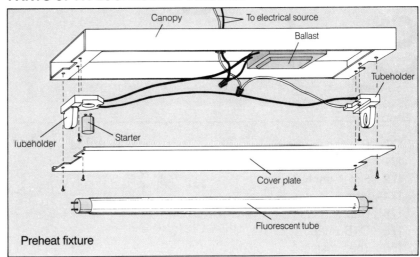

Preheat fixture

## REPLACING A TUBEHOLDER

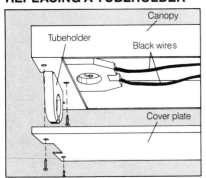

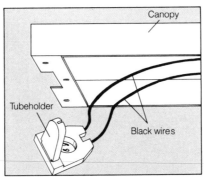

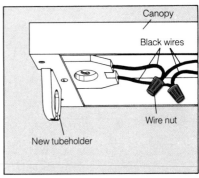

1) **To remove the old tubeholder,** first turn off the power to the circuit. Remove the fixture's cover plate and fluorescent tube.

2) **Unscrew or unsnap the tubeholder** from the end of the fixture's canopy. Cut or disconnect the wires connecting the tubeholder to the fixture.

3) **Connect the wires** to the new tubeholder with wire nuts. Attach the new tubeholder, install the cover plate and tube; turn on the power.

## REPLACING A BALLAST

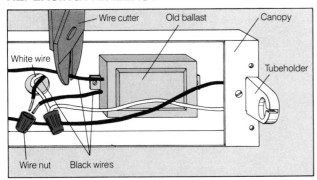

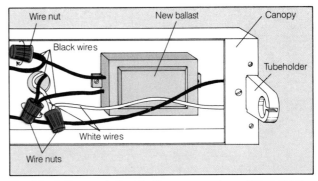

1) **To remove the old ballast,** turn off the power to the circuit; remove the cover plate and fluorescent tube. Cut or disconnect the wires. Remove the ballast from the canopy.

2) **Attach the new ballast to the canopy.** Connect the ballast wires to the existing wires with wire nuts. Install the fluorescent tube and cover plate; turn on the power.

# Heating & Cooling Systems

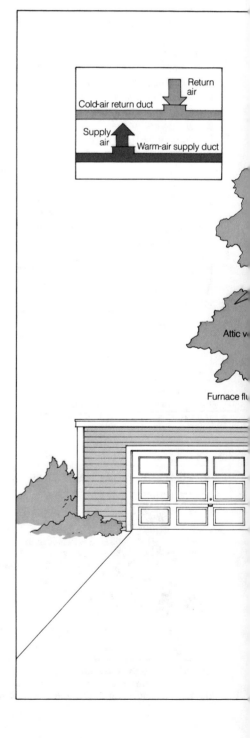

Return air

Cold-air return duct

Supply air — Warm-air supply duct

Attic v

Furnace fl

Your home may be heated by steam, hot water, or warm air—and cooled by air conditioning or fans. In this house, a basement furnace heats cold air drawn from the rooms above, then returns it via ducts and registers. An attic fan exhausts hot air through one side, allowing cooler air to enter through vents in the other side. For details on common heating and cooling systems, read on.

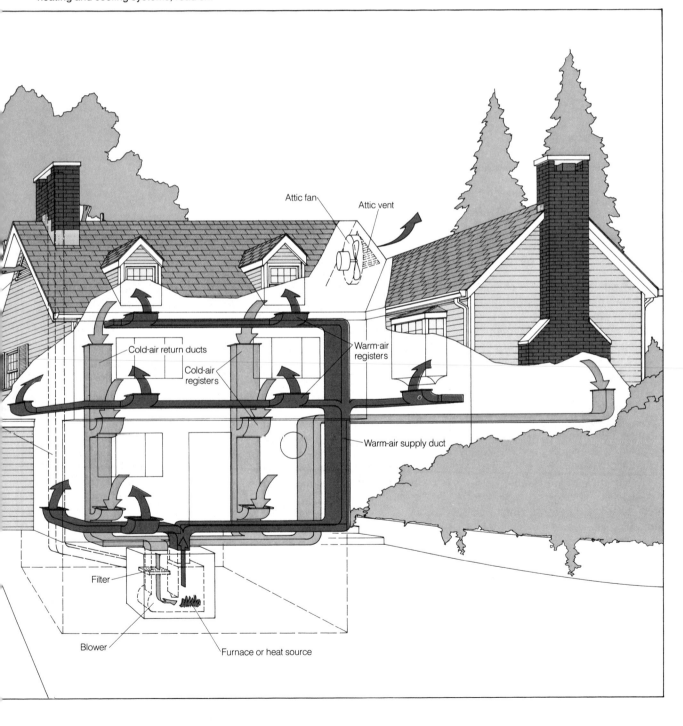

Attic fan

Attic vent

Cold-air return ducts

Cold-air registers

Warm-air registers

Warm-air supply duct

Filter

Blower

Furnace or heat source

# Heating Systems

Heating systems can vary enormously, but all work toward the same goal—ensuring comfort in your home.

Most homes today are heated by forced warm air or hot water. Steam heat, found in older homes, is rarely installed now. Electric heat and heat pumps (see below) are the choice in some situations.

## Understanding heating systems

Steam, hot water, forced warm-air, and electric heating systems all function in the same basic way. Each system is equipped with a control, a heat producer, a heat exchanger, and a heat distributor.

The control, called a thermostat, signals a need for heat. The signal turns on the heat producer, usually an oil or gas burner or an electric heating element; the heat warms the transfer medium—air, water, or steam—in the heat exchanger: a furnace if it heats air, a boiler if it heats water or produces steam.

The transfer medium moves by gravity or is forced through ducts (warm air) or pipes (water or steam) to the heat distributors located in the living areas. These heat distributors are registers in a forced warm-air system and convectors or radiators in a hot water or steam system. In a hot water radiant heating system, the water moves through tubing concealed in the ceiling, walls, or floor.

Return ducts or pipes carry the medium back to the heat exchanger. When the temperature of the living area reaches the level set on the thermostat, the thermostat automatically shuts down the system.

## Caring for your system

In general, heating systems operate reliably for years, providing they're carefully maintained. Most routine maintenance, minor repairs, and simple adjustments are well within the capability of the homeowner. But other repairs, either those too dangerous or too technical for the do-it-yourselfer, require professional help.

Whether you're performing routine maintenance or trying to solve a problem, you'll find much valuable information, as well as a description of the different heating systems and their major components, burners and thermostats, on the following pages.

## USING ELECTRIC HEAT

In areas where electricity is cheaper than either gas or oil, or when a remodeling project results in an increased demand for heat without increasing the capacity of the existing heating system, electric heat makes good sense.

Several options are available, including electric-fired boilers for hot water systems (pages 172–173) and electric-fired furnaces for forced warm-air systems (pages 174–175). Neither type requires a flue.

Other choices are electric heaters installed in existing warm-air ducts, baseboard heaters, small wall and ceiling heaters, and electric radiant heating panels. Heat pumps (page 181) are also a source of electric heat.

**Electric boilers and furnaces.** In an electric boiler or furnace, the heating elements are immersed directly in the transfer medium, either water or air. Maintenance of such a system is similar to that required for a gas or oil-fired boiler or furnace; problems with the electric heating elements are best left to a professional.

**Duct heaters.** Designed for installation in the ducts of an existing forced warm-air heating system (pages 174–175), duct heaters can be turned on at the same time as the blower or can be operated by a separate thermostat located in an area requiring supplemental heat. The heaters must be controlled so they don't turn on unless the blower is running.

**Baseboard heaters.** These heaters require no pipes or ducts—they connect directly to the electrical system in the house. A good choice for a room addition or a hard-to-heat area, a baseboard heater has its own thermostat and safety thermal cutoff switch. Most baseboard heaters are very reliable; if you do have a problem, you'll have to call in an electrician.

Some baseboard heaters use resistance coils that glow red hot; others have a resistance wire that heats a ceramic tube; still others have the heating element immersed in a sealed tube. The tubes are surrounded by fins that radiate heat into the room.

**Wall and ceiling heaters.** Suitable for bathrooms and other small areas, these resistance-heated units are mounted in a wall or ceiling and are wired directly into the electrical system. Clean the heater occasionally; replace a defective one.

**Radiant heating panels.** These may be electrically heated glass panels mounted in walls or ceilings or special gypsum board panels embedded with electric resistance wires and installed in place of regular gypsum board. Both kinds are wired into the electrical system and are controlled by a thermostat. Once installed, they provide trouble-free service for years.

# Steam Heat

A hallmark of many older homes, steam heat begins in a boiler fueled by gas, oil, or electricity. The boiler turns water into steam, which rises through pipes to radiators or convectors. There the steam gives up its heat and condenses into water, which returns to the boiler.

To maintain a steam heating system in good condition, periodically check the safety valve, steam pressure gauge, and water level gauge, as explained below. Be sure to regularly inspect your burner (pages 176–179) and thermostat (page 180) as well.

Some adjustments to a steam heating system are within the scope of the homeowner; others must be performed by a professional. The chart below describes problems you may encounter and how to remedy them.

**Safety valve.** Located on top of the boiler, the safety valve allows steam to escape if the pressure in the boiler exceeds safe levels. Test the valve every month during the heating season by depressing the handle (stand clear of valve pipe); if steam doesn't come out, have the valve replaced.

**Steam pressure gauge.** Check that the pressure of the steam in the boiler, as shown on the gauge, is within normal bounds—typically 2 to 10 pounds per square inch (psi). If not, shut off the boiler and call for service.

## A STEAM HEATING SYSTEM

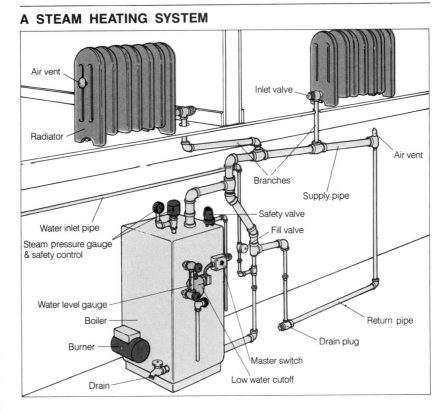

Air vent · Radiator · Water inlet pipe · Steam pressure gauge & safety control · Water level gauge · Boiler · Burner · Drain · Inlet valve · Air vent · Branches · Supply pipe · Safety valve · Fill valve · Master switch · Low water cutoff · Return pipe · Drain plug

**Water level gauge.** Once a month, open the valves at each end of the sight glass in the gauge—the water level should be in the middle of the glass. (Be sure to close the valves after checking.) If water is not visible, immediately shut off the boiler and let it cool; then add water by opening the fill valve on the water inlet pipe, unless your system has an automatic water fill valve. In that case, call for service.

To remove the sight glass for cleaning or replacement, shut off the valves and undo the collar nuts at each end of the glass. Install new gaskets when you reassemble the unit.

## TROUBLESHOOTING A STEAM HEATING SYSTEM

| Problem | Possible Causes | Remedies |
|---|---|---|
| **No heat** | No power | Check master switch and fuse or circuit breaker (pages 152–153) |
| | Not enough water in boiler | Add water by opening fill valve; or adjust automatic fill valve* |
| | Defective thermostat | Clean thermostat or replace (page 180) |
| **Cold radiator** | Closed inlet valve | Open valve completely |
| | Radiator out of adjustment | Adjust thermostatic air vent or thermostatic inlet valve; if none, install thermostatic air vent* |
| **Hammering noises** | Radiator not sloped | Check radiator with a level; if not sloped slightly toward outflow end, shim opposite end |

*This repair is best left to a professional
Some problems may be burner related; see pages 176–179

# Hot Water Heat

In a hot water heating system, water heated in a boiler travels through a network of pipes to the heat distributors (usually convectors or radiators) where the heat is given off. The cooled water then returns to the boiler through the return pipe.

In older homes, the movement of water is governed by gravity—warmer, lighter water rises and takes the place of heavier, cooler water. The more modern hydronic systems employ a circulating pump to move the water under pressure; a thermostat governs the operation of the pump as well as the burner.

An expansion tank, usually mounted above the boiler, contains air and water; the air acts as a cushion to maintain heated water at the proper pressure.

With routine maintenance, a modern hot water heating system will give you many years of trouble-free service. Check the system periodically; at the same time, take a look at the burner (pages 176–179) and the thermostat (page 180).

If some parts of the house are too cold or too hot, follow the directions on the facing page to balance the system. Other problems you may encounter are discussed in the troubleshooting chart on the facing page.

### Maintaining the system

With regular maintenance and inspection, especially during the heating season, you can correct problems with a boiler that's not operating properly or with heat distributors that aren't working to capacity because air is trapped inside.

**Checking the gauges.** Mounted on the boiler are two gauges, one for water temperature and another for pressure, or altitude (sometimes they're combined in a single housing, as illustrated above).

Water temperature is determined by the design of the system and the settings of the limit controls on the boiler.

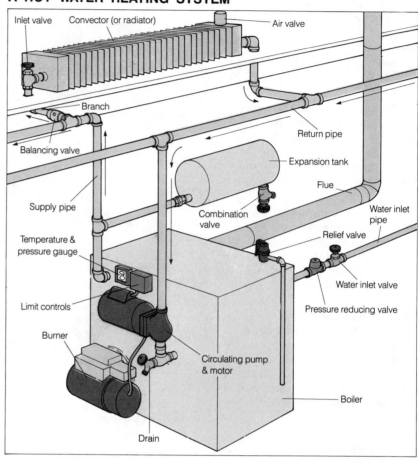

**A HOT WATER HEATING SYSTEM**

Inlet valve • Convector (or radiator) • Air valve • Branch • Balancing valve • Supply pipe • Temperature & pressure gauge • Limit controls • Burner • Drain • Return pipe • Expansion tank • Flue • Water inlet pipe • Combination valve • Relief valve • Water inlet valve • Pressure reducing valve • Circulating pump & motor • Boiler

Adjusting the temperature is a job for a professional.

The pressure gauge (illustrated on facing page) provides a check on the water level. The fixed pointer, set when the system was installed, is a reference point for water level. The moving pointer indicates current water level and should align with the fixed one when the water is cold.

If the moving pointer reads higher, drain some water from the expansion tank (see facing page). If it's lower and you have no pressure reducing valve, add water through the water inlet valve until the pointers are aligned.

In a system equipped with a pressure reducing valve, water level should be maintained automatically. If draining the expansion tank doesn't work or if the water level is too low, consult a professional.

**Draining the expansion tank.** A pressure gauge that reads high or a tank that feels hot indicates there's too little air in the expansion tank. Draining some of the water from the tank, as shown on the facing page, will restore the proper air-water ratio. You can do the job yourself, unless you have a diaphragm tank; in that case, call for service.

To drain the tank, turn off the power and the water to the boiler; let the water in the tank cool. Attach a hose to the combination valve and open it. Let water flow out until the pointers on the pressure gauge coincide. Close the valve and restore power and water.

**Checking the relief valve.** This valve releases excess pressure. Once a month, lift the valve lever; if no water flows from the valve, replace it.

**Bleeding the convectors or radiators.** Convectors and radiators won't heat properly if air is trapped inside. If your units don't have automatic air valves, you'll need to bleed the air from them (see illustration) at the beginning of each heating season, whenever you add water to the system, or if a convector or radiator remains cold when it shouldn't.

Depending on the type of valve, use a wrench, screwdriver, or special key to open the valve. When water spurts out, close the valve.

## Balancing the system

Unless your system has zone controls that automatically control water temperature in specific areas, you may need to balance your system to compensate for overly cold or overly warm rooms.

Turn the system on and let room temperatures stabilize before you start. To adjust a convector or radiator, gradually open or close the balancing valve on that branch or the inlet valve on the affected convector or radiator (see at right). Be patient—it may take several days of adjustments to bring the system into balance.

## FOUR ADJUSTMENTS TO THE SYSTEM

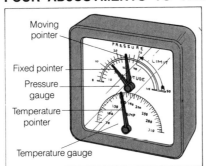

To align the pressure gauge pointers, drain the expansion tank if the moving pointer is higher than the fixed one; add water if it's lower.

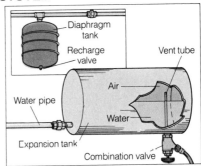

To drain an expansion tank, close the water inlet valve and open the combination valve (attach hose first). Let a professional drain a diaphragm tank (see inset).

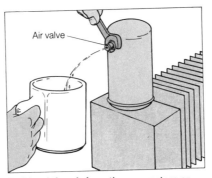

To bleed the air from the convectors or radiators, open each air valve. Close the valve when water spurts out (use a cup to catch water).

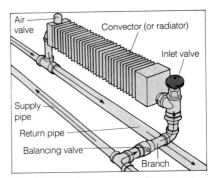

To adjust the temperature of a convector or radiator, open or close the inlet valve or alter the water flow by adjusting the balancing valve in that branch.

## TROUBLESHOOTING A HOT WATER HEATING SYSTEM

| Problem | Possible Causes | Remedies |
|---|---|---|
| **No heat** | No power | Check master switch and fuse or circuit breaker (pages 152–153) |
| | Closed fuel supply valve | Open oil or gas inlet valve |
| | Dirty or defective thermostat | Clean thermostat or replace (page 180) |
| **Cold convector or radiator** | Air in convector or radiator | Bleed convector or radiator (see text) |
| **Leaking inlet valve stem** | Worn stem packing | Drain water in system below level of valve and replace packing as for a faucet (page 114); then refill system and bleed convector or radiator (see text) |
| **Leaking circulating pump** | Defective seal or impeller | Replace seal or impeller* |
| **Noisy circulating pump** | Broken coupling | Replace coupling* |
| **Water dribbling from relief valve** | Too much water in expansion tank | Drain expansion tank to restore proper air-water ratio (see text) |

*This repair is best left to a professional
Some problems may be burner related; see pages 176–179

# Forced Warm-Air Heat

Low installation cost, fast heat delivery, and reliability make forced warm-air systems a popular heating choice. The system is also very versatile, lending itself to the addition of central air conditioning (page 183).

In this system, a blower pulls air from the rooms into the cold-air return and return duct, through a filter, and into the furnace. There the air is heated. It then flows back to the rooms through the warm-air ducts and registers.

For maximum efficiency, clean the system (see below) and inspect the burner (pages 176–179) and thermostat (page 180). A system that's working inefficiently can be adjusted, as explained on the facing page. For other problems, see the chart .

## Caring for the system

To ensure trouble-free operation, service the system as follows:

- **Clean or replace the filter** monthly during the heating season.

- **Brush and vacuum heat exchanger surfaces** annually (see owner's manual for instructions).

- **Clean the blower blades** at the start of each heating season; add a few drops of motor oil to each oil cup if your blower is equipped with them.

## A FORCED WARM-AIR HEATING SYSTEM

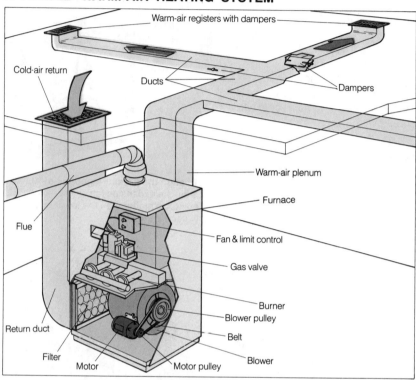

- **Check and adjust the belt alignment and tension** (see illustrations below) if your furnace has a belt-driven blower. To replace a worn belt, loosen the motor adjustment bolt, remove the old belt, and attach a new one. Adjust as shown.

- **Examine the ducts** annually for leaks; seal any leaks with duct tape.

## Balancing the heat

If some rooms are too hot or too cold, try adjusting the dampers in the registers and, if your system has them, the dampers in the warm-air ducts.

Leaving the thermostat at one setting, let the system run for 3 hours to stabilize the temperatures. Open the

## THREE BLOWER ADJUSTMENTS

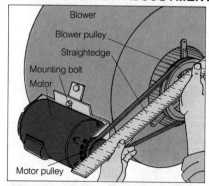

**Check the pulley alignment** by placing a straightedge against the pulley faces. If they're not aligned, loosen the mounting bolts and adjust the motor pulley.

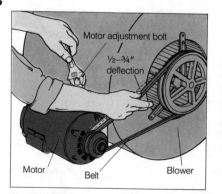

**To check belt tension,** push the belt — it should deflect ½ to ¾ inch. Turn the adjustment bolt and move the motor away to tighten the belt, closer to loosen it.

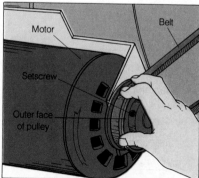

**To speed up the blower** and increase air flow, loosen the setscrew and turn the outer pulley face clockwise; turn it counterclockwise to slow down the blower.

dampers wide in the coldest rooms. Then adjust the dampers room by room until temperatures are balanced. Wait half an hour after each adjustment before rechecking or readjusting.

Speeding up the blower may help heat chronically cold rooms. Adjust the motor pulley of a belt-driven blower (see facing page, bottom) or, for a direct-drive blower, change the electrical connections (see owner's manual).

### Setting the fan control

If you're chilled by a blast of cool air when the blower turns on, try adjusting the fan control (see at right). A word of

caution: If your furnace has a combination fan and limit control, do *not* touch the pointer on the limit control side. This pointer turns off the furnace if the maximum allowable air temperature is exceeded.

As the blower turns on, hold your hand in front of the warm-air register farthest from the furnace. Ideally, your hand should feel neither cooler nor warmer. If it feels cooler, uncover the control and move the fan control's ON pointer a few degrees higher. Check and readjust as necessary.

Conduct a similar test to increase fuel efficiency, but check the air just before the blower shuts off. If your hand feels warmer, move the OFF pointer a few degrees lower.

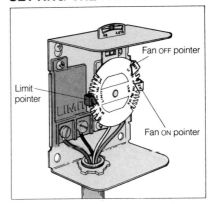

### SETTING THE FAN CONTROL

**To adjust the temperature** of the air coming out of the registers, move the ON pointer to set the temperature at which the blower turns on, the OFF pointer to set the temperature at which it turns off.

## TROUBLESHOOTING A FORCED WARM-AIR HEATING SYSTEM

| Problem | Possible Causes | Remedies |
|---|---|---|
| **No heat** | No power | Check master switch and fuse or circuit breaker (pages 152–153) |
|  | Defective thermostat | Clean thermostat or replace (page 180) |
| **Insufficient heat** | Clogged filter | Clean or replace filter |
|  | Dirty heat exchanger | Brush and vacuum (see owner's manual) |
|  | Leaking air ducts | Seal leaks with duct tape |
|  | Blower operating too slowly | Adjust blower speed (see text) |
|  | Loose blower belt | Tighten belt (see text) |
| **Blower doesn't operate** | Broken belt | Replace belt (see text) |
|  | Fan control too high | Adjust fan control (see text) |
|  | Defective blower motor | **Repair or replace motor*** |
| **Noisy blower** | Insufficient lubrication | Put oil in oil cups if any |
|  | Loose or worn blower belt | Tighten or replace belt (see text) |
| **Blower cycles too rapidly** | Fan control differential too low | Adjust fan control (see text) |
|  | Blower operating too fast | Adjust blower speed (see text) |
|  | Defective fan and limit control | **Replace fan and limit control*** |
| **Room temperature exceeds thermostat setting** | Thermostat improperly located | **Move thermostat*** |
|  | Thermostat improperly installed | Install thermostat properly (page 180) |
| **Room temperature doesn't reach thermostat setting** | Thermostat improperly located | **Move thermostat*** |
|  | Thermostat improperly installed | Install thermostat properly (page 180) |
|  | Dirty thermostat contacts | Clean contacts (page 180) |
|  | Clogged filter | Clean or replace filter |
|  | Blower operating too slowly | Adjust blower speed (see text) |
|  | Fan control too low | Adjust fan control (see text) |
|  | Thermostat improperly calibrated | **Recalibrate thermostat*** |

*This repair is best left to a professional
Some problems may be burner related; see pages 176–179
Furnace models vary; see your owner's manual for specifics

# Gas Burners

Extremely common for home heating use, gas burners can fuel warm-air, hot water, or steam heating systems.

When the thermostat in the system calls for heat, the burner's automatic gas valve opens, allowing gas to flow into a manifold and then into venturi tubes where it mixes with air. When the air-gas mixture emerges from the burner ports, the pilot ignites it and heat is created. A thermocouple adjacent to the pilot closes the gas valve if the pilot isn't working.

Whether fueled by natural, manufactured, or bottled or liquefied petroleum gas, gas burners are generally reliable and require little routine maintenance. Problems you may encounter are discussed below and in the chart on the facing page.

## Solving pilot problems

Pilots in gas burners may be electric or gas. For problems with electric pilots, call in a professional. Gas pilots can be relit and cleaned by the homeowner.

**Lighting a gas pilot.** Before you try to relight a pilot that has gone out, read the instructions usually printed on the front of the boiler or furnace. If there are none, have your utility company light it or follow these steps:

Use the manual control knob on the automatic gas valve to turn off the

### A TYPICAL GAS BURNER

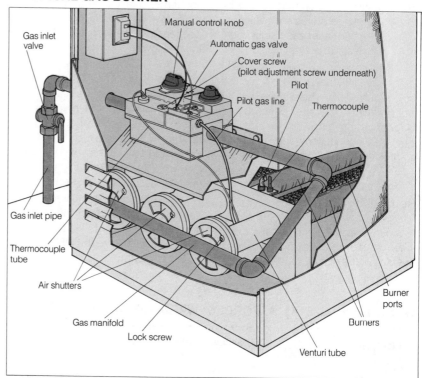

gas to the main burner and pilot. Allow at least 5 minutes for accumulated gas to dissipate before proceeding. Use extreme caution—and take more time—if your fuel is bottled gas; it doesn't dissipate readily.

When the gas has dissipated, set the thermostat well below room tem-

perature. Turn the manual control knob to PILOT and light the pilot, holding the knob there for a minute. Release the knob and turn it to ON. If the pilot doesn't stay on, refer to the chart on the facing page or call the gas company. (Remember to reset the thermostat when the pilot's relit.)

## ADJUSTING THE PILOT

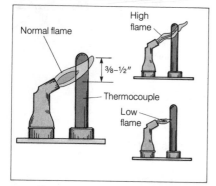

**To adjust the pilot flame** to the normal position, turn the pilot adjustment screw (under cover screw) clockwise to reduce the flame, counterclockwise to increase it.

## REPLACING A THERMOCOUPLE

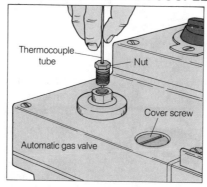

**1)    To replace the thermocouple,** turn the manual control knob to OFF; then unscrew the nut that secures the thermocouple tube to the automatic gas valve.

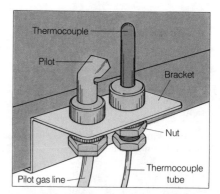

**2)    Unscrew the nut** holding the thermocouple to the bracket; remove the thermocouple and tube. Attach the new unit to the bracket and gas valve; relight the pilot.

**Adjusting the pilot flame.** The pilot flame should be blue and should cover the thermocouple. Before adjusting the flame (see facing page, bottom), turn the thermostat down; reset it when you're done.

**Cleaning the pilot orifice.** If you have trouble lighting the pilot, the orifice may be plugged. To clean it, first shut off the gas supply by turning the gas inlet valve handle so it's at a right angle to the pipe. Next, disconnect the thermocouple tube and the pilot gas line from the automatic gas valve. Then remove the bracket holding the pilot and the thermocouple.

Use stiff wire to clean the orifice (be careful not to chip it). Reattach the bracket, pilot gas line, and thermocouple tube. Turn on the gas and relight the pilot.

## Cleaning the burners

Clogged gas burners and ports heat inefficiently. Clean them at the start of the heating season.

To reach the ports, shut off the gas inlet valve and remove the bracket holding the pilot and thermocouple. Remove any screws or nuts holding the burners and maneuver them out of the combustion chamber.

To clean the burners, scour them with a stiff wire brush; clean the burner ports with stiff wire that's slightly smaller than the diameter of the openings.

After cleaning, reassemble the burners in the combustion chamber, replacing any screws or nuts that secured the burners. Then mount the bracket holding the pilot and thermocouple. Turn on the gas and relight the pilot (see facing page). Be sure to adjust the air-gas ratio, as explained below.

## Adjusting the burners

For maximum efficiency, burners fueled with natural gas should burn with a bright blue flame that has a soft blue green interior and no yellow tips. (Check with your gas company for the correct colors for other types of gas.)

To correct the air-natural gas ratio, you'll need to adjust the air shutters. Turn up the thermostat so the burners light and loosen the lock screws. Slowly open each shutter until the flames are bright blue, then close the shutters gradually until yellow tips appear. Slowly reopen the shutters until the yellow tips just disappear; tighten the screws.

## TROUBLESHOOTING A GAS BURNER

| Problem | Possible Causes | Remedies |
| --- | --- | --- |
| **Burner doesn't operate** | No power | Check master switch and fuse or circuit breaker (pages 152–153) |
| | Closed gas inlet valve | Open valve so handle is parallel to pipe |
| | Closed automatic gas valve | Turn manual control knob to ON |
| | Improperly set or defective thermostat | Check thermostat setting and, if automatic setback type, check clock setting; replace if defective (page 180) |
| | Pilot extinguished | Relight (see text) |
| **Pilot won't light** | Dirty pilot orifice | Clean orifice with stiff wire (see text) |
| | Loose or defective thermocouple | Tighten nut; or replace thermocouple (see text) |
| **Pilot won't stay lit** | Pilot not heating thermocouple | Increase flame (see text) or reposition pilot |
| | Excessive draft | **Install draft diverter\*** |
| **Insufficient heat** | Burner flame not properly adjusted | Fully open gas inlet valve (handle parallel to pipe); adjust air shutters on burners (see text) |
| | Clogged burner ports | Clean burners and ports (see text) |
| **Delayed burner ignition** | Clogged burner ports near pilot | Clean ports with stiff wire (see text) |
| | Pilot not properly adjusted | Increase flame (see text) or reposition pilot and thermocouple |
| **Burner won't turn off** | Short circuit or defective automatic gas valve or furnace limit switch | IMMEDIATELY close gas inlet valve, leaving electric power on, and call utility company |
| **Gas odor** | Gas leak, loose connection, or broken gas line | IMMEDIATELY get everyone out of house, close main gas supply to house, and call utility company |

\*This repair is best left to a professional
Some problems may be furnace or boiler related; see pages 171–175

# Oil Burners

Two types of oil burners are used to produce heat in warm-air, hot water, and steam heating systems for the home. The most common is the pressure, or gun-type, burner; the vaporizing, or pot-type, burner is used only in small furnaces.

Most oil burners run for years with few problems. For maximum efficiency, call in a professional every year to service your burner. Check a pressure-type burner regularly during the heating season and clean it as necessary; for the causes and remedies of common burner problems, see the chart on the facing page. Most problems with vaporizing burners are best left to a professional.

## How oil burners work

When the thermostat of a heating system equipped with a pressure-type burner demands heat, the burner motor turns on, pumping filtered fuel oil under pressure through a nozzle, forming a mist. At the same time, the burner's blower forces air through the draft tube where it mixes with the oil mist. As the mixture enters the combustion chamber, it's ignited by a high-voltage spark between two electrodes located at the end of the draft tube.

When a vaporizing burner is turned on, the oil control valve opens, allowing oil to pool in the pot. An electric spark ignites the oil, and the heat of the burning oil causes more oil to vaporize. These vapors combine with a blower-induced or natural air draft and the mixture burns in the combustion chamber.

If the oil in either type of burner does not ignite, the burner is turned off by a flame sensor in the burner or by a heat sensor on the stack control attached to the flue. This prevents the boiler or furnace from being flooded by oil.

## TWO TYPES OF OIL BURNERS

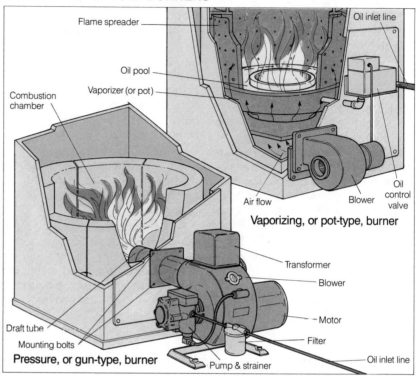

Vaporizing, or pot-type, burner

Flame spreader · Oil inlet line · Oil pool · Vaporizer (or pot) · Combustion chamber · Air flow · Blower · Oil control valve

Pressure, or gun-type, burner

Draft tube · Mounting bolts · Transformer · Blower · Motor · Filter · Pump & strainer · Oil inlet line

## CLEANING THE BLOWER & STRAINER

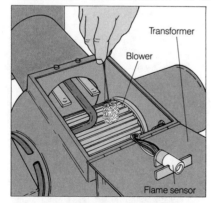

**Clean the blades of the blower** with a small brush after lifting the cover (the transformer may be attached to the cover).

Transformer · Blower · Flame sensor

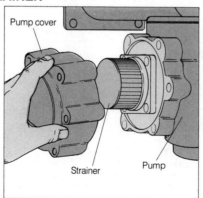

**To reach the fuel pump strainer,** unscrew the pump cover. Remove the strainer and clean it in mineral spirits or kerosene.

Pump cover · Strainer · Pump

## REPLACING THE FILTER

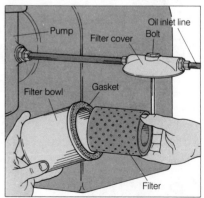

**To replace the filter and gasket,** shut off the valve between the filter and tank; unscrew the bowl from the cover and change the filter and gasket.

Pump · Filter cover · Oil inlet line · Bolt · Filter bowl · Gasket · Filter

## Servicing your burner

Professional service that includes a thorough inspection and cleaning of your burner, as well as a check of its efficiency, should be carried out annually.

To keep repair and fuel bills at a minimum, inspect and clean your pressure-type burner several times between service calls. Lubricate the motor and blower bearlngs by pouring oil in the oil cups if the motor and blower are equipped with them. Clean the blower, oil strainer, and sensors and, when necessary, replace the filter and gasket (see at right and on facing page). Be sure to turn off the power to the burner before you begin work.

## CLEANING THE SENSORS

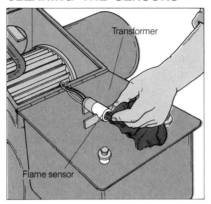

**Clean the flame sensor** with a soft cloth after lifting the blower cover. If your flame sensor is located at the end of the draft tube, rely on a professional.

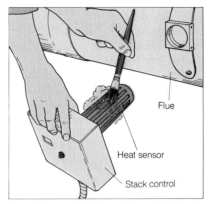

**Clean the heat sensor** on the stack control with hot soapy water and a brush after removing the control from the flue; dry and replace the control.

## TROUBLESHOOTING AN OIL BURNER

| Problem | Possible Causes | Remedies |
|---|---|---|
| **Burner doesn't operate** | No power | Check master switch and fuse or circuit breaker (pages 152–153) |
| | Defective thermostat | Clean thermostat or replace (page 180) |
| | Tripped stack control | Reset twice; then call for service |
| | Tripped motor relay | Reset twice; then call for service |
| | Open furnace limit control | Reset twice; then call for service |
| | Defective motor or motor relay | **Repair or replace motor or motor relay\*** |
| **Burner operates but doesn't light** | Low oil level | Fill tank |
| | Dirty electrodes | **Clean or replace electrodes\*** |
| | Cracked electrode insulators | **Replace insulators\*** |
| | Loose electrode wiring connections | Shut off power and tighten connections |
| | Defective transformer | **Replace transformer\*** |
| | Dirty oil filter or strainer | Clean or replace filter, or clean strainer (see text) |
| | Clogged nozzle | **Clean or replace nozzle\*** |
| **Burner runs intermittently** | Dirty oil filter or strainer | Clean or replace filter, or clean strainer (see text) |
| | Air leaks | Tighten connections and valve packings in oil inlet line; tighten filter and strainer covers |
| | Water in oil | **Repair leak in oil line outside foundation or pump out tank and clean or repair\*** |
| | Poor flame | **Check nozzle, nozzle size, air adjustment, and oil pressure\*** |
| **Smoky flame** | Incorrect air-oil ratio | **Open air shutters to increase air flow\*** |
| **Noisy burner** | Air in oil inlet line | Tighten all connections and valve packings in inlet line; tighten filter and pump covers |
| | Misaligned motor and fuel pump | **Realign motor and pump\*** |
| | Noisy pump | **Replace pump\*** |
| | Loose mounting bolts | Tighten bolts |

\*This repair is best left to a professional
Some problems may be furnace or boiler related; see pages 171–175

# Thermostats

Modern thermostats for heating or air conditioning systems rarely break down. The only maintenance required is an occasional light cleaning. Don't attempt to repair a defective thermostat; instead, replace the entire unit with a new one. Be sure the replacement is the correct voltage and type for your system.

To install a new thermostat, follow the illustrations below.

**How thermostats work.** Thermostats are switches that are turned on by a temperature-sensitive device that, in turn, activates the switch controlling the operation of a boiler, furnace, electric heater, air conditioner, or other heating or cooling device. Low-voltage and millivolt thermostats are the most common types.

The three principal parts of a thermostat are the heat sensor, the switch, and, in low-voltage types only, the heat anticipator. The sensor, usually a bimetal coil, contracts as it cools, tripping the switch to "on," and expands as it warms, tripping the switch to "off."

The switch may have open contacts (in older models) or a mercury-type contact enclosed in an airtight glass tube. The anticipator prevents the living area from overheating by shutting off the boiler or furnace just before the desired temperature is reached.

**Cleaning a thermostat.** Gentle cleaning will help keep a thermostat operating efficiently.

First, you'll need to remove the cover of the thermostat. Then follow the instructions below to dust the heat sensor and, if your thermostat has them, exposed contact points and switch contacts.

## CLEANING A THERMOSTAT

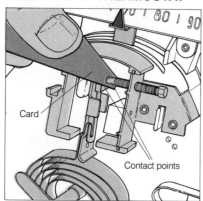

**To clean the contact points,** turn the thermostat up until the points close; remove the cover and wiggle a strip of thin card between the points. Blow clean.

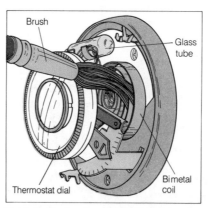

**To clean the heat sensor's bimetal coil** (or element), remove the cover and brush the coil with a soft brush; blow the thermostat clean.

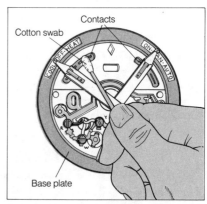

**To clean the switch contacts,** if your thermostat is equipped with them, remove the cover and clean the contacts with a cotton swab moistened with alcohol.

## INSTALLING A THERMOSTAT

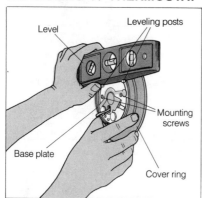

**1) After removing the old thermostat,** feed the wires through the hole in the new base plate and insert the screws. Level the plate, then tighten the screws.

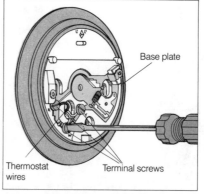

**2) Strip the ends of the wires** if needed, or scrape them clean; wrap the ends clockwise around the terminal screws and tighten the screws.

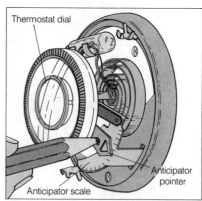

**3) Mount the thermostat** on the base plate; using a pencil, set the anticipator pointer to match the current value marked on the gas valve.

# Air Conditioning Systems

Air conditioners are a blessing in hot climates. Not only do they cool the air, but many dehumidify and filter the air as well. The two most common types of air conditioning systems for the home are evaporative and refrigerated. Both can cool just a single room or an entire house; most types are controlled by a thermostat.

Evaporative air conditioners, also called swamp coolers, work well in dry desert regions. Refrigerated units, though more expensive to purchase than evaporative ones, are the only way to cool air in other than desert climates. Included in the category of refrigerated units are both room air conditioners, fitted into a wall or window, and central air conditioning (page 183). Another type of refrigerated system, a heat pump, cools and heats a house (see below).

The energy cost of most air conditioning systems is high. For this reason, it's important that your system be properly maintained and, if necessary, serviced by a professional.

The descriptions below and on the next pages will help you become familiar with the different systems. To ensure long, reliable operation, be sure to follow the few simple maintenance steps outlined for your particular system.

## Evaporative Air Conditioners

In hot, dry areas, evaporative air conditioners are the most efficient way to cool a home. The unit is mounted in full sun on the roof or beside the house.

Inside the unit, water is sprayed on porous, absorbent blankets. Hot outside air pulled through the blankets by a blower causes the water to evaporate, cooling the air. The cool air then enters the house, forcing stale air out through open windows.

With conscientious maintenance, you can expect few problems. At the beginning of each cooling season, and more often if you see a mineral buildup from the evaporated water, thoroughly clean the unit, oil the pump and blower, and replace the blankets. Also, check and adjust the blower belt; if it's cracked or worn, replace it as for a belt in a warm-air furnace (page 174).

### A TYPICAL EVAPORATIVE AIR CONDITIONER

Blankets — Distribution pipes — Belt — Blower motor — Pump — Overflow — Reservoir — Float valve — Blower

## HOW A HEAT PUMP WORKS

Basically, a heat pump is a refrigerated air conditioning system in which the air flow is instantly reversible.

During warm weather, the pump draws heat from the air inside the house, cooling it and transferring the heat to the outside or to a large solar mass. During cool weather, the flow is reversed—heat extracted from the outside air or from a large solar mass heats the air inside the house. Once the thermostat is set at the desired temperature, the heat pump automatically heats or cools your house as required.

In climates where temperatures below 0°F are common, either electric heating elements or some other supplemental heat source is required. Whenever the heat pump cannot extract enough heat from the outside air, the supplemental system turns on.

If you add an electric air cleaner and, to compensate for dry winter air, a humidifier, your heat pump system will provide clean air at the correct temperature and humidity for 24 hours a day.

Be sure to keep the outdoor portion of the heat pump free of snow and debris. Occasionally check the blower and filter, and replace the filter monthly when in use.

# ... Air Conditioning Systems

## Refrigerated Air Conditioners

All refrigerated air conditioners, whether individual room units or central systems, operate according to the same principle: they extract heat and moisture from the room air, cooling and dehumidifying it, then return the air to the room. Refrigerant, the same substance that's used in a refrigerator, circulates through the system.

**How refrigerated systems work.** Inside a refrigerated air conditioner are a compressor, evaporator or cooling coils, a condenser, and connecting tubing; all are filled with refrigerant. Liquid refrigerant forced through a nozzle expands and partially vaporizes into a gas. The gas then flows through the evaporator coils, cooling the coils so they extract heat and moisture from the room air (the moisture condenses on the coils).

The warm gas then flows into the compressor, where the gas is heated by compression so it exceeds the outside temperature. From the compressor, the hot gas enters the condenser. There, the hot condenser coils dissipate heat to the outside, and the gas condenses into a liquid, ready to repeat the cycle.

**Types of refrigerated air conditioners.** One type, a room air condi-

### A TYPICAL ROOM AIR CONDITIONER

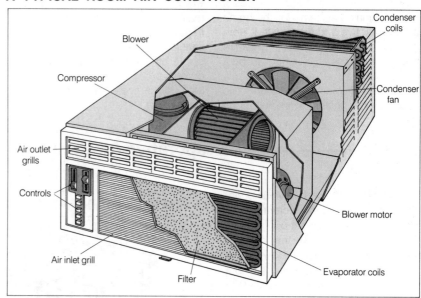

tioner, is very easy to operate; units can be installed in as many rooms as needed. Another type is central air conditioning, which either can be an independent system with its own blower and ducts or can be combined with a forced warm-air heating system (pages 174–175), in which case it uses the same blower and ducts as the heating system.

### Room air conditioners

A room air conditioner is mounted in a window or wall; most of the unit projects outside the house.

A blower in the unit sucks warm room air through a filter protected by a large inlet grill on the front of the unit; cool, dehumidified air returns to the room through outlet grills. Water con-

### CLEANING THE FILTER

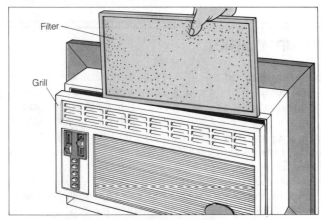

**To clean the filter,** first remove it from the unit (filter is accessible from top or side or, if necessary, by lifting off grill). Brush and vacuum the filter and replace it.

### CLEANING THE CONDENSER COILS

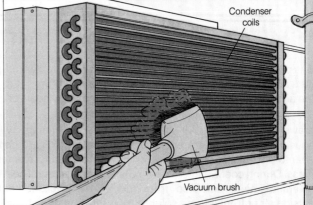

**To clean the condenser coils,** expose them by removing the access panels or the cover at the back of the unit; brush and vacuum the coils. Reassemble.

densing on the evaporator coils drains outside, and a fan blows outside air around the condenser coils to dissipate heat.

Little maintenance is required. During the cooling season, clean the filter and condenser coils every month (see facing page, bottom); replace the filter as necessary. You can reach the filter either through a slot on the side or top or by removing the grill. To reach the condenser, remove the back of the outside housing. Problems with the refrigeration system are best left to a professional.

## Central air conditioners

Though the initial expense is higher, central air conditioning is generally more efficient, quieter, and less costly in the long run than individual room units.

In a house without forced warm-air heat, a central air conditioner can be a single unit installed next to the house or a split unit, with the condenser and compressor outdoors and the evaporator and blower inside.

For a house heated with forced warm air, the most economical installation is a split system (see at right). The evaporator is mounted in the plenum of the furnace, and the condenser and compressor are located outside the house.

### A SPLIT-TYPE CENTRAL AIR CONDITIONER

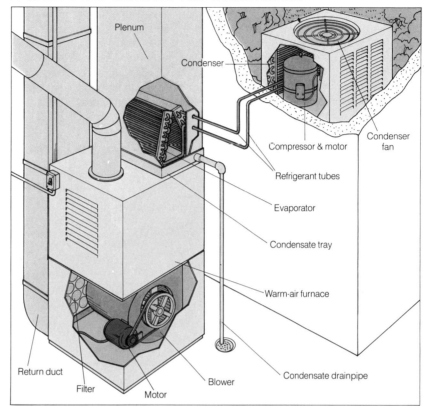

Plenum
Condenser
Compressor & motor
Condenser fan
Refrigerant tubes
Evaporator
Condensate tray
Warm-air furnace
Condensate drainpipe
Return duct
Filter
Motor
Blower

To ensure efficient operation, clean the filter every month during the cooling season; replace the filter as necessary. Check that the condensate drain is clear and that the condenser and evaporator coils are clean. When you vacuum the coils, be careful not to damage or deform the fins.

For problems with the operation of your air conditioning system, see the chart below. Call in a professional to repair the refrigeration system.

## TROUBLESHOOTING A REFRIGERATED AIR CONDITIONER

| Problem | Possible Causes | Remedies |
| --- | --- | --- |
| **Air conditioner doesn't operate** | No power | Check fuse or circuit breaker (pages 152–153) |
| | Defective room unit power cord | Replace cord |
| **Air conditioner doesn't cool or cools inefficiently** | Insufficient air flow | Clean or replace filter and clean evaporator and condenser coils (see text) |
| | Defective thermostat | Clean thermostat or replace (page 180) |
| | Defective compressor | **Repair compressor\*** |
| | Dirty or bent evaporator or condenser fins | Clean or straighten fins |
| | Frost on evaporator coils | Don't operate in temperatures below 60° F |
| **Air conditioner excessively noisy** | Dirty or bent fan blades | Clean or straighten fan blades |
| | Loose blower motor | Tighten mounting bolts |
| | Insufficient lubrication in motor | Place oil in oil cups if any |

*This repair is best left to a professional

# Ventilation

Proper ventilation in a home can replace warm air with cool, remove odors and excess moisture from the kitchen, bathroom, and laundry room, and reduce the level of heat and humidity in an attic as well as in a basement or crawl space.

Passive ventilators are simply openings in the walls and roof that al-low heat to escape. Since these may be inadequate, mechanical ventilators—whole-house fans, attic fans, and exhaust fans—are often installed in homes. Mechanical ventilators, also referred to as ventilating fans, remove hot, moist, or stale air and replace it with fresh air from the outside or from another part of the house.

With proper care, you can expect years of trouble-free service from your mechanical ventilator. Maintenance and repair procedures are uncomplicated and well within the skills of most homeowners. If you experience a problem with your ventilator, the chart on the facing page will help you determine the cause and remedy.

## Whole-House Fans

Even though the outside air may be cooler after the sun goes down, the heat accumulated in a house during the day dissipates slowly, and the living areas may remain uncomfortably hot. Within a few hours, a whole-house fan can reduce the temperature inside the house by 15° to 25°F.

**How whole-house fans work.** These fans pull hot air from the house through a ceiling opening and exhaust the air through attic vents. Louvers on a shutter under the fan open automatically when the fan turns on and close, sealing the opening, when the fan stops. The air exhausted by the fan is replaced by cooler outside air entering through open windows and doors.

Usually, whole-house fans are mounted in a central location on the attic floor. But sometimes this type of fan is mounted in a gable. In this case, for the fan to be effective, all other attic vents must be sealed so air is pulled only from the living area.

A switch or timer conveniently located in the living area controls the operation of the fan. For safety, a limit switch should be provided so the high temperature caused by a fire will shut off the fan and close the shutter.

When you turn on the fan, make sure enough doors and windows are open to provide a free flow of air—the openings should at least equal the area of the fan, twice the area if the doors and windows are screened.

Because you probably won't want to turn on the fan during the heat of the day, this type of fan will not prevent the attic from overheating as does an attic fan (see facing page).

### A TYPICAL WHOLE-HOUSE FAN

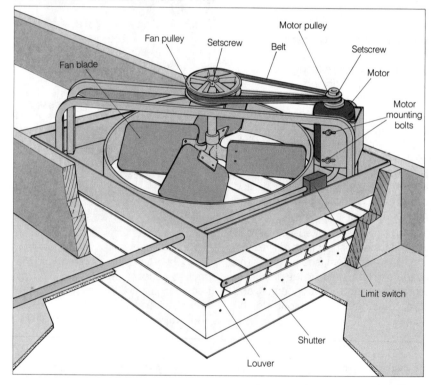

Fan pulley · Motor pulley · Setscrew · Belt · Setscrew · Motor · Fan blade · Motor mounting bolts · Limit switch · Shutter · Louver

**Maintaining a whole-house fan.** Generally, whole-house fans operate reliably for years, providing they're looked after at least once during the year. The best time to perform the routine maintenance procedures described below is at the beginning of each cooling season.

■ **Clean the fan blades** and shutter louvers.

■ **Lubricate the fan and motor bearings** (unless they're sealed) by pouring oil in the oil cups.

■ **Tighten all screws and bolts,** especially the setscrews securing the pulleys to the motor and fan shafts.

■ **Check the belt;** replace it as you would a blower belt if it's cracked or worn (page 174).

■ **Check the belt tension** by pressing in on the middle of the belt—it should deflect ½ to ¾ inch. If it doesn't, loosen the mounting bolts and reposition the motor until the tension is correct.

■ **Clean all the screens** covering the vents in the attic.

# Attic Fans

Though most attics have openings for ventilation, these usually are not enough to prevent the attic temperature from reaching 140°F or higher on a hot day. This heat seeps into the living areas below, causing discomfort for the occupants or increasing the load on the air conditioner. With an attic fan (also called a roof fan), you can substantially reduce the temperature of the attic air.

**How attic fans work.** Mounted as high as possible in a gable or roof surface, an attic fan exhausts hot attic air and pulls in cooler outside air through vents in the eaves or soffits and the other gables. Such a fan can reduce the attic temperature 20 percent or more and room temperatures as much as 10°F.

During the winter months, the same fan equipped with a humidity control can remove excess moisture from the attic, reducing the possibility that damaging ice dams will form on the roof.

Smaller than a whole-house fan, an attic fan also moves much less air. The fan blade is mounted directly on the motor shaft. A thermostat in the fan housing or nearby in the attic turns the fan on at a preset temperature and turns it off when the attic temperature returns to normal.

**Caring for an attic fan.** Perform the following routine maintenance (work on the fan from the attic or, after removing the protective cover, from the roof) at the beginning of each cooling season:

- **Clean the housing** and fan blades.
- **Clean the screens** on the fan and on the attic vents.

## A TYPICAL ATTIC FAN

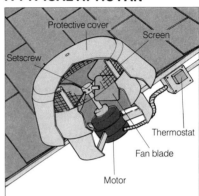

Protective cover
Screen
Setscrew
Thermostat
Fan blade
Motor

- **Tighten all screws and bolts,** especially the setscrew securing the blade assembly to the motor shaft.
- **Lubricate the motor bearings** (unless they're sealed) by pouring oil in the oil cups.

# Exhaust Fans

Exhaust fans remove moisture, heat, and odors from kitchens, bathrooms, basements, and laundry rooms. They also help remove grease particles from kitchens. Quite small compared to attic and whole-house fans, exhaust fans are installed in a wall or ceiling, except for the fan in a range hood.

**How exhaust fans work.** A wall-mounted fan exhausts to the outside. A ceiling-mounted fan exhausts into the attic or through a duct to the outside. A fan in a range hood may exhaust through a duct or only recirculate the air through a charcoal filter without removing heat or moisture.

**Caring for exhaust fans.** Clean the grill and fan blades of a regular exhaust fan once or twice a year. Every 2 months wash the grease filter in a range hood fan; every 6 months wash the fan blades and housing. Replace the pellets in a recirculating fan's charcoal filter annually.

## TROUBLESHOOTING A MECHANICAL VENTILATOR

| Problem | Possible Causes | | Remedies | |
|---|---|---|---|---|
| **Fan doesn't operate** | ⓦⒶ | No power | ⓦⒶ | Check fuse or circuit breaker (pages 152–153) |
| | | | ⓦ | Replace switch (pages 158–159) or timer |
| | | | Ⓐ | Replace thermostat* |
| | ⓦ | Tripped limit switch | | Reset limit switch |
| | ⓦⒶ | Defective motor | | **Replace motor or fan*** |
| **Motor operates but no air flow** | ⓦ | Broken belt | | Replace belt as for blower (page 174) |
| **Insufficient air flow** | ⓦ | Loose belt | | Tighten belt (see text) |
| | ⓦⒶ | Clogged exhaust vents | | Clean vents |
| | ⓦⒶ | Inadequate intake openings | ⓦ | Open some doors or windows |
| | | | Ⓐ | Clean attic vents |

ⓦ Whole-house fan    Ⓐ Attic fan
*This repair is best left to a professional

# Year-round Maintenance Chart

The saying "an ounce of prevention is worth a pound of cure" may be a cliché, but it's useful advice. Preventive maintenance is the best way to keep your home in good repair. Often, such maintenance routinely carried out will ward off major repairs.

Below is a list of the most common maintenance work you should do around the home. The chart is merely a guide; if you notice a problem developing, take care of it immediately. Repairing a fine crack in a wall as soon as it appears may keep it from widening into a gaping split; stopping a minor plumbing leak *now* can prevent water damage later on.

Repairs and additional maintenance information for specific systems, parts of the house, and appliances are discussed throughout the book. In all cases, the final authority for maintenance or repairs should be the owner's manual supplied by the manufacturer.

CAUTION: Before inspecting, cleaning, or making any repairs to the electrical system or to any device connected to it, shut off the power (pages 152–153) or unplug the device. For maintenance of or repairs to plumbing fixtures or water-using appliances, you may need to shut off the water (page 7). To turn off the gas, see page 9.

| When | Where to Check | What to Do |
| --- | --- | --- |
| **Every month (when in use)** | Fire extinguisher | Check that it's fully charged and recharge if necessary |
| | Smoke detector | Test batteries and replace if necessary |
| | Sink and tub stoppers | Clean out debris |
| | Garbage disposer | Flush with hot water and baking soda |
| | Steam heating system | Check safety valve and steam pressure gauge, and have replaced if necessary; check water level gauge and add water if needed; drain water until clear to eliminate sediment |
| | Hot water heating system | Test relief valve and replace if necessary; check pressure gauge and drain expansion tank if necessary |
| | Forced warm-air heating system | Clean or replace air filter; vacuum registers |
| | Evaporative air conditioner | Replace blankets; check air flow and clean or repair unit if necessary |
| | Heat pump | Clean or replace air filter; clean condenser and evaporator coils and condensate drain; remove snow and/or debris from outdoor portion of unit |
| | Refrigerated air conditioner | Clean or replace filter; clean condenser and evaporator coils and condensate drain |
| **Every 2 months (when in use)** | Oil burner (pressure type) | Inspect and clean |
| | Wall furnace | Clean grills |
| | Range hood fan | Clean grease filter |
| **Every 3 months** | Faucet | Clean aerator |
| | Tub drain assembly | Clean out debris; inspect rubber seal and replace if necessary |
| | Floor drain strainer | Clean out debris and scrub strainer |
| | Dishwasher | Clean strainer, spray arm, and air gap |
| **Every 6 months** | Basement and foundation | Check for cracks and moisture, and repair if necessary |
| | Toilet | Check for leaks and repair if necessary |
| | Interior caulking | Inspect caulking around tubs, showers, and sinks, and replace if deteriorating |
| | Water heater | Drain water until clear to eliminate sediment; inspect flue assembly (gas heater) |
| | Garbage disposer | Tighten drain connections and fasteners |
| | Clothes washer | Clean water inlet filters; check hoses for leaks and replace if necessary |
| | Clothes dryer | Vacuum lint from ducts and surrounding areas |
| | Refrigerator | Clean drain hole and pan (more often in warm weather); wash door gasket; vacuum condenser coils |
| | Wiring | Check for frayed cords and wires and repair if necessary |
| | Exhaust fan | Clean grill and fan blades |
| | Range hood fan | Wash fan blades and housing |

| When | Where to Check | What to Do |
|---|---|---|
| **Every spring** | Roof | Inspect roof surface, flashings, eaves, and soffits, and repair if necessary |
| | Gutters and downspouts | Clean out (more frequently if necessary); inspect and repair weaknesses; check for proper drainage and adjust if necessary |
| | Siding | Inspect and clean siding and repair if necessary |
| | Exterior caulking | Inspect caulking and replace if deteriorating |
| | Window sills, door sills, and thresholds | Fill cracks, caulk edges, and repaint; replace if necessary |
| | Window screens and screen doors | Clean screening and repair or replace if damaged; tighten or repair loose or damaged frames and repaint if necessary; replace broken, worn, or missing hardware; tighten and lubricate door hinges and closers |
| | Drain-waste and vent system | Flush out system |
| | Hot water heating system | Lubricate circulating pump and motor |
| | Evaporative air conditioner | Clean unit; check belt tension and adjust if necessary; replace cracked or worn belt |
| | Heat pump | Lubricate blower motor |
| | Refrigerated air conditioner | Lubricate blower motor |
| | Whole-house or attic fan | Clean unit; check belt tension and adjust if necessary; replace cracked or worn belt; tighten screws and bolts; lubricate motor bearings |
| **Every autumn** | Roof | Inspect roof surface, flashings, eaves, and soffits, and repair if necessary |
| | Gutters and downspouts | Clean out (more frequently if necessary); inspect and repair any weaknesses; check for proper drainage and adjust if necessary |
| | Chimney/stovepipe | Clean flue (more frequently if needed); repair any cracks in flue or any loose or crumbling mortar |
| | Siding | Inspect and clean siding and repair if necessary |
| | Exterior caulking | Inspect caulking |
| | Storm windows and doors | Replace any cracked or broken glass; tighten or repair loose or damaged frames and repaint if necessary; replace broken, worn, or missing hardware; tighten and lubricate door hinges and closers |
| | Window and door weatherstripping | Inspect and repair or replace if deteriorating |
| | Drain-waste and vent system | Flush out system |
| | Hot water heating system | Lubricate pump and motor; bleed air from radiators or convectors |
| | Forced warm-air heating system | Vacuum heat exchanger surfaces; clean and lubricate blower blades and motor; check fan belt tension and adjust if necessary; replace cracked or worn belt; check for leaks in ducts and repair if necessary |
| | Gas burner | Clean burners and ports |
| | Oil burner | Have professionally serviced |
| | Thermostat | Clean heat sensor, contact points, and contacts; check accuracy and replace if necessary |
| **Annually** | Garage doors | Clean and lubricate hinges, rollers, and tracks; tighten screws |
| | Septic tank | Have a professional check tank (watch for back-up throughout the year) |
| | Water heater | Test temperature-pressure relief valve and replace if necessary; clean burner ports (gas heater) |
| | Refrigerator | Test door seal (replace gasket about every 6 years); check temperature and adjust if necessary |
| | Recirculating fan (range hood) | Replace pellets in charcoal filter |

# Glossary

**Abrasive.** Substance, such as sandpaper, that wears away a surface by scraping or friction.

**Ampere.** Measurement of electrical current. Many elements in an electrical system and devices connected to it are rated in amperes for the greatest amount of electrical current they can safely carry (abbreviated "amp").

**Bevel.** To angle an edge (usually 45°) on a piece of wood or other material.

**Blind nail.** To drive a nail into a piece of material (such as flooring or paneling) so the nail will be hidden when the next piece is installed.

**Blower.** Motor-driven fan that moves air through the ducts of a heating or cooling system or through vents.

**Bond.** Adhesion of glue or other adhesive to materials being joined; pattern formed in laying brick or other masonry units.

**Circuit.** Two or more wires that provide a path for electrical current from a source through some device using electricity (such as a light) and back to the source.

**Circuit breaker.** Automatic safety switch installed in a circuit to break the flow of electricity when the current exceeds a predetermined safe amount.

**Cleanout.** Opening that provides access to a drainpipe or to a trap under a sink and that's sealed with a threaded plug.

**Combustion chamber.** Fireproof compartment in a boiler or furnace that contains the flame of an oil or gas burner.

**Convector.** Type of radiator (used in a hot water heating system) that transfers heat to a room by air convection.

**Cope.** To saw the end of a piece of molding so it conforms exactly to the face of another piece of molding to form a right-angle joint.

**Counterbore.** To drill a hole for a screw so the head will be below the surface.

**Countersink.** To drill a hole for a flathead screw so the head will be flush with the surface; to install a nail so its head is below the surface.

**Coupling.** Fitting used to connect two lengths of pipe.

**Course.** Horizontal row of shingles or shakes, brick or other masonry units, siding materials, ceramic wall tiles, or ceramic, wood, or resilient floor tiles.

**Damper.** Flat plate that opens and closes to control amount of air flowing through a heating duct, exhaust vent, flue, or chimney.

**Dowel.** Cylindrical wood peg fitted into a hole drilled through two pieces of wood.

**Duct.** Large channel through which air passes in a heating, cooling, or exhaust system.

**Escutcheon.** Decorative metal piece that fits over or around a pipe protruding from a wall, or over a faucet body, or around a lockset on the face of a door.

**Face nail.** To nail into the face of a piece of wood or other building material.

**Flange.** Projecting rim or collar, such as on a skylight, that aids attachment or increases stiffness.

**Furring strips.** Thin, narrow pieces of wood fastened to studs or joists to even out a surface and/or provide a nailing base for finish materials.

**Fuse.** Safety device in an electric circuit designed to blow or open and stop flow of electricity when current exceeds a predetermined safe amount.

**Gasket.** Material (often rubber) that is installed between two parts to make a joint leakproof.

**Glazier's points.** Small metal pieces used to hold a glass pane in a window sash until putty is applied.

**Graphite.** Fine black lubricating powder used dry or mixed with oil.

**Ground.** To connect any part of an electrical wiring system to a ground, either a cold water pipe or a long metal rod driven solidly into the soil, to keep metal parts of wiring system at zero volts.

**Gypsum board.** Large panel composed of a fire-resistant gypsum core sandwiched between two layers of heavy paper and used as a finish for walls and ceilings, or as a backing for other wall and ceiling materials.

**Joint compound.** Plasterlike material used along with wallboard tape to fill and finish joints between gypsum board panels.

**Joists.** Evenly spaced, horizontal lengths of lumber that provide structural support for floors and ceilings.

**Level.** To determine if a surface is exactly horizontal or if two or more points are exactly the same height.

**Locknut.** Nut used to hold a threaded part in position or to prevent another nut from turning on a screw or bolt.

**Masonry.** Brick, stone, concrete, or concrete block building material used for walls, floors, and pavings.

**Milling.** Process that imparts a smooth surface to a piece of lumber; process that lends decorative shape to a piece of wood, such as molding.

**Miter.** To cut ends of two pieces of wood at an angle so they can be joined to form a corner.

**Molding.** Milled piece of lumber used to hide a joint or add a finished look.

**Mortar.** Mixture of cement, sand, water, and sometimes lime used as an adhesive for laying brick, stone, ceramic tile, and concrete block.

**Mortise.** Recess made in a piece of wood to receive a lockset, hinge, or other piece of hardware.

**Penetrating oil.** Oil used to loosen joints—particularly rusted ones—between metal parts.

**Pilot flame.** Small gas flame or electric spark that ignites a gas burner in a range, water heater, dryer, furnace, or boiler.

**Pilot hole.** Starter hole drilled into wood or metal before inserting a screw or nail to prevent fastener from splitting wood. Diameter of hole must be smaller than fastener.

**Pilot orifice.** Small hole in a pilot through which gas passes before igniting.

**Plenum.** Enclosed chamber in furnace where warm air is distributed to ducts.

**Plumb.** To determine if a vertical surface is exactly perpendicular (90°) to a horizontal plane.

**Prime.** To apply an undercoat of paint or sealer to seal pores of wood and provide a surface to which finish coats can adhere.

**Pulley.** A wheel grooved to receive a cord, cable, or belt, such as in a window sash, roll-up garage door, or blower.

**Receptacle.** Device in an electric wiring system to which a lamp, appliance, or extension cord is connected by means of a plug on the end of a cord.

**Refrigerant.** Substance used in a refrigerator or air conditioner that absorbs and releases heat.

**Register.** Grill at end of a supply or return duct in a forced warm-air heating system or refrigerated air conditioning system through which air enters or leaves a room.

**Roofing ocment.** Black elastic waterproofing compound used in flashing and roofing installations, and for repairs.

**Roofing felt.** Thick, fibrous paper impregnated with asphalt used between roof deck and some roofing materials.

**Sash.** Part of a window that holds the glass and is supported by the frame.

**Score.** To cut or scribe a fine line on a surface in order to facilitate cutting or to mark a cutting or location line.

**Screed.** To bring a fill material flush with the surrounding surface.

**Self-tapping screw.** Screw that cuts its own thread in metal when driven into a pilot hole.

**Setscrew.** Headless screw used to hold two metal parts together, such as a pulley on a shaft, a handle on some faucets, or a socket on a light fixture.

**Shim.** Small, thin piece of wood, cardboard, or metal; to use these pieces to adjust level, plumb, or alignment.

**Shutoff valve.** Device that controls flow of water or gas to an individual fixture or appliance or to the entire system.

**Soil stack.** Large drain-waste and vent pipe that connects toilet and branch drains to main house drain and extends out of the roof.

**Solar mass.** Large amount of material such as water, rock, or masonry in a solar-heated home that absorbs and stores heat from the sun and releases it when needed.

**Splice.** To join wires by twisting and soldering or with solderless connectors such as wire nuts.

**Stucco.** Plaster made from a mixture of cement, sand, and water applied over wood or metal lath, wire mesh, or masonry as an exterior finish.

**Studs.** Vertical pieces of lumber usually spaced on 16 or 24-inch centers and attached to top and sole plates, forming the structural core of interior and exterior walls of a house.

**Subfloor.** Boards, planks, or plywood nailed to floor joists to provide structural rigidity and a base for finish flooring.

**Texture.** To form a patterned, raised surface on stucco, plaster, gypsum board, or paint.

**Thermocouple.** Device in a gas burner which by converting the heat of a pilot flame into electricity controls a gas valve that assures the gas is shut off if the pilot is extinguished.

**Thumbscrew.** Screw with a special head that can be turned with thumb and forefinger.

**Toenail.** To drive a nail at an angle through a vertical piece of lumber, such as a stud, into a horizontal piece, such as a sole or top plate.

**Tool.** To finish a mortared joint in masonry, leaving an impression of the finishing tool.

**Transformer.** Electrical device that raises or lowers voltage in a circuit.

**Trap.** U-shaped section of pipe located between a fixture or appliance and a branch drain that holds water, forming a seal to prevent sewer gas from entering through fixture drain.

**Undercut.** To cut away inner edges of a crack or hole in the shape of an inverted V in order to provide a stronger base for patching material.

**Valve.** Device in a heating or plumbing system that controls the flow of a liquid or gas.

**Vaporize.** To convert a liquid into a gas, usually by application of heat.

**Vent stack.** Pipe that rids plumbing system of sewer gas and prevents pressure buildup in pipes.

**Volt.** Unit of measurement denoting electrical pressure or potential (usually abbreviated "V").

**Voltage.** Electric potential or pressure at which a circuit or device operates, expressed in volts.

**Washer.** Flat disc with a center hole used under a screw, bolt, or nut.

**Wet-sanding.** Using water and fine sandpaper with a waterproof backing, known as wet-or-dry paper, to achieve a smooth finish on joint compound without clogging the sandpaper's abrasive grains.

**Wire nut.** Plastic or plastic and metal connector used to splice two or more wires without solder.

**Wood preservative.** Chemical applied to wood to protect it from insects, dry rot, and moisture.

**Worm gear.** Toothed gear and screw combination found in casement window operators and in tilt mechanisms of venetian blinds.

# Index